# MILTON: MAN AND THINKER

# MILTON
## MAN AND THINKER

*By*

### DENIS SAURAT

*Docteur ès Lettres: Directeur de l'Institut Français
du Royaume Uni: formerly Professor of English
at the University of Bordeaux*

**HASKELL HOUSE PUBLISHERS** Ltd.
*Publishers of Scarce Scholarly Books*
**NEW YORK. N. Y. 10012**

First Published 1925


HASKELL HOUSE PUBLISHERS LTD.
Publishers of Scarce Scholarly Books
280 LAFAYETTE STREET
NEW YORK. N. Y. 10012


Library of Congress Catalog Card Number: 76-121151


Standard Book Number 8383-1093-1


Printed in the United States of America

# PREFACE

A FEW details on the history of this book will, I think, help the reader to come to his own conclusions about the questions which it raises.

In 1920, I presented for the degree of Docteur ès lettres at the Sorbonne what constitutes now the first three parts of this work, under the title *La pensée de Milton*. That book was favorably reviewed, but the upper strata of the " scholarly " critics refused to admit the originality of Milton's thought — without, however, suggesting any adequate sources. Indeed, I had been led into insisting upon the absolute originality of the poet's ideas (the relative originality I shall always insist upon) by that very absence of sources. Neo-Platonism offered much too easy, and much too loose, an explanation: it accounted for none of the traits that seemed to me peculiarly Miltonic. Professor S. B. Liljegren, of Lund, Sweden, whom I feel honored to count among my friends, has since investigated the Italian Renaissance, and particularly the works of Giordano Bruno (see *Revue de littérature comparée*, October–December, 1923), with equally negative results.

That perspicuous critic, A. R. Orage, came nearest to a solution, in his review of my *Blake and Milton*, by asking: Was it possible after all that the " Puritan " Milton and the " Swedenborgian " Blake belonged to the same school? I am now in a position to answer that they did, that they were both kabbalists, and that this fact explains their common stock of ideas.

I state all this in order to plead " not guilty." I did not start on the hypothesis that Milton used the Kabbalah, and then try to find kabbalistic notions in Milton. My analysis of Milton's thought was done first, at a time when I believed it to be original; consequently without any presuppositions as to its origins. I cannot but feel that this gives a sort of objective scientific value to the results obtained later.

Further study of the relationship between Milton and Blake brought me to the conclusion that a common influence had necessarily been at work. I had already singled out in 1920 the passage on " retraction " in *Paradise Lost* (VII, 170–73) as holding the kernel of Milton's thought; and therefore when, in 1921, while studying the *Zohar* for sources of Blake's ideas,[1] I came upon a similar passage in the *Tikunē*, I felt that I held the solution. There remained the task of locating the influence in Milton's intellectual surroundings: Fludd then became inevitable, as well as the Mortalists, who ought long ago to have attracted the attention of all who knew that Milton did not believe in the survival of the soul.

One lesson comes obviously from this adventure in scholarship: perhaps the biggest gap in our scientific equipment for research in the history of literature and philosophy is the lack of a thorough study of Arabic and Jewish philosophy and its influence in Europe, not only in the Middle Ages, but well on into the modern period.

May I point out also that my work has been done independently — indeed, in ignorance, till 1920 — of the results obtained since 1918 in Sweden by Professor Liljegren, and in America by Professors Greenlaw, Hanford,

[1] A fruitful search, as is shown by the independent studies of Professor Fehr, of Zurich (*Englische Studien*, 1920).

and others.  That the conclusions arrived at in three separate lines of research should be, on the whole, harmonious, is, it seems to me, a fair proof of their soundness.

This book is in part a translation or adaptation of the
following books or papers:

*La pensée de Milton.*  Paris, Alcan, 1920.

" Les sources anglaises de la pensée de Milton " [on the
    Mortalists].  (In *Revue germanique,* October, 1921.)

" Milton et le *Zohar.*"  (In *Revue germanique,* Janu-
    ary, 1922; in English, in *The Quest,* January, 1922,
    and in *Studies in Philology,* April, 1922.)

" La Cabale et la philosophie de Milton."  (In *Revue
    des études juives,* September, 1921.)

The chapter on Fludd is entirely new; and of the rest,
much is revised, particularly the section on the Mortalists.

I therefore give here, besides the analysis of Milton's
thought contained in my previous book, the results of my
subsequent attempt to solve the problem of the origin of
this thought.

                                                D. S.

Bordeaux, 1924.

# CONTENTS

PAGE

Introduction........................................... xiii

## PART I. THE MAN

I. The Elements of Milton's Character in Youth...    1
   1. Character and family.........................    1
   2. The University and Horton....................    6
   3. Early poems.................................   13

II. The Man of Action and of Passion...............   21
   1. Milton, man of action......................   21
   2. The struggle against the bishops.............   32
   3. The first shock: private life and the conception of the
      Fall........................................   49
   4. The second crisis: the break with the Presbyterians   70
   5. The political struggle and the conception of evil..   80
   6. Failure....................................   94
   7. The problem................................  104

## PART II. THE SYSTEM

I. Ontology........................................  113
   1. The Absolute...............................  113
   2. God non-manifested.........................  117
   3. Individual beings: the "retraction"..............  123
   4. The total plan of being: the decree of God.......  125
   5. The aims of creation.........................  131

II. Cosmology......................................  134
   1. The Son...................................  134
   2. The Holy Spirit.............................  134
   3. Matter....................................  136
   4. Death and resurrection......................  143

III. Psychology and Ethics..........................  149
   1. The origin of evil and the duality of man........  149
   2. The Fall...................................  150
      a. The Fall in general: the triumph of passion
         over reason...........................  150
      b. The Fall in particular: sensuality...........  152

ix

PAGE

3. The normal state.............................. 155
   a. Legitimate sensuality....................... 155
   b. The conception of woman.................. 159
   c. Reason triumphant......................... 170

IV. RELIGION............................................ 172
   1. The second creation.......................... 172
   2. Christ: Intelligence triumphant over passion...... 173
   3. Christ: the greater man...................... 174

V. POLITICS........................................... 181
   1. Liberty...................................... 181
      a. Moral liberty: no law...................... 181
      b. Religious liberty: no priests................. 182
      c. Intellectual liberty: no censors.............. 183
      d. Political liberty: no tyrants................. 185
   2. Destiny: God and history...................... 192

VI. CONCLUSION: A GENERAL VIEW OF MILTON'S PHIL-
    OSOPHY.......................................... 198


PART III.  THE GREAT POEMS

I. FAITH, PHILOSOPHY, AND POETRY IN MILTON'S WORK.. 203

II. PARADISE LOST ..................................... 213
   1. Milton in Paradise Lost...................... 213
   2. God in Paradise Lost: the divine irony.......... 229

III. PARADISE REGAINED and SAMSON AGONISTES............ 233


PART IV.  THE SOURCES

SECTION I

THE MYTH OF THE FALL: SOURCES AND INTERPRETATION

I. HEBRAIC SOURCES.................................... 251
   1. The fall of man.............................. 251
   2. The fall of the angels ....................... 253

II. THE CHRISTIAN ERA................................. 259
   1. Paul........................................ 259
   2. Later Judaism............................... 261

PAGE

III. THE FATHERS....................................... 264
   1. Milton's opinions of the Fathers................ 264
   2. The Fathers before Augustine................... 269
   3. Augustine....................................... 273

SECTION II
CONTEMPORARY SOURCES AND INFLUENCES

I. THE *ZOHAR* AND THE KABBALAH ..................... 281

II. ROBERT FLUDD (1574–1637) ......................... 301

III. THE MORTALISTS, 1643–1655......................... 310

CONCLUSION............................................. 323

APPENDICES

A. MILTON'S BLINDNESS................................. 329

B. THE NEW CONCEPTION OF MILTON: A CRITICAL BIBLI-
   OGRAPHY........................................... 342
   1. The American Group ........................... 342
   2. European Critics .............................. 348

INDEX ................................................ 355

# INTRODUCTION

THE aim of this study is to determine the human and lasting element in Milton's thought.

Milton has been studied too much in connection with his century, or at least with the wrong side of his century. We have been taught to see in him the stiff Puritan figure; and that has taken much of our interest away from him. Only too often do we feel half inclined to forgive Milton both his character and his ideas for love of the irresistible beauty of his art. Only too often do we open and read his poems with half-smothered prejudice against him; and thus we lose much that is important and interesting in them. There is, however, in Milton's work a permanent interest, outside the religious and political squabbles of his time, outside even dogma and religion proper — a philosophical interest susceptible of universal appeal, and fully as important for our own time as for Milton's.

Milton's thought is most attractive when studied in connection with its intimate sources in his character and emotional experience. His abstract ideas are mostly generalizations of conceptions acquired in his personal experience, in the conflict between his temperament and the circumstances, private and political, of his life. His ideas are an interpretation of life which has not been built in the abstract by speculation, but which has been the result of the passing through life of a highly sensitive man — a man of high intelligence also — to whom life brought revelations about himself, his ambitions, and his cause.

An abstract study of his ideas, therefore, would be insufficient. In his great poems, Milton gives us a picture of life as he understood it after having lived. It is necessary to throw on the poems the light which comes from a study of his abstract ideas; many details rise then into significance, many peculiarities of the works are explained. But, inversely, many gaps in the thought are filled in by the poetry. I mean to try to show Milton as one, to reveal the unity of his private and political and literary life, the unity of the man himself. For it is not right even to say that the private man or the political man in him influenced the poet or the thinker. Quite as often it was the poet who influenced the politician in him, or the private man, by giving him a magnificent but impossible ideal to carry out into deeds. And the failures of the practical man again set his problems to the thinker. In a word, Milton was one in all his activities: his complex sensitiveness is found in his poems as in his life; his clear imperious will is seen in his philosophy as in his actions; his penetrating and systematic intellect dominates his political life as well as his theology or his poems.

In a first part, I shall study Milton's character in his youth and show how that character brought him into conflict with the realities of private or public life; what problems the conflict presented to his intelligence; what conceptions of life it engraved deeply into his very being.

A second part will analyze the abstract ideas that arose out of his experience, first as a solution to the problems set by his life to a man of his temperament, but also as the outcome of as wide an intellectual culture as a man ever had.

In a third part, I shall study the essential rôle played

in the great poems by the ideas and tendencies thus revealed.

And finally, in the last part, I shall try to fasten on the important and peculiar points of that culture of which he took advantage to express his ideas. In studying the sources of his conceptions, I see in external inspiration only an occasion which helped and clarified the workings of his own peculiar thought. This fourth part will make clear also with what side of his own time he is to be connected.

The book as a whole will thus link Milton's art to his thought, and both art and thought to his life, one in itself, varied in its expressions, political, private, philosophical, or artistic. And in doing so, it will endeavor to reveal his permanent value for us, to show that he was a man who suffered and fought, who sang and thought in such wise that he can bring comfort in all the struggles of man in all times, and not only the pleasure of mere artistic dilettantism.

The very center of Milton's personality seems to me to consist in a powerful feeling of egotism and pride, in the fullest self-consciousness of a tremendous individuality. And yet nothing mean or petty mixes here, and Trelawny, who, with all his faults, was a man and a judge of men, could permit himself to say: "The greatest man, although not the greatest poet, John Milton." [1] This is because there was deeply rooted in Milton a tendency to look upon himself not as an exception in the romantic manner, but as a normal representative of human nature. His high opinion of himself is also a high opinion of man. In the divorce pamphlets as well as in the letter on edu-

[1] *Records of Shelley, Byron, and the Author* (London, 1878), p. 215.

cation, in politics as well as in religion, he always tried to apply to others such rules and methods as he found good for himself.

Moreover, Milton always knew how to place above himself the Impersonal, the Cause. Great as he felt himself to be, he never forgot that he was first of all a great Servant. Hence a noble humility in his pride. He could sacrifice himself: to a Cause, he sacrificed at one time all his literary ambition, at another his eyesight; personal interest and the gratification of vanity had no place in his life. He often boasted of what he had done, but he had never undertaken anything in order solely to derive glory or profit from it; the mark of the Impersonal is on all that he did. This fact places him high above the great lords of literature, above Byron as above Hugo. Hence his exquisite courtesy towards his friends, hence his admirations — Galileo, for instance. He knew his peers; he could treat as equals all men of intelligence and culture. Hence again the balance of his character, that self-possession so rarely found in company with excessive pride. Whereas Byron probably thought himself fit to be king of Greece, Milton did not believe himself worthy of a commission in the Civil War.[2]

This legitimate pride, in the full and fair knowledge of his capacities, as a representative of mankind, is the center of Milton's personality. His intelligence works with this feeling behind it always. Hence his fundamental idea that human nature is good and great, and, in essence, divine. Hence the necessity of liberty for man. But this pride is implanted in an intelligent and sensitive nature, which sees failure clearly and suffers deeply from it.

[2] *Cf.* Masson, *The Life of John Milton* (London, 1871–1880), II, 472–86.

Hence his theories of the Fall. And the same feeling of pride allows him no thought that places outside man either fall or regeneration. Clearly and pitilessly, Milton makes man responsible for his failure and his shame.

We shall find in Milton, then, not only a supreme poetical genius and an incomparable master of expression, but a clear and powerful intellect and will, a deep and quick sensitiveness, and, towering above all other traits, pride — pride tremendous and yet worthy of respect because it does not separate Milton from his fellow-men, but rather unites him to them in sublime aspiration towards an ideal common to all mankind.

Milton's thought comes from all these elements. The distinction between feeling and idea is purely fictitious, for Milton in any case. In his most abstruse ideas, apparently the work of the purest intellect, we find his feelings, elaborated and transposed into the refining, analyzing forms of language and art.

PART **I**

THE MAN

# MILTON: MAN AND THINKER

## CHAPTER I

## THE ELEMENTS OF MILTON'S CHARACTER IN YOUTH

### I. CHARACTER AND FAMILY

TWO essential traits of character can be discerned in Milton from his youth onwards. The first is a varied, lively, and deep sensitiveness, such as is expected in a poet. The second is a sort of moral intractableness, which led Milton to sacrifice every practical or sentimental consideration to a high ideal of purity and truth, in private or public life.

This latter trait, generally referred to as Milton's puritanism of character, is the one which has most impressed the public and the majority of the biographers. It is at the basis of the ordinary conception of Milton as a rigid Puritan, upright no doubt, but on the whole unlovable, lacking in that good warm human feeling which creates sympathy in men — and in readers.

There is no doubt an element of truth in this popular conception of the poet; but there is also an element of exaggeration, and above all a large element of injustice in ignoring the human side of his character. Some critics, however — and those most in sympathy with Milton — have protested against the prejudices that mar the personal reputation of the poet. Richard Garnett, in his admirable preface to his extracts from Milton's prose, compares him aptly to Rousseau and to Shelley. " The chief lesson," he says, " to be drawn from Milton's prose works . . . is the recognition of his position as the great idealist, the Rousseau or the Ruskin of his generation. The current view of his character does him great injustice, while in itself natural and almost inevitable. A man of strict and austere life, living in a Puritan age and siding with Puritanism in almost all the questions at issue between it and contending tendencies, can hardly be taken for anything but a Puritan. . . . It requires study to discover that, like the great Protestant cathedral, the great Protestant epic descends from the Renaissance. Even as his poetry reveals Milton in the character of a humanist, so the more important of his prose works display him as a revolutionist, eager to sweep away everything obstructive of an ideal existing solely in his own mind. . . . He took Puritanism up partly, no doubt, because it embodied his favourite virtues of fortitude and temperance, but also because it was the only organized force in that age which, by overthrowing the old order, would offer a chance for the realization of his ideals. . . . The spiritual kinship with Shelley would be more evident if the younger poet's exuberant fancy had not veiled his figure in a radiant mist, which conceals the real Shelley as the Genevan habit conceals the real Milton." [1]

Milton came from a family in which religious passion seems at first sight to run deep. But on looking more closely into the question, it appears that this passion was hardly as religious as one might expect. There was, at bottom, in Milton himself, very little religious fury; his vehemence was always directed against some form of reli-

---

[1] *The Prose of Milton Selected* (London, 1893), pp. xi-xiii.

gion he disapproved of, and never supported any precise religious dogma. He attacked; he never praised. He founded no sect; he followed none. And the passion he brought to the attack on Episcopalian or Presbyterian was not the zeal of the fanatic that wanted to destroy a rival sect, but that of the intellectual who was fighting for liberty of thought.

The poet's grandfather, Richard Milton, was a Catholic. In July, 1601, he was fined sixty pounds for not having attended service in the Established Church for more than three months, and in October of the same year, the fine was renewed for the same offense.[2] Richard's son became a Protestant, and was consequently turned out of his home and disinherited. Both the father and the grandfather of our John Milton show thus the same intractableness as the poet himself in matters of conscience. But were these cases of fanaticism, or merely of the need of asserting personal opinion, a rebellion to conquer liberty for a Catholic in a Protestant community, for a Protestant in a Catholic family? Richard Milton had held some position in an Anglican church;[3] his son, as we shall see, was never conspicuous for fanaticism. It seems probable that in both father and son a strong dose of pride and obstinacy mingled with religious feeling, if indeed the need to get one's own way was not the essential motive of rebellion for both. Thus in Milton himself the feeling for personal independence is much stronger than religious zeal.

We know the poet's father, John Milton, much better than his grandfather. There was nothing of the pedantic and narrow-minded Puritan about him. He had been

[2] Masson, I, 17–18.     [3] *Ibid.*, I, 23.

given a liberal education, and had perhaps studied at Oxford.[4] Love of music was in him already, and he was known as a composer, being one of twenty-five who set to music a series of madrigals in honor of Queen Elizabeth: *The Triumphs of Oriana* — essentially non-religious music.[5] The scrivener had literary ambitions too, and a sonnet from his pen survives; his modesty and good taste are proved by the fact that he did not try to force the Muse's favors, and desisted after that attempt. His literary ambition centered in his son, and his discernment and disinterestedness cannot be overpraised. He was convinced from the first of the extraordinary merits of his son, and grudged no sacrifice to make him a great man. He had thought of the Church for him, but rather in order to give him an opportunity than out of religious zeal; in the dreams by the family fireside, the young Milton did not appear as a future Calvin, but as a second Homer; and surely here is the most intimate proof that there was nothing of the fanatic about John Milton the father: an over-religious family would have coveted the fame of a reformer for such a richly gifted son; Milton's family brought him up for poetical glory. When Milton decided he could not enter the Church, his father does not seem to have been hard to win over, and he went on allowing the young poet, for culture and travel, the use of a laboriously acquired fortune.

The retired business man had a calm and happy old age in his eldest son's house, " without the least trouble imaginable," says Phillips: [6] no sign of violent religious zeal, considering the fact that at the time there lived in the same house the royalist, and possibly Catholic, family

---

[4] *Ibid.*, I, 23.    [5] *Ibid.*, I, 51–54.    [6] Quoted by Masson, II, 508.

of Milton's wife. Besides, this same John Milton, who
had left his father's house over a religious quarrel, lived in
perfect harmony with his son Christopher for several years
— and Christopher was destined to become a Catholic.
This family changed religion a little too often; their ideas
were evidently broad enough, since Christopher, a royalist, found shelter in his brother's home when the royalist
cause was lost; and we do not know that good harmony
was ever broken among the three men.[7] All this confirms
the hypothesis that what was the matter with this family
was not fanaticism, but the need for personal independence. When they agreed to respect each other's rights
to think as they liked, they lived quite happily in spite
of all their divergences of opinion — an impossible thing
for fanatics to do.

As for our John Milton, he wrote verses which were
considered marvelous in the home circle when he was
about ten years old, and he was henceforward brought
up deliberately to be a man of genius.[8] What colossal
pride must have been latent in a family where such a
thing was accepted as normal, where such an enterprise
was carried through successfully, to the complete satisfaction of all participants in this unique conspiracy! The
habit of looking upon himself as a great man was thus
acquired by the poet in early childhood. He came to
accept it as a simple and natural thing. His greatness
was taken for granted, first of all by himself. During the
whole course of his life, he was to make candid and stu-
pendous admissions concerning his own genius. He did
not boast of it; it was a natural, well known fact, which
needed not to be insisted upon in itself; but it was an

[7] *Ibid.*, II, 490, 508.    [8] Masson, I, 65.

advantage of which he would deprive neither his cause nor his ideas. The form of his exhortations to the people or to the great was always, more or less: Ἀμὴν ἀμὴν λέγω ὑμῖν Verily, I, Milton, say unto you! Another characteristic of his pride may also have come from its home origin. Milton never clearly perceived that the world was not made of Miltons. Anticipating the Kantian formula, he legislated as though what was valid for him was valid for the universe. He appraised man's powers too high, judging by himself. No doubt this tendency came from the time when he accepted in all good faith his family's cult, and probably believed that every family was similarly educating a young Milton.

## II.   The University and Horton

Milton went to Cambridge in 1625. His proud and sensitive nature seems to have been put at first to a severe test. The students were not likely to surround him with the affection of the home circle, and his delicacy must have rebelled against the grossness and indifference of his new companions. Anyhow he succeeded in acquiring neither the good opinion of his teachers, as the quarrel between him and his tutor Chappell proves, nor that of his comrades, as is visible in the opening sentences of the first of his *Prolusiones*. And yet, when he left the University in 1632, he had conquered: he went regretted by many, admired by all.[9]

This change in public opinion is a sure proof of the amiability of his character: a stiff Puritan, having once made an unfavorable impression, would never have gained his companions' affection. This human side of his nature

[9] See Masson, I, 159–61, 276–77, 307.

is evident above all in his friendship with Charles Deodati, a school friend from pre-university days, a precious
comrade till his death in 1639, Milton's most intimate
friend, it would seem. Their correspondence, in turns
gay or serious, is normally in the tone of affectionate
banter. The Latin elegy sent to Deodati in 1626 reveals
the lighter side of Milton's soul: his love for the stage,
and also his intense susceptibility to feminine charm. The
poet was good-looking and elegant in his dress; it was
in the order of things that he should be himself attracted
by beauty. Thus he duly went into raptures over the
charms of the London girls. In May 1628 (he was
twenty), he was violently in love — so he says in his
seventh Latin elegy — with a young girl he had seen by
chance in a crowd and would never see again.

These two productions are no doubt, partly at least, literary exercises, full of cold rhetoric and false mytholog-
ical allusions. Yet they contain some lively traits. First
of all, a young Puritan would have avoided the subject
altogether. Then the second poem is based on a true
incident: the young man caught sight in the street of a
beautiful woman, lost as soon as seen; this ordinary hap-
pening must have been real, since many less thin subjects
were at hand for artificial love poetry. But we have even
better proof of Milton's feelings at this period, since the
keenest of Milton's biographers, Dr. Smart of Glasgow,
has set in their true light the Italian sonnets.[10] These
were probably written about Milton's twenty-third year.
They are "a record of his first love" — that is, if we
leave out of count the unknown young London girl. "The
person addressed in these poems was a lady of Italian

[10] *The Sonnets of Milton*, by John S. Smart (Glasgow, 1921), pp. 133 ff.

descent, having a foreign type of beauty, new to the poet, with a dark complexion and dark eyes. . . . His regard for her was something more than a passing admiration. . . . It is also evident that she was aware of his feelings, and was not unwilling to make some response; for the sonnets were composed in Italian, rather than English, at her own request, she having said: ' It is the language of love.' "

But there is more in these earliest poems of Milton. With the rise of amorous feeling, there awakens in Milton a marvellous sympathy with Nature, in which he feels and recognizes immense forces of well-nigh voluptuous desire. This feeling was later developed in some of Comus's speeches and fully expressed in the Creation book of *Paradise Lost;* it then became a sort of sense of universal fruitfulness, which gives life to lines like

> Reptile with spawn abundant, living soul.

No other poet has been so close to a feeling of Nature's fecundity, and, as we shall see later, this conception has a high philosophical importance in Milton's subsequent work.[11] Already in his *In Adventum Veris* (1629) we find the promise of future splendor:

> Look, Phœbus; loves, easy to reach, call to thee; the breezes of Spring send forth their prayers sweet as honey. . . . Not without presents does the Earth seek thy love. . . . If precious things, dazzling offerings touch thy soul (for love is often bought with presents), she spreads before thee all the wealth she keeps hidden under the vast seas and inside the mountains.[12]

United to this exquisite sensibility, from youth through the whole of life, is the mastery of self, especially in that form which appeals most to the imagination of a pure

[11] See below, pp. 141-43.    [12] Ll. 67-78.

though passionate young man: chastity. Milton had been called by the Cambridge students the "lady of Christ's"; this homage to his good looks was also a sarcasm on his purity.[13] But he was proud of his chastity. He boasts of it in the epistle to Deodati we have quoted above: "Shunning far on my path false Circe's infamous mansions." We shall find this pride again in the *Apology for Smectymnuus*.[14] Let us note here the chief reason for this chastity. It is not religious in our sense, though it is in a more fundamental meaning; like the great ascetics of primitive magic, Milton was chaste in order to acquire supernatural powers. He explains it quite clearly, both in verse and prose: "He who would not be frustrate of his hope to write well hereafter in laudable things" — for the powers he wishes to acquire are those of the bard — ought to be chaste. And in the sixth elegy:

> Additur huic scelerisque vacans, et casta juventus,
> Et rigidi mores, et sine labe manus.

*Comus* was to be the glorification of the magic powers of chastity.

We discern several feelings that uphold Milton's purity. No doubt there comes first his hatred of all compromise when an ideal is at stake, the clear, hard domination of intelligence over passion; but there comes also pride: moral pride, as a sense of his own worth which is not to be degraded; intellectual pride also — Milton thinks so highly of his reason, has such trust in his intellect, that he wants his reason to be mistress absolute in himself. He takes himself too seriously — he takes his genius and his mission too seriously — to allow passion to rule in him. His amorous tendencies, real and deep as they are,

[13] Masson, I, 311.      [14] See below, pp. 45–46.

remain, for the time being, well in hand, reasonable and
obedient almost to the sovereign will.   Literary ambition
and pride of intellect are the dominant factors in Milton's
youth.

Meanwhile, great plans were being meditated.   At nine-
teen, in a college exercise, the poet rises for one moment
above grotesque Latin and buffoon English, and binds
himself by his first oaths to his future Muse:

> Hail, native language. . . .
> Yet I had rather, if I were to choose,
> Thy service in some graver subject use, . . .
> Such where the deep transported mind may soar
> Above the wheeling poles, and at Heaven's door
> Look in, and see each blissful deity
> How he before the thunderous throne doth lie,
> Listening to what unshorn Apollo sings. . . .
> Then sing of secret things that came to pass
> When beldam Nature in her cradle was. . . .

The subject of *Paradise Lost* is not yet found, but the
plans are drawn:  the poet foresees vaguely a universal
epic, describing the origin of the world and revealing the
secret aims and occupations of divinity.   In any religion,
Milton would have sung, and his poem would have been
substantially what it is.   Here we see him ready to write
*Paradise Lost* out of Greek mythology.   His subject is inevitable; he is driven by the great force of his sublime
pride to the largest and deepest theme imaginable:  what
else can he sing but the All, the World, the Gods?   The
compass of his genius is that of the whole Cosmos; he
cannot choose a smaller subject.

In 1632, he retired to Horton, where, with the full approval of his father, he devoted himself to deliberate preparation for his high mission.   A few years later he wrote

to Deodati: " Do you ask what I am meditating? By
the help of Heaven, an immortality of fame." [15]

Milton's pride and his plans naturally went together
with an imperious need for personal liberty; and that,
naturally also, kept him out of the Church his father had
meant him to enter. We know well enough what his
opinions were about 1632: he was a liberal Anglican,
probably without any very definite convictions on points
of dogma.[16] Thus he remained for many years still. It
was neither fanaticism nor even deep religious feeling
that kept him out of orders; it was his need to be free to
think and do as he liked. His pride would not be curbed
under the yoke of the Church. Years later, in the *Reason
of Church Government* he wrote: [17]

> . . . coming to some maturity of years, and perceiving what
> tyranny had invaded the church, that he who would take orders
> must subscribe slave, and take an oath withal, which, unless he
> took with a conscience that would retch, he must either straight
> perjure, or split his faith; I thought it better to prefer a blame-
> less silence before the sacred office of speaking, bought and begun
> with servitude and forswearing.

From this time onward there entered into his very soul
the hatred of priesthood. The Roman Catholic religion,
in particular, seemed to him the very type of intolerance
and priestly domination. Rome was to him, during the
whole of his life, the Whore of Babylon; even in 1673,
in his last pamphlet in favor of toleration, he excluded
Catholicism from it " as being idolatrous, . . . not to be
tolerated, either in public or in private." [18] This attitude
is all the more characteristic as on many points, as we
shall see, Milton came quite near to Roman Catholic

---

[15] *Prose Works*, Bohn ed., III, 495.      [17] *Prose Works*, II, 482.
[16] *Cf.* Masson, I, 323, 326.      [18] *Ibid.*, II, 514.

ideas; and that on such important points as, for instance,
the freedom of the will.  It was not Catholic dogma or
ideas that shocked him, but the political and intellectual
tyranny he associated with the Church of Rome.

His long stay in Horton was occupied by reading, social
intercourse with neighboring wealthy and educated families, and the writing of *L'Allegro, Il Penseroso, Arcades,
Comus,* and *Lycidas*.  He went up to London frequently,
took lessons in mathematics and music, and altogether
enjoyed himself as fully as he could.  His nephew Phillips tells us that in 1640 Milton frequented the beaux of
the capital, dressed as elegantly as any of them, and allowed himself " a gaudy-day " in their company once or
twice a month.[19]   In the country, the Countess of Derby,
the Earl of Bridgewater, Sir Henry Wotton were among
his friends; for their entertainment *Arcades* and *Comus*
were written and performed.

We are far in all this from the Puritan of popular imagination.  We find here an elegant young man, fond of
music and of mixing in the choicest society, well known
among his friends as a promising poet, keenly alive to all
worldly charm, and especially to feminine charm, pure
in behavior as in mind.[20]   But in himself, he has devoted
his whole life to a supreme poetical enterprise, and he
looks upon the world as from a tower in his pride, strength,
and seriousness — a perfect master of himself, his mind
set with a sort of grimness on getting out of his great
gifts all they can produce.

[19] Masson, II, 209.
[20] *Cf.* his letter to Deodati (1637): " . . . whatever the Deity may have
bestowed upon me in other respects, he has certainly inspired me, if any
ever were inspired, with a passion for the good and fair.  Nor did Ceres,
according to the fable, ever seek her daughter Proserpine with such un-
ceasing solicitude, as I have sought this τοῦ καλοῦ ἰδέαν, this perfect model
of the beautiful in all the forms and appearances of things. . . . I am wont
day and night to continue my search " (*Prose Works*, III, 494).

Such was Milton, as we listen to him in his first poems, as we see him on his travels in Italy.

## III. EARLY POEMS

Milton's early poems were only, in his opinion, a trial of his strength, a promise to the world. He published them at a time (1645) when he had given up literature for less familiar but, as he thought, more pressing duties. The modest way in which he presented them, under the Virgilian warning,

—— Baccare frontem
Cingite, ne vati noceat mala lingua futuro,

tells us that he did not look upon them as a very important work. In his pamphlets, too, on several occasions, he records his promise to do great things yet in literature, without so much as mentioning his early poems. Yet in the history of Milton's ideas, these poems give us a very solid starting-point; at a time when his religion was more or less orthodox, they reveal his dominant characteristics, those general tendencies of his temperament which, acting on his first conceptions, were to dissolve his orthodoxy in the following fifteen years.

For one thing, the poems display an extremely varied sensibility. It is necessary to insist on this variety and, so to speak, "humanity" of the poet's soul. He feels sympathy for all feelings of the human heart, even encompassing apparently contradictory ones. Now Milton is the least dramatic of the poets; he has no skill in creating character; he is essentially lyrical; what he sings is still and ever Milton. And this is quite in harmony with his self-centered character. But it also shows that the poet who has been made out to be a narrow Puritan was in reality gifted with an extraordinary wealth of feeling and sympathy for everything human.  Thus *L'Allegro* and *Il Penseroso* represent two alternate states of soul familiar to Milton as to all men.

> . . . Laughter holding both his sides. . . .
> The mountain nymph, sweet Liberty; . . .
> . . . The spicy nut-brown ale, . . .
> The hidden soul of harmony;

are as familiar to him as

> The cherub Contemplation,

or that

> Sweet bird that shunn'st the noise of folly,

or the

> Lamp at midnight hour,

or

> The hairy gown and mossy cell.

He can equally well

> Sing to those that hold the vital shears,

and lead the dancing troop

> O'er the smooth enamel'd green
> Where no print of step hath been.[21]

In particular, the poems are full of amorous and more than half voluptuous feeling.  Milton could muse in his youth in this wise:

> Alas!  What boots it with uncessant care
> To tend the homely slighted shepherd's trade,
> And strictly meditate the thankless Muse?
> Were it not better done as others use,
> To sport with Amaryllis in the shade,
> Or with the tangles of Neæra's hair? [22]

[21] *Arcades*, ll. 65, 84–85          [22] *Lycidas*, ll. 64–69.

Nor was it any Puritan poet who saw the exuberance of
Nature as Comus celebrates it in that astounding passage
in which we feel in full maturity that peculiar love for
Mother Earth already suggested in the Latin poems: a love
internal, so to speak, that describes but little, but consists
in a sort of sympathy for the very growth of all beings,
as though Milton recognized in himself the same generous
forces as in vegetation and the luxuriance of animal
generation:

O foolishness of men! that lend their ears
To those budge doctors of the Stoic fur,
And fetch their precepts from the Cynic tub,
Praising the lean and sallow Abstinence.
Wherefore did Nature pour her bounties forth,
With such a full and unwithdrawing hand,
Covering the earth with odours, fruits, and flocks,
Thronging the seas with spawn innumerable,
But all to please, and sate the curious taste?
And set to work millions of spinning worms,
That in their green shops weave the smooth-hair'd silk
To deck her sons; and that no corner might
Be vacant of her plenty, in her own loins
She hutched th' all-worshipp'd ore, and precious gems,
To store her children with: if all the world
Should in a pet of temp'rance feed on pulse,
Drink the clear stream, and nothing wear but frieze,
Th' All-giver would be unthank'd, would be unpraised,
Not half his riches known, and yet despised;
And we should serve him as a grudging master,
As a penurious niggard of his wealth;
And live like Nature's bastards, not her sons,
Who would be quite surcharged with her own weight,
And strangled with her waste fertility;
Th' earth cumbered, and the wing'd air dark'd with plumes,
The herds would over-multitude their lords,
The sea o'erfraught would swell, and th' unsought diamonds
Would so emblaze the forehead of the deep,

And so bestud with stars, that they below
Would grow inured to light, and come at last
To gaze upon the sun with shameless brows.[23]

Out of this feeling for Nature, an idea is arising which
will play a great part in Milton's philosophy. Nature
comes from God; natural instincts are good; to follow
them is to fulfil God's will. The line

Th' All-giver would be unthank'd, would be unpraised

contains in germ the thought which will later be clearly
expressed in

Our Maker bids increase, who bids abstain
But our destroyer, foe to God and man? [24]

In this feeling for Nature is the ultimate source of Milton's pantheistic ideas. He will never admit that Nature,
or matter, or the flesh are evil. His deepest sympathy
goes out to all that grows, reproduces itself, spreads out
into beautiful rich shapes. He loves Nature in a twofold
way: through his senses for her external beauty, and
through this inner feeling of sympathy with Life.

Comus, speaking thus, is a part of Milton's soul, even
as Satan will be later. But, ruling high above these
deeper powers of feeling, which are but half-awakened
as yet, sits Reason. *Comus* is one long praise of temperance, self-mastery, chastity. I have already pointed out
the strictly non-Christian character of this value given to
chastity. There is little that is Christian about *Comus*.
Chastity has a value of its own, and gives powers in the
supernatural world by its own magic forces:

[23] *Comus*, ll. 706–36. In the *Times Literary Supplement* for January 19,
1922, Dr. Smart points out a curious source for this passage in Randolph.
But the feeling as well as the poetry have been put in by Milton.
[24] *Paradise Lost*, IV, 748–49.

'Tis chastity, my brother, chastity:
She that has that, is clad in complete steel,
And like a quiver'd nymph with arrows keen
May trace huge forests, and unharbour'd heaths,
Infamous hills, and sandy perilous wilds,
Where, through the sacred rays of chastity,
No savage fierce, bandit, or mountaineer
Will dare to soil her virgin purity;
Yea, there where very desolation dwells,
By grots, and caverns shagg'd with horrid shades,
She may pass on with unblench'd majesty,
Be it not done in pride, or in presumption.
Some say no evil thing that walks by night,
In fog, or fire, by lake, or moorish fen,
Blue meager hag, or stubborn unlaid ghost,
That breaks his magic chains at curfew time,
No goblin, or swart faery of the mine,
Hath hurtful power o'er true virginity.[25]

Curious as this passage is, the following, woven round a few sentences of Plato's *Phœdo*, is more important still, as showing the beginnings of some of Milton's later and most original conceptions:

So dear to heav'n is saintly chastity,
That when a soul is found sincerely so,
A thousand liveried angels lacky her,
Driving far off each thing of sin and guilt,
And in clear dream, and solemn vision,
Tell her of things that no gross ear can hear,
Till oft converse with heav'nly habitants
Begin to cast a beam on th' outward shape,
The unpolluted temple of the mind,
And turns it by degrees to the soul's essence,
Till all be made immortal: but when lust,
By unchaste looks, loose gestures, and foul talk,
But most by lewd and lavish act of sin,
Lets in defilement to the inward parts,
The soul grows clotted by contagion,

[25] *Comus*, ll. 420–37.

> Imbodies, and imbrutes, till she quite lose
> The divine property of her first being.
> Such are those thick and gloomy shadows damp
> Oft seen in charnel vaults, and sepulchres,
> Ling'ring and sitting by a new-made grave,
> As loath to leave the body that it loved,
> And linked itself by carnal sensualty
> To a degenerate and degraded state.[26]

As yet the poet is only playing with Platonic conceptions. But here is the idea that in certain circumstances the body becomes soul,

> And turns . . . by degrees to the soul's essence,
> Till all be made immortal. . . .

What is here an exception in favor of chastity will become later, in the poet's mind, the normal rule: body and spirit will become one, will all become immortal; all distinction between them will disappear. Here already the essential distinction is weakened: the body can become spirit through chastity; the soul materializes itself through lust. No impassable barrier separates the two orders. It is typical of Milton's mind and temperament that it is through meditation on sensual desire that he comes to the conception of the fundamental unity between body and soul, no doubt because of the intensity of desire he felt in himself, possessing him. We shall see how the passionate introspection which followed his unhappy marriage made the idea grow in him, and how one of the most important conceptions of his philosophy thus came inevitably from his temperament.

But this high appreciation of chastity was to remain with him to the end. The fall, in a certain sense, was always to be lust, " the deed of darkness." Only, when

[26] *Ibid.*, ll. 453–75.

Milton ceased to believe in a separate soul, the body became sacred, and its instincts also. His hymn to chastity became a hymn to wedded love, and the horror and degradation of sensuality came to attach only to illegitimate love.[27]

Milton's personal experience thus worked upon his early conceptions, but the philosophical working of his mind molded these first materials, which were only half-poetical fancies, in harmony with the poet's character. In *Lycidas*, in *Comus*, can be found already the essential principle of Milton's ethics:

> To triumph in victorious dance
> O'er sensual Folly, and Intemperance.[28]

Such is the lesson of *Comus:* the triumph of reason over passion, the inner freedom of man, secured by virtue:

> Love virtue, she alone is free.[29]

The chief passion to be conquered is sensuality, in *Comus* as later in *Paradise Lost*. The theme of *Comus* is no artificial choice; it corresponds to one of the deepest needs in the poet: the need to triumph over sensuality, which in itself implies sensuality. These two feelings, passion and the desire to conquer it, produced in the end two of the most important ideas of Milton's philosophy: first, the legitimacy of passion, since Milton felt it in himself, normal and powerful; then the necessity of keeping harmony between passion and reason, for passion is only legitimate when its ends are approved by the intellect. Thus we find in *Comus* the germs of Milton's conception of good. One phrase in the invective in *Lycidas* gives us similarly the aptest expression of his conception of evil.

[27] See below, pp. 155–59.    [28] *Comus*, ll. 974–75.    [29] *Ibid.*, l. 1019.

Never did Milton express more powerfully what evil was for him than in the celebrated words " blind mouths ": [30] " blind," that is to say, without intelligence; " mouths," that is to say, full of avidity; men whose passions only live in them, and whose reason is blind. For it is the domination of passion in man that is the source of all evil and creates slaves as well as tyrants.

These ideas were elaborated and systematized during the passionate struggles from 1641 to 1658, under the Long Parliament and Commonwealth; they were applied to politics and to theology, and became the center of an explanation of the Cosmos. But they existed from 1637 onwards, growing unavoidably from the deeper strata of Milton's character, amid the interplay of his fundamental tendencies — a passionate sensibility and pride of intellect.

When Milton returned from Italy, in August, 1639, he was ready to face the problems of public life. All his powers were about to be tested in furious action, in real experience — tested and broken. In his trials and failures, the Miltonic conception of life was definitely molded.

[30] Line 119.

## CHAPTER II

### THE MAN OF ACTION AND OF PASSION

#### I.   MILTON, MAN OF ACTION

THE religious situation in England had called Milton back from his travels. Two great parties divided the country.

The Puritan party had been gradually developing since the time of Elizabeth. At the Reformation, the Bible had spread through all classes, and a new culture had thus been acquired by part of the English people. Englishmen had learned that all men were equals before God and that every man had a right to think for himself, with the sole help of the Holy Word. They had acquired a passion for discussing religious questions, and a horror of the Roman Catholic Church, which was to them as the bondage of Egypt, from which they had just escaped. Their external appearance had hardened, but their inner life had grown tenfold. Family life had become dearer to them than before, and had taken on a sacred character: the head of the family was a priest who read and explained the Book. The expression " holy wedlock " came to have a real meaning. The great Puritan ideal was the domination of the soul over the flesh, the mastery of one's self, and, in public life, Justice inexorable.

Such were the best among the Puritans, and many of their traits are in Milton. But in inferior minds, and largely among the masses that came, more or less, to the party when it triumphed, these precious qualities changed into unloveable faults; hypocrisy, fanaticism, austerity, and narrow-mindedness spread only too rapidly among the Puritans.  Milton consequently soon parted company with the majority who wanted to set up in England a tyranny worse than the Episcopalian rule.  Cromwell had to govern against the Puritan majority and practically with the sole backing of his army, and it was owing to Cromwell that intolerance and fanaticism did not completely conquer the country.

The other party — the party of the King and of Laud — was, at bottom, though often unconsciously, turned toward the Catholic ideal.  For Laud, ecclesiastical discipline was the essence of religion, and the basis of the Church was the apostolic succession that took all bishops back to Peter.  The clergy was encouraged to remain celibate; a fixed ritual and complicated and pompous ceremonies (which reminded the Puritans of the Whore of Babylon) flourished in the Church.  The Anglican establishment was completely separated from the Protestants on the Continent, and had a tendency to become an insular and but slightly modified branch of the Church of Rome.  The Puritans, who read the Bible instead of receiving instructions from their superiors, and who hated surplices, were driven out of their churches.  Calvinism was openly combated, and Arminianism — the belief in free-will — encouraged.  Passive obedience to the King in all things was taught; Laud and his Church became a powerful instrument at the disposal of the Crown.

On the other hand, a spirit of toleration reigned in the King's party, both as to ideas and morals.  As long as you obeyed the King and the Bishop, you were free to think and to act as you pleased.  On many points, Milton was at one with these enemies of his party.  He also ended by rejecting predestination, and made of free-will the very center of his system.  He also fought for toleration, like Chillingworth, like Hales, like the Anglican liberals. He also inclined to think that people ought to be allowed to enjoy themselves on Sundays, instead of being driven into the churches.

But Milton rebelled first of all against the Episcopalian tyranny, and the majority of his countrymen went with him.  The fear of a return to Catholicism made Scotland and England rise against the Crown.  Charles I waged two ridiculous wars to force Bishops on Scotland, and succeeded only in wrecking his finances.  The English, who feared the King's plans of personal domination perhaps even more than his Church policy, took their opportunity and obliged Charles to call the Parliament of 1640, which was to become the Long Parliament.  This Parliament first attacked the political enemy, and in 1641, Strafford, abandoned by a master he had served not without genius, perished on the scaffold.  Then came the onslaught on the Bishops.  But the King, who had not been able to defend Strafford, fought for the Church, and found a party to fight for it.  In 1642, the Civil War began.  Before that, Milton had already published five pamphlets on the Parliamentary side; leaving alone for the time being the political question, he had joined with his whole soul in the struggle against the Bishops.

Milton's pamphlets must not be looked upon as literature, but as action.

The Puritan ideal was shaping into a generous vision that attracted invincibly the noblest minds of England.

Those that went farthest were awaiting the Fifth Monarchy, the triumphant coming of Christ on earth —
" shortly expected," as Milton says — and the foundation
of an earthly Kingdom of Christ, that was to last a thousand years and end with the world itself.[1]  Milton certainly held this view at the end of his life,[2] and possibly
from 1640, though we cannot tell precisely.  But the
Millenarians were only expressing in a more precise manner the sublime hope of the great Puritan party.  Who
could tell whether or when Christ would come?  Meanwhile, the English were going to set to work; they were
going to suppress tyranny, political and ecclesiastical;
they were going to reorganize their country on a rational
basis in harmony with the will of God.  The English were
the people chosen of God, who reveals Himself, says Milton, " first to his Englishmen." [3]  They were devoted to
His service, from 1643, by a Solemn League and Covenant; they were going to found on earth the visible Kingdom of God.

Milton fully shared that hope, that pride, that enthusiasm.  And besides his high idea of the English people,
he had his high idea of himself.  He believed himself
capable of real and decisive action; he felt in himself a
great power that was to weigh heavily in the destiny of
the Church and of the country.  His pride rose to sacrifice.  He gave up the aims which had so far filled his
life.  What mattered literature now?  The will of God
had to be carried out; the Earthly Paradise was to be
founded, and *Paradise Lost* or *Paradise Regained* could
wait.  That same ardor which had urged Milton towards
what had then seemed to him the highest aim of man,

[1] See Masson, III, 152.
[2] See below, pp. 196–97.
[3] *Areopagitica*, in *Prose Works*, II, 91.

poetry, now urged him to a greater and more real aim when such a one appeared to him. Behind Milton's literary ambition, there was a higher one: to be great. When greatness seemed to lie elsewhere than in literature, he sought for it elsewhere. There is therefore no contradiction, no inconsistency, between the two parts of Milton's life. They are not two; they come together from his character; they are one: the search for the glory of God, which is the same as the search for the glory of Milton. But Milton, in his pride, preferred the inner glory of his own approbation to the applause of the literary public.

It is fine and noble to sing the ways of God; it is finer and nobler to fulfil them. Therefore, in that earnest soul of Milton's, there was little hesitation. And he knew perfectly well — and this is all-important — that he was sacrificing himself. He knew well enough he was not made for that struggle; there was but little of the sort of glory he cared for to be acquired from it. He said it openly: " I should not choose this manner of writing, wherein knowing myself inferior to myself, led by the genial power of nature to another task, I have the use, as I may account, but of my left hand." [4] And again: " If I hunted after praise, by the ostentation of wit and learning, I should not write thus out of mine own season when I have neither yet completed to my mind the full circle of my private studies. . . ." [5] But the work was urgent and needed all hands. And Milton gave up his throne of poetical glory, and eagerly became an obscure workman in the service of God. " When God commands to take the trumpet, and blow a dolorous or a jarring

[4] *The Reason of Church Government*, in *Prose Works*, II, 477.
[5] *Ibid.*, II, 476.

blast, it lies not in man's will what he shall say, or what he shall conceal." [6]    He foresaw clearly, from the very start, the consequences of a failure to respond:

But this I foresee, that should the church be brought under heavy oppression, and God have given me ability the while to reason against that man that should be the author of so foul a deed; or should she, by blessing from above on the industry and courage of faithful men, change this her distracted estate into better days, without the least furtherance or contribution of those few talents, which God at that present had lent me; I foresee what stories I should hear within myself, all my life after, of discourage and reproach.    Timorous and ungrateful, the church of God is now again at the foot of her insulting enemies, and thou bewailest. What matters it for thee, or thy bewailing?    When time was, thou couldst not find a syllable of all that thou hast read, or studied, to utter in her behalf.    Yet ease and leisure was given thee for thy retired thoughts, out of the sweat of other men.    Thou hast the diligence, the parts, the language of a man, if a vain subject were to be adorned or beautified; but when the cause of God and his church was to be pleaded, for which purpose that tongue was given thee which thou hast, God listened if he could hear thy voice among his zealous servants, but thou wert dumb as a beast; from henceforward be that which thine own brutish silence hath made thee. Or else I should have heard on the other ear: Slothful, and ever to be set light by, the church hath now overcome her late distresses after the unwearied labors of many her true servants that stood up in her defence; thou also wouldst take upon thee to share amongst them of their joy: but wherefore thou?    Where canst thou shew any word or deed of thine which might have hastened her peace? Whatever thou dost now talk, or write, or look, is the alms of other men's active prudence and zeal.    Dare not now to say or do anything better than thy former sloth and infancy; or if thou darest, thou dost impudently to make a thrifty purchase of boldness to thyself, out of the painful merits of other men; what before was thy sin is now thy duty, to be abject and worthless.    These, and suchlike lessons as these, I know would have been my matins duly, and my even-song.[7]

[6] *Ibid.*, II, 474.
[7] *Ibid.*, II, 475–76.

Thus, in the fullest consciousness of what he was doing, Milton gave up the aims of his life. He trusted in God, and, so to speak, ran up a debit account against God's name, hoping that one day God would pay up. He trusted that once the work was done God would grant him life and force and courage to sing of the great triumph, and would allow him to be the trumpet of victory as he had been the trumpet of the fighting. In the middle of his pamphlets, he takes aside " the elegant and learned reader " and makes his private arrangements for the future — for " after the war." And surely such trust was as sublime as the pride that inspired it, as the spirit of sacrifice that made it necessary:

Neither do I think it shame to covenant with any knowing reader, that for some few years yet I may go on trust with him toward the payment of what I am now indebted, as being a work not to be raised from the heat of youth, or the vapors of wine; like that which flows at waste from the pen of some vulgar amourist, or the trencher fury of a rhyming parasite; nor to be obtained by the invocation of dame memory and her siren daughters, but by devout prayer to that eternal Spirit, who can enrich with all utterance and knowledge, and sends out his seraphim, with the hallowed fire of his altar, to touch and purify the lips of whom he pleases: to this must be added industrious and select reading, steady observation, insight into all seemly and generous arts and affairs; till which in some measure be compassed, at mine own peril and cost, I refuse not to sustain this expectation from as many as are not loth to hazard so much credulity upon the best pledges that I can give them. Although it nothing content me to have disclosed thus much beforehand, but that I trust hereby to make it manifest with what small willingness I endure to interrupt the pursuit of no less hopes than these, and leave a calm and pleasing solitariness, fed with cheerful and confident thoughts, to embark in a troubled sea of noises and hoarse disputes, put from beholding the bright countenance of truth in the quiet and still air of delightful studies, to come into the dim reflection of hollow an-

tiquities sold by the seeming bulk, and there be fain to club quotations with men whose learning and belief lies in marginal stuffings,
who, when they have, like good sumpters, laid ye down their horse-
loads of citations and fathers at your door, with a rhapsody of
who and who were bishops here or there, ye may take off their
packsaddles, their day's work is done, and episcopacy, as they
think, stoutly vindicated.  Let any gentle apprehension, that can
distinguish learned pains from unlearned drudgery imagine what
pleasure or profoundness can be in this, or what honor to deal
against such adversaries.  But were it the meanest under-service,
if God by his secretary conscience enjoin it, it were sad for me
if I should draw back. . . .[8]

Milton proved to be right; his trust in destiny was not
vain.  From that struggle which was so bitter to his heart,
he drew the very substance of *Paradise Lost*.  Without
knowing it, he prepared in his sacrifice the richest harvest
of his future glory.  His ideas shaped themselves in the
rough and painful contact with reality.  The greatness
of *Paradise Lost*, like that of the *Divina Commedia*, lies
in this, that neither of the two European epics was written by mere literary men, but by men who had fought
and suffered in the greatest enterprises of their time, and
through many years, and who put into their poetry the
result of their experience of life and struggle, problems
and hopes, passions and despair and ultimate certainty.
That is why *Paradise Lost*, like the *Divina Commedia*, is
a universal and human poem and not merely a work of
rhetoric.

Milton desired, above everything else, the coming of
the Kingdom of the Saints.  He wanted to help God; he
believed he was able to.  His pamphlets have been judged
as literature and found wanting.  That is a complete
error.  They are deeds, and must be judged as such.  He

[8] *Prose Works*, II, 481-82.

adapted his form to the end in view, which was to impress his contemporaries. Hence, first of all, the negligence of his style; he had to produce quickly, at the proper moment; the only quality he looked for was forcibleness. Hence also the personalities, the insolence, the frequent grossness and vulgarity of his attacks: such were the weapons which left a mark on the adversary, even more than argument or erudition, highly valued as these were. Hence again his pedantry: the opponent had to be crushed under texts and authorities, and proved wrong before a tribunal which admitted that sort of proof. Milton believed in the efficacy of his efforts in this field; his contemporaries did also, and therefore he was right: he produced much of the impression he wanted to produce. In after life, he looked back upon his pamphleteering career as a success. *Eikonoklastes* and the *Defences* gave him fame. Much of his work was done at the request of the best political heads of his time. It is not therefore for us to decide that he lost his pains as a man of action. Such was not the opinion of his century, which surely knew best.

Besides, this character of being a deed, an action in the world of real fact, is found in *Paradise Lost*. After the fall of all his hopes and his country's hopes, the problem was, no longer for an ignorant public, but for the very conscience of mankind itself, not to give way to despair, but to find out the causes of the failure, and to discern therein reasons for eternal hope. Between 1642 and 1657, Milton learned that reality only too often refuses to adapt itself to abstract ideas; he learned what stuff human nature was made of. The great question and the great answer became clear to him. It was Milton's turn of

mind to reason from one particular case to the general.
Just as in the divorce pamphlets he does not mention his
own case, so in *Paradise Lost* he does not speak of the
failure of the Commonwealth; yet it was his marriage
that made him write the treatises on divorce, and it was
the ruin of the Commonwealth that set the problem for
*Paradise Lost.* It was still the same old Milton that had
written a violent pamphlet *pro populo Anglicano. Paradise Lost* is only a sublime pamphlet for the defence of
God:

To justify the ways of God to men.

I shall now examine the pamphlets solely from the
point of view of the formation of Milton's ideas, in order
to find in them evidences of his philosophical tenets and
also of the state of his feelings.

The study of the pamphlets falls naturally into several
periods. First comes the period of ecclesiastical controversy, 1641–1642, which produced *Of Reformation in
England, Of Prelatical Episcopacy, Animadversions on the
Remonstrant's Defence, The Reason of Church Government urged against Prelacy,* and *An Apology for Smectymnuus.* During this period Milton is with the Presbyterians. Then comes the group of treatises on divorce,
from 1643 to 1645: *The Doctrine and Discipline of Divorce, Tetrachordon, Colasterion.* Here Milton parts
from the Presbyterians and joins the Independents.
During this same period, in 1644, he publishes two works
which have remained the most interesting in his prose for
the public in general: *Areopagitica* and *On Education.*
From 1649 to 1655 comes the struggle over the King's
trial and execution. Milton publishes in 1649 *The Tenure
of Kings and Magistrates* and *Eikonoklastes.* Then come

the three *Defences* in Latin: *Defensio pro populo Angli-cano* (1651), *Defensio secunda* (1654), and *Defensio pro se* (1655).  Lastly, from 1658 to 1660, Milton, conscious of the failure of his cause, makes a last effort, first against the prelates again in *A Treatise of Civil Power in Ec-clesiastical Causes* and *Considerations on the likeliest Means to remove Hirelings out of the Church,* and then against monarchy in *The Ready and Easy Way to estab-lish a Free Commonwealth.*  This is the last of Milton's pamphlets; the cause is lost; action has become useless; Milton goes back to literature.  In 1673, just before his death, he gives a last word of advice to his contemporaries about their religious quarrels, and in a few pages speaks *Of True Religion, Heresy, Schism, Toleration, and what best Means may be used against the Growth of Popery.*

This division of the pamphlets is not a mere list of titles; it makes up, could we but discover it, the deeply human tale of Milton's hopes and disillusions.  A noble heart and a high intelligence were thrown into the struggle in 1641; in 1660, there came out of the fighting a bitterly pessimistic man, conscious of complete failure.

During the struggle against the Bishops, Milton was young, full of ardor and of pride, and did not for one moment doubt of himself or of his cause.  His marriage brought him the first great shock of his life.  At one blow, he saw one of his noblest ideals shattered, and ap-parently through his own fault:  he had allowed passion to blind him.  He knew now that there were evil powers in him; he knew also that his party would help him not one bit in his struggle for his own inner liberty.  But his youth and his pride rebelled.  He resolved to free himself

and so to free the world. The *Areopagitica* and *On Education* are two hymns of certainty, of faith in the final
triumph of liberty, in the divine mission of England, in
the powers of the human mind. Then Milton grew
calmer. His home life was established on a compromise;
he lived through the civil wars. Then again he rushed
into battle; Cromwell and the Saints had come; the Kingdom was coming. Milton struggled against political evil,
and realized, with disgust and indignation, that passion
and self-interest rule in the world, and that the corrupt
individual could not but corrupt society. His conception
of universal evil, the triumph of passion, settled in his
mind. Soon he saw that evil was in his own party. Cromwell himself was not satisfactory, and at Cromwell's
death, the small number of the Saints was all too insufficient against the upheaval of blind popular passion. All
of his hopes had failed. The problem of evil had appeared to him in all the bitterness and despair of personal
failure and of vain suffering and vain sacrifice.

## II.   The Struggle Against the Bishops

In January, 1641, Bishop Hall published his *Humble
Remonstrance* against the revolutionary projects of the
Parliament in the matter of ecclesiastical discipline. The
famous pamphlet against the Bishops signed " Smectymnuus," came out in March of the same year. Thomas
Young, who had been preceptor to Milton, was the chief
author. Milton was still in connection with him, and
Masson thinks that the poet even collaborated on the
pamphlet.[9] However this may be, in June, 1641, Milton

---

[9] II, 219, 221, 238, 260.  Masson's unruly imagination, however, frequently makes him an untrustworthy guide.

published anonymously his first contribution to the struggle: *Of Reformation in England and the Causes that hitherto have hindered it.*

The interest of this work is but small if the subject-matter alone is considered. The general idea, which is endlessly repeated in Milton's pamplets, is that any sort of true reformation has been made impossible in England by the ambition and the caste-selfishness of the Bishops. Milton goes through the history of the Church — in a very unmethodical fashion — from the time of Henry VIII and, in a way, from early Christian times, looking for proofs. No properly equipped historian seems to have tackled the enormous quantity of historical matter in Milton's pamphlets, and I dare say the work is not worth doing. But from our point of view — the study of Milton's ideas in 1641 — *Of Reformation in England* is interesting.

Milton attaches himself from the first to the religious aspects of the quarrels of the time. Politics proper interest him less. This will be a permanent trait: even when he comes to pass judgment on his hero Cromwell, he will consider first his religious undertakings, and though approving of his general policy, will condemn him because of his religious measures.

Sir, — Amidst those deep and retired thoughts, which, with every man Christianly instructed, ought to be most frequent of God, and of his miraculous ways and works amongst men, and of our religion and works, to be performed to him; after the story of our Saviour Christ, suffering to the lowest bent of weakness in the flesh, and presently triumphing to the highest pitch of glory in the spirit, which drew up his body also; till we in both be united to him in the revelation of his kingdom, I do not know of anything more worthy to take up the whole passion of pity on the one side, and joy on the other, than to consider first the foul and sudden corruption, and then, after many a tedious age, the long deferred, but much more wonderful and happy reformation of the church in these latter days.[10]

This is a starting-point of Milton's thought; we shall see that at his latter end he did not think the Reformation worth mentioning in *Paradise Lost*.[11] In his stand against the clergy, Milton is the champion of a very exalted conception of God. We find here already one of the chief tendencies of his philosophy, one that will lead him to Arianism, and further: the notion that God is boundless, without form, and incomprehensible. He charges the Church with having desired too precise a God; in this he sees the origin of all superstition:

. . . as if they could make God earthly and fleshly, because they could not make themselves heavenly and spiritual; they began to draw down all the divine intercourse betwixt God and the soul, yea, the very shape of God himself, into an exterior and bodily form, urgently pretending a necessity and obligement of joining the body in a formal reverence and worship circumscribed; they hallowed it, they fumed up, they sprinkled it, they bedecked it, not in robes of pure innocency, but of pure linen, with other deformed and fantastic dresses, in palls and mitres, gold, and gewgaws fetched from Aaron's old wardrobe or the flamins vestry. . . .[12]

The idea also appears for the first time that England is a nation specially chosen of God, and that England must prove worthy of that choice:

The pleasing pursuit of these thoughts hath oftimes led me into a serious question and debatement with myself, how it should come to pass that England (having had this grace and honour from God, to be the first that should set up a standard for the recovery of lost truth, and blow the first evangelic trumpet to the nations, holding up, as from a hill, the new lamp of saving light to all Christendom) should now be last and most unsettled in the enjoy-

[10] *Prose Works*, II, 364.    [11] See below, p. 196.    [12] *Prose Works*, II, 365.

ment of that peace, whereof she taught the way to others; although indeed our Wickliffe's preaching, at which all the succeeding reformers more effectually lighted their tapers, was to his countrymen but a short blaze, soon damped and stifled by the pope and prelates for six or seven kings' reigns; yet methinks the precedency which God gave this island, to be first restorer of buried truth, should have been followed with more happy success, and sooner attained perfection. . . .[13]

Already, too, Milton feels scant respect for the early Christians and the Fathers:

How little therefore those ancient times make for modern bishops hath been plainly discoursed; but let them make for them as much as they will, yet why we ought not to stand to their arbitrament, shall now appear by a threefold corruption which will be found upon them. 1. The best times were spreadingly infected. 2. The best men of those times foully tainted. 3. The best writings of those men dangerously adulterated. These positions are to be made good out of those times witnessing of themselves.[14]

The part played in the State by the clergy is compared to that of a wen on a man's head:

Upon a time the body summoned all the members to meet in the guild, for the common good: (as Æsop's chronicles aver many stranger accidents:) the head by right takes the first seat, and next to it a huge and monstrous wen, little less than the head itself, growing to it by a narrower excrescency. The members, amazed, began to ask one another what he was that took place next their chief? None could resolve. Whereat the wen, though unwieldy, with much ado gets up, and bespeaks the assembly to this purpose: "That as in place he was second to the head, so by due of merit; that he was to it an ornament, and strength, and of special near relation; and that if the head should fail, none were fitter than himself to step into his place: therefore he thought it for the honour of the body, that such dignities and rich endowments should be decreed him, as did adorn and set out the noblest members." To

---

[13] *Ibid.*, II, 368.
[14] *Ibid.*, II, 378. See below, pp. 264 ff. I shall no longer point out in this Part I the innumerable proofs of Milton's contempt for the early church.

this was answered, that it should be consulted. Then was a wise and learned philosopher sent for, that knew all the charters, laws, and tenures of the body. On him it is imposed by all, as chief committee, to examine, and discuss the claim and petition of right put in by the wen; who soon perceiving the matter, and wondering at the boldness of such a swoln tumour, "Wilt thou," quoth he, " that art but a bottle of vicious and hardened excrements, contend with the lawful and freeborn members, whose certain number is set by ancient and unrepealable statute? Head thou art none, though thou receive this huge substance from it. What office bearest thou? what good canst thou shew by thee done to the commonweal?" The wen, not easily dashed, replies that his office was his glory; for so oft as the soul would retire out of the head from over the steaming vapours of the lower parts to divine contemplation, with him she found the purest and quietest retreat, as being most remote from soil and disturbance. "Lourdan," quoth the philosopher, " thy folly is as great as thy filth: know that all the faculties of the soul are confined of old to their several vessels and ventricles, from which they cannot part without dissolution of the whole body; and that thou containest no good thing in thee, but a heap of hard and loathsome uncleanness, and art to the head a foul disfigurement and burden, when I have cut thee off, and opened thee, as by the help of these implements I will do, all men shall see." [15]

Violent as he is against the Bishops, Milton as yet finds nothing wrong with the monarchic constitution of England:

There is no civil government that hath been known, no, not the Spartan, not the Roman, though both for this respect so much praised by the wise Polybius, more divinely and harmoniously tuned, more equally balanced as it were by the hand and scale of justice, than is the commonwealth of England; where, under a free and untutored monarch, the noblest, worthiest, and most prudent men, with full approbation and suffrage of the people, have in their power the supreme and final determination of highest affairs. [16]

The pamphlet ends with a prayer and a curse in the grandest Miltonic style. In the final triumph of the

15 *Ibid.*, II, 398.          16 *Ibid.*, II, 408.

Saints, the poet figures as the bard who will sing the victorious anthem. The prayer is interesting also as a proof that Milton already held the theory that God intervenes at every moment in history, and always as a liberator. Another point to be noted: God is still the orthodox Trinity:

> Thou, therefore, that sittest in light and glory unapproachable, parent of angels and men! next, thee I implore, omnipotent King, Redeemer of that lost remnant whose nature thou didst assume, ineffable and everlasting Love! and thou, the third subsistence of divine infinitude, illumining Spirit, the joy and solace of created things! one Tripersonal godhead! look upon this thy poor and almost spent and expiring church, leave her not thus a prey to these importunate wolves, that wait and think long till they devour thy tender flock; these wild boars that have broke into thy vineyard, and left the print of their polluting hoofs on the souls of thy servants. O let them not bring about their damned designs, that stand now at the entrance of the bottomless pit, expecting the watchword to open and let out those dreadful locusts and scorpions, to reinvolve us in that pitchy cloud of infernal darkness, where we shall never more see the sun of thy truth again, never hope for the cheerful dawn, never more hear the bird of morning sing. Be moved with pity at the afflicted state of this our shaken monarchy, that now lies labouring under her throes, and struggling against the grudges of more dreaded calamities.
>
> O thou, that, after the impetuous rage of five bloody inundations, and the succeeding sword of intestine war, soaking the land in her own gore, didst pity the sad and ceaseless revolution of our swift and thick-coming sorrows; when we were quite breathless, of thy free grace didst motion peace, and terms of covenant with us; and having first well nigh freed us from antichristian thraldom, didst build up this Britannic empire to a glorious and enviable height, with all her daughter-islands about her; stay us in this felicity, let not the obstinacy of our half-obedience and will-worship bring forth that viper of sedition, that for these fourscore years hath been breeding to eat through the entrails of our peace; but let her cast her abortive spawn without the danger of this travailing and throbbing kingdom: that we may still remember in our solemn thanksgivings,

how for us, the northern ocean even to the frozen Thule was scattered with the proud shipwrecks of the Spanish armada, and the very maw of hell ransacked, and made to give up her concealed destruction, ere she could vent it in that horrible and damned blast.

O how much more glorious will those former deliverances appear, when we shall know them not only to have saved us from greatest miseries past, but to have reserved us for greatest happiness to come! Hitherto thou hast but freed us, and that not fully, from the unjust and tyrannous claim of thy foes; now unite us entirely, and appropriate us to thyself, tie us everlastingly in willing homage to the prerogative of thy eternal throne.

And now we know, O thou our most certain hope and defence, that thine enemies have been consulting all the sorceries of the great whore, and have joined their plots with that sad intelligencing tyrant that mischiefs the world with his mines of Ophir, and lies thirsting to revenge his naval ruins that have larded our seas: but let them all take counsel together, and let it come to nought; let them decree, and do thou cancel it; let them gather themselves, and be scattered; let them embattle themselves, and be broken; let them embattle, and be broken, for thou art with us.

Then, amidst the hymns and hallelujahs of saints, some one may perhaps be heard offering at high strains in new and lofty measure to sing and celebrate thy divine mercies and marvellous judgments in this land throughout all ages; whereby this great and warlike nation, instructed and inured to the fervent and continual practice of truth and righteousness, and casting far from her the rags of her whole vices, may press on hard to that high and happy emulation to be found the soberest, wisest, and most Christian people at that day, when thou, the eternal and shortly expected King, shalt open the clouds to judge the several kingdoms of the world, and distributing national honours and rewards to religious and just commonwealths, shall put an end to all earthly tyrannies, proclaiming thy universal and mild monarchy through heaven and earth. . . .

But they contrary, that by the impairing and diminution of the true faith, the distresses and servitude of their country, aspire to high dignity, rule, and promotion here, after a shameful end in this life, (which God grant them,) shall be thrown down eternally into the darkest and deepest gulf of hell, where, under the despiteful control, the trample and spurn of all the other damned, that in the anguish of their torture, shall have no other ease than to exercise a raving and bestial tyranny over them as their slaves and negroes, they shall remain in that plight for ever, the basest, the lowermost, the most dejected, most underfoot, and downtrodden vassals of perdition.[17]

Here is no longer the cold and artistic man of letters, the author of *Comus;* there is passion here; Milton has thrown himself wholly into the struggle, with his whole pride and power of hatred and vision, in the service of a great ideal. He is certain of victory: victory on Earth first, and soon after, the eternal reign of Christ, " shortly expected."

In that day of triumph, Milton expected to reassume his natural rôle and become again a poet. And he did again become a poet, but it was in the failure and ruin of all his ambitions, and not as he had dreamt. But the generous dream reveals the unity of his soul and life, the inevitable relationship between his political career and his literary aims, the part he wished to play when entering the struggle. We see here also the deeper source of his epic poetry: it was to be the song of triumph. In defeat, the source of inspiration will be the same: *Paradise Lost* will be the song of hope and comfort to the vanquished. From 1641, Milton understood whence his poem was to come to him — from the very struggle for which he seemed to be giving it up.

Milton's second pamphlet, published in July, 1641, was an answer to a pamphlet by Archbishop Usher, and has but little interest. It is short, and the full title is sufficient to give an idea of its subject-matter, the form calling for no remarks: *Of Prelatical Episcopacy, and whether it may be deduced from the apostolical times, by virtue of*

[17] *Ibid.*, II, 417-19.

*those testimonies which are alleged to that purpose in*
*some late Treatises, one whereof goes under the name of*
*James, Archbishop of Armagh.*  Milton naturally comes
to the conclusion that it may not, and shows a fine contempt for the Fathers of the Church and any authorities
generally that may seem to be against him.

Meanwhile, Bishop Hall had replied to " Smectym-
nuus " in a defence of his *Humble Remonstrance.*
Thereupon Milton retorted in July, 1641, with his
*Animadversions upon the Remonstrant's Defence against*
*Smectymnuus.*  In his preface, Milton apologizes for the
violence of his language; that is, however, the only inter-
est we can discover in the pamphlet, which takes up the
Bishop's arguments one by one, in this form:

Remonst.  It is God that makes the bishop, the king that gives
the bishopric: what can you say to this?
Answ.  What you shall not long stay for: we say it is God that
makes a bishop, and the devil that makes him take a prelatical
bishopric; as for the king's gift, regal bounty may be excusable in
giving, where the bishop's covetousness is damnable in taking.
Remonst.  Many eminent divines of the churches abroad have
earnestly wished themselves in our condition.
Answ.  I cannot blame them, they were not only eminent but
supereminent divines, and for stomach much like to Pompey the
Great, that could endure no equal. . . .
Remonst.  No one clergy in the whole Christian world yields
so many eminent scholars, learned preachers, grave, holy, and accomplished divines, as this church of England doth at this day.
Answ.  Ha, ha, ha! [18]

A passage in section V shows that Milton felt no more
respect for modern than for ancient authorities.  " You
think," he says, " you are fairly quit of this proof, because
Calvin interprets it for you, as if we could be put off with

[18] *Ibid.*, III, 85, 87.

Calvin's name, unless we be convinced with Calvin's reason! " [19]  But Spenser is quoted at length and considered as of much weight.[20]

In the beginning of 1642, Milton published a fourth pamphlet in which he explains more methodically and more soberly than in the previous ones his arguments against the Bishops: *The Reason of Church Government urged against Prelaty.* This short treatise and the following *Apology for Smectymnuus* are among the most interesting prose works of Milton, not through their main subject-matter, which is the usual polemic stuff, but through the wealth of information they contain on their author.

Milton is at this time a whole-hearted Presbyterian. In the preface to the *Reason of Church Government,* he gives us warning thus:

> . . . I shall . . . hope through the mercy and grace of Christ, the head and husband of his church, that England shortly is to belong, neither to see patriarchal nor see prelatical, but to the faithful feeding and disciplining of that ministerial order, which the blessed apostles constituted throughout the churches; and this, I shall essay to prove, can be no other than that of presbyters and deacons.[21]

Milton again brings forward an idea he has already harped upon, and uses one of his favorite methods of attack. What he combats, he says, has been established by the devil; later on, as we shall see, the devil will be the first king; here he appears as the first bishop. Some prelate having said that Adam was the first prelate, Milton muses thus:

> To which assertion, had I heard it, because I see they are so insatiable of antiquity, I should have gladly assented, and confessed

19 *Ibid.,* III, 73.     20 *Ibid.,* III, 84-85.     21 *Ibid.,* II, 440-41.

them yet more ancient: for Lucifer, before Adam, was the first prelate angel. . . .[22]

Although a Presbyterian, Milton is already an apostle of toleration; his heart leans towards " sects and schisms," and he finds in their favor an ingenious and artistic argument:

> . . . it best beseems our Christian courage to think they are but as the throes and pangs that go before the birth of reformation, and that the work itself is now in doing. For if we look but on the nature of elemental and mixed things, we know they cannot suffer any change of one kind or quality into another, without the struggle of contrarieties. And in things artificial, seldom any elegance is wrought without a superfluous waste and refuse in the transaction. No marble statue can be politely carved, no fair edifice built, without almost as much rubbish and sweeping.[23]

However, in 1642, Milton still admits of excommunication, although he insists on the necessity of the greatest precautions before coming to it.[24]   In conclusion, he declares that the prelates are the best instruments of tyranny. The Anglican Church has used the Gospel as a weapon against liberty, and as a means to satiate avarice and ignoble ambition:

> But when they have glutted their ungrateful bodies, at least, if it be possible that those open sepulchres should ever be glutted, and when they have stuffed their idolish temples with the wasteful pillage of your estates, will they yet have any compassion upon you, and that poor pittance which they have left you; will they be but so good to you as that ravisher was to his sister, when he had used her at his pleasure; will they but only hate ye, and so turn ye loose. No, they will not, lords and commons, they will not favour ye so much. . . .[25]   That if it should happen that a tyrant (God turn such a scourge from us to our enemies) should come to grasp the sceptre, here were his spearmen and his lances, here were his

---

[22] *Ibid.*, II, 450.
[23] *Ibid.*, II, 469.
[24] *Ibid.*, II, 497-98.
[25] The allusion is to II Samuel 13:18.

firelocks ready, he should need no other pretorian band nor pensionary than these, if they could once with their perfidious preachments awe the people.[26]

## And again:

. . . prelaty, whom the tyrant custom begot, a natural tyrant in religion, and in state the agent and minister of tyranny, seems to have had this fatal gift in her nativity, like another Midas, that whatsoever she should touch or come near either in ecclesial or political government, it should turn, not to gold, though she for her part could wish it, but to the dross and scum of slavery, breeding and settling both in the bodies and the souls. . . .[27]

## Here is Milton's opinion of the Universities, ten years after he had left Cambridge:

Which makes me wonder much that many of the gentry, studious men as I hear, should engage themselves to write and speak publicly in her defence; but that I believe their honest and ingenuous natures coming to the universities to store themselves with good and solid learning, and there unfortunately fed with nothing else but the scragged and thorny lectures of monkish and miserable sophistry, were sent home again with such a scholastic bur in their throats, as hath stopped and hindered all true and generous philosophy from entering, cracked their voices for ever with metaphysical gargarisms. . . .[28]

## And here is a sample of Milton's forcible rhetoric:

. . . outrageous desire of filthy lucre. Which the prelates make so little conscience of, that they are ready to fight, and if it lay in their power, to massacre all good Christians under the names of horrible schismatics, for only finding fault with their temporal dignities, their unconscionable wealth and revenues, their cruel authority over their brethren, that labour in the word, while they snore in their luxurious excess. . . . More like that huge dragon of Egypt, breathing out waste and desolation to the land, unless he were daily fattened with a virgin's blood . . . this mighty sail-winged monster, that menaces to swallow up the land unless her bottomless gorge may be satisfied with the blood of the king's daughter, the

[26] *Prose Works*, II, 501-02.    [27] *Ibid.*, II, 503.    [28] *Ibid.*, II, 504.

church; and may, as she was wont, fill her dark and infamous den
with the bones of the saints.[29]

But Milton is still loyal to the King, as were most Englishmen at the time.  The King, as well as England, is to
be liberated from the prelates' yoke.  Let us notice by
the way that the subject of *Samson* has already caught
Milton's attention:

> I cannot better liken the state and person of a king than to that
> mighty Nazarite Samson; who being disciplined from his birth in
> the precepts and the practice of temperance and sobriety, without
> the strong drink of injurious and excessive desires, grows up to a
> noble strength and perfection with those his illustrious and sunny
> locks, the laws, waving and curling about his godlike shoulders.
> And while he keeps them about him undiminished and unshorn, he
> may with the jawbone of an ass, that is, with the word of his
> meanest officer,[30] suppress and put to confusion thousands of those
> that rise against his just power. But laying down his head among
> the strumpet flatteries of prelates, while he sleeps and thinks no
> harm, they wickedly shaving off all those bright and weighty tresses
> of his law, and just prerogatives, which were his ornament and
> strength, deliver him over to indirect and violent counsels, which,
> as those Philistines, put out the fair and far-sighted eyes of his
> natural discerning, and make him grind in the prisonhouse of their
> sinister ends and practices upon him: till he, knowing this prelatical
> rasor to have bereft him of his wonted might, nourish again his
> puissant hair, the golden beams of law and right; and they sternly
> shook, thunder with ruin upon the heads of those his evil counsellors,
> but not without great affliction to himself.[31]

Early in 1642, Bishop Hall and his son attacked Milton
(on the occasion of his *Animadversions*) in a most scurri-
lous and violent pamphlet.  Milton answered in April with
his *Apology for Smectymnuus*, and thus we owe to the
Halls some of the most beautiful pages of Milton's prose.
These are so well known and so easily accessible — unlike

[29] *Ibid.*, II, 505.
[30] Milton's sense of humor seems somewhat in abeyance here, as often
happens to him.                    [31] *Prose Works*, II, 506.

many others in the pamphlets — that I shall only repro-
duce here a few passages which will be useful to us as
landmarks in the evolution of Milton's ideas.

First let us hear him on love and chastity:

. . . and above them all, [I] preferred the two famous renowners
of Beatrice and Laura, who never write but honour of them to
whom they devote their verse, displaying sublime and pure thoughts,
without transgression. . . .

Next, (for hear me out now, readers,) that I may tell ye whither
my younger feet wandered; I betook me among those lofty fables
and romances, which recount in solemn cantos the deeds of knight-
hood founded by our victorious kings, and from hence had in
renown over all Christendom.   There I read it in the oath of
every knight, that he should defend to the expense of his best
blood, or of his life, if it so befell him, the honour and chastity of
virgin or matron. . . . So that even these books, which to many
others have been the fuel of wantonness and loose living, I cannot
think how, unless by divine indulgence, proved to me so many
incitements, as you have heard, to the love and steadfast observation
of that virtue which abhors the society of bordelloes.

Thus, from the laureat fraternity of poets, riper years and the
ceaseless round of study and reading led me to the shady spaces
of philosophy; but chiefly to the divine volumes of Plato, and his
equal Xenophon: where, if I should tell ye what I learnt of
chastity and love, I mean that which is truly so, whose charming
cup is only virtue, which she bears in her hand to those who are
worthy; (the rest are cheated with a thick intoxicating potion, which
a certain sorceress, the abuser of love's name, carries about;) and
how the first and chiefest office of love begins and ends in the soul,
producing those happy twins of her divine generation, knowledge and
virtue.   With such abstracted sublimities as these, it might be
worth your listening, readers, as I may one day hope to have ye in
a still time, when there shall be no chiding; not in these noises, the
adversary, as ye know, barking at the door, or searching for me at
the bordelloes, where it may be he has lost himself and raps up
without pity the sage and rheumatic old prelates, . . . to inquire
for such a one. . . .

. . . But having had the doctrine of holy scripture unfolding
those chaste and high mysteries, with timeliest care infused, that

" the body is for the Lord, and the Lord for the body "; thus also
I argued to myself, that if unchastity in a woman, whom St.
Paul terms the glory of man, be such a scandal and dishonour,
then certainly in a man, who is both the image and glory of God,
it must, though commonly not so thought, be much more deflouring
and dishonourable; in that he sins both against his own body, which
is the perfecter sex, and his own glory, which is in the woman; and,
that which is worst, against the image and glory of God, which is
in himself. Nor did I slumber over that place expressing such high
rewards of ever accompanying the Lamb, with those celestial songs
to others inapprehensible, but not to those who were not defiled
with women, which doubtless means fornication; for marriage must
not be called a defilement.[32]

" *For marriage must not be called a defilement* ": this is
the corrective to *Comus*, to the hymn to total chastity;
and also the distinction, inherited from the Elizabethans,
which will play so great a part in Milton's life and
thought, between love commanded and love forbidden,
love and lust; and lust is counted already as the lowest degradation of men; it will later become *the fall*,
essentially.

" *The body is for the Lord, and the Lord for the body.*"
Here are the first germs of the fundamental doctrine of
*Paradise Lost* and of the *Treatise of Christian Doctrine*,
that the body is not only *from*, but *of* the Lord: the body
is a part of God, matter is a part of the Divinity. The
passage shows us how Milton was driven to pantheism by
his pride and chastity: his body was holy in his eyes;
his body will be of the substance of God; matter will be
of the substance of God.

Here is now Milton's good opinion of the lower classes,
a good opinion that was destined not to survive the
Restoration:

[32] *Ibid.*, III, 117–22.

Which of these three will the confuter affirm to exceed the capacity of a plain artisan?  And what reason then is there left, wherefore he should be denied his voice in the election of his minister, as not thought a competent discerner?

It is but arrogance therefore, and the pride of a metaphysical fume, to think that " the mutinous rabble " (for so he calls the Christian congregation) " would be so mistaken in a clerk of the university," that were to be their minister.  I doubt me those clerks, that think so, are more mistaken in themselves; and what with truanting and debauchery, what with false grounds and the weakness of natural faculties in many of them, (it being a maxim in some men to send the simplest of their sons thither,) perhaps there would be found among them as many unsolid and corrupted judgments, both in doctrine and life, as in any other two corporations of like bigness. This is undoubted, that if any carpenter, smith, or weaver were such a bungler in his trade, as the greater number of them are in their profession, he would starve for any custom.[33]

The pamphlets against the Bishops show us Milton at the starting-point of his thinking: he is still the orthodox believer who prays to the Trinity; he is still a Presbyterian and a royalist.

One passion is dominant in him, the passion for liberty, and at bottom that is only the pride of his individual development.  But this passion, expressed here by the violence of his polemics, will draw him out of all bonds — out of dogmatic orthodoxy, which will be in contradiction with his high idea of himself and of human nature; out of Presbyterianism, too narrow for him, as it holds its adherents to a creed and a discipline; out of royalism also, since in the next few years this will prove incompatible with the spirit of liberty.

We must note also that Milton, in his first pamphlets, has no doctrine to defend.  He is incessantly attacking. It is only through chance allusions that we discover what

[33] *Ibid.,* III, 154–55.

he believes, or what he thinks he believes. For, in truth, he has not, as yet, examined his beliefs. He has identified himself with a cause without looking into it very closely. What he is really fighting for is not Presbyterianism, which he is going to abandon, but his own personality, his right to think as he likes.

The personal character of these polemics of Milton is not therefore only a matter of form; it is in the substance of his work. It is Milton's egotism which happens to be, for the time, the champion of the Presbyterians. But a crisis is coming which will show him that the Presbyterians also do not acknowledge his right to think and live as he likes. Then he will forsake the party, unhesitatingly, without even meaning to, or doing it intentionally. He will think at first of converting the party to his views. But he will soon have to give that up. His pamphlets in favor of divorce will be personal in substance, even more than his pamphlets in favor of the Presbyterians. Indeed, it was by a mere coincidence that in these he found himself at one with a party; and the illusion was short-lived.

But Milton's egotism will not remain limited to itself. Because of his peculiar pride, his egotism will always need to be identified with something great. We have just seen him identifying himself with a cause, and nobly vindicating his character so that the cause may not be spotted. But once that cause is given up as, after all, narrow and mediocre, Milton will not consent to be only Milton. He will put himself into the service of the Republic, and, last of all and most of all, into the service of God. And Milton will end by identifying himself with God, being the spokesman and indeed a very part of the Divinity.

But he will then confer the same privilege on all men

worthy of it.  His unconscious egotism is never narrow;
it would otherwise appear as mere selfishness, which Milton's high moral conscience — and Milton's pride —
would not bear.  Thus the philosophical idea of the unity
of man and God will grow gradually in Milton out of
his pride and high ambition.  Disappointed in all parties
on Earth, he will belong only to God's party.  But then
he will be a part of God, a temple of the Spirit.  This
ultimate ambition, which will lead him to write *Paradise
Lost* and the *Treatise of Christian Doctrine,* is only a
development of the ambition which caused him to take
up his pen in 1641 in the attack against Episcopacy.

### III.  The First Shock: Private Life and The Conception of The Fall

Milton was about to enter upon a crisis which taught
him two things: the power of passion in himself, and the
legitimacy of passion.  And these two conceptions, deeply
driven into his soul by suffering, were destined to become
two of his most fundamental ideas.

Milton married Mary Powell.[34]  It would seem that he
must have been carried away solely by physical passion,
since no other adequate cause has ever been brought forward. Whatever historians may discover, I refuse to believe that Milton ever married in order to facilitate a mere
money arrangement.  He avowedly was not attracted
either by Mary Powell's brilliancy of wit or gentleness of
temper; there are some texts in the divorce pamphlets
against that.

It would also seem that the marriage remained a nom-

---

[34] The date usually given is 1643, but that is not by any means certain,
or even likely.

inal one and that Milton's wife shortly left him, after having refused herself to him.[35]   This seems to me to be indubitable, in view of a few passages in the pamphlets, one of which is as follows:

The soberest and best governed men are least practised in these affairs; and who knows not that the bashful muteness of a virgin may ofttimes hide all the unliveliness and natural sloth which is really unfit for conversation?   Nor is there that freedom of access granted or presumed, as may suffice to a perfect discerning till too late; and where any indisposition is suspected, what more usual than the persuasion of friends, that acquaintance, as it increases, will amend all?   And lastly, it is not strange though many, who have spent their youth chastely, are in some things not so quick-sighted, while they haste too eagerly to light the nuptial torch; nor is it, therefore, that for a modest error a man should forfeit so great a happiness, and no charitable means to release him, since they who have lived most loosely, by reason of their bold accustom-ing, prove most successful in their matches, because their wild af-fections unsettling at will, have been as so many divorces to teach them experience.   Whenas the sober man honouring the appearance of modesty, and hoping well of every social virtue under that veil, may easily chance to meet, if not with a body impenetrable, yet often with a mind to all other due conversation inaccessible, and to all the more estimable and superior purposes of matrimony useless and almost lifeless. . . .[36]

This amounts to a confession of our first point: that Milton married, or, as he puts it, " hasted too eagerly to light the nuptial torch " without knowing anything of his future wife but her external appearance.   As to the sec-ond point, is there anything more piteously humorous, and more grotesquely convincing, than that a man, im-mediately after his marriage, should harp upon the means of preserving chastity, at this moment of all moments, for

[35] Mark Pattison (*Milton*, New York, 1880, p. 55) and Sir Walter Raleigh (*Milton*, New York, 1900, p. 48) both support this hypothesis.
[36] *Prose Works*, III, 190.

the only time in his life?  Yet this Milton does: listen to
his anger against the rebellious flesh which entrapped him
and now is not to be appeased:

> As for that other burning, which is but as it were the venom of
> a lusty and over abounding concoction, strict life and labour, with
> the abatement of a full diet, may keep that low and obedient
> enough. . . .[37]
> The flesh hath other mutual and easy curbs which are in the
> power of any temperate man.[38]
> . . . a sublunary and bestial burning, which frugal diet, without
> marriage, would easily chasten.[39]

And who will believe that it was merely the desire of
intellectual companionship — of which Milton had plenty
at the time — that could drive him to envisage despair
and loss of faith?  No, it was the awful dilemma in which
he found himself, married after a swelling wave of physical passion, and yet unmarried:

> . . . repining, even to atheism. . . .[40]
> . . . therefore when human frailty surcharged is at such a loss,
> charity ought to venture much, and use bold physic, lest an over-
> tossed faith endanger to shipwreck.[41]

And whence the fear which underlies that other passage,
in which the whole of psycho-analysis is anticipated?

> To these considerations this also may be added as no improbable
> conjecture, seeing that sort of men who follow Anabaptism,
> Familism, Antinomianism, and other fanatic dreams, (if we under-
> stand them not amiss), be such most commonly as are by nature
> addicted to religion, of life also not debauched, and that their opin-
> ions having full swing, do end in satisfaction of the flesh; it may be-
> come with reason into the thoughts of a wise man, whether all this
> proceed not partly, if not chiefly, from the restraint of some lawful
> liberty, which ought to be given men, and is denied them?  As

---

[37] *Ibid.*, III, 192.
[38] *Ibid.*, III, 192–93.
[39] *Ibid.*, III, 205.
[40] *Ibid.*, III, 205.
[41] *Ibid.*, III, 194.

by physic we learn in menstruous bodies, where nature's current hath been stopped, that the suffocation and upward forcing of some lower part affects the head and inward sense with dotage and idle fancies. . . . This may be worth the study of skilful men in theology, and the reason of things.[42]

Or this in his conclusion?

Let not, therefore, the frailty of man go on thus inventing needless troubles to itself, to groan under the false imagination of a strictness never imposed from above; enjoining that for duty which is an impossible and vain supererogating. " Be not righteous overmuch," is the counsel of Ecclesiastes; "why shouldst thou destroy thyself? " Let us not be thus overcurious to strain at atoms, and yet to stop every vent and cranny of permissive liberty, lest nature, wanting those needful pores and breathing-places, which God hath not debarred our weakness, either suddenly break out into some wide rupture of open vice and frantic heresy, or else inwardly fester with repining and blasphemous thoughts, under an unreasonable and fruitless rigour of unwarranted law.[43]

And if the lack of intellectual culture in his wife was the reason of his tremendous outburst, why then did he take her back? Her culture could hardly have increased during the months she spent with her parents. What was the submission she could offer him — " Creature so fair his reconcilement seeking " — in that famous scene at his relative's when she threw herself at his feet? Hardly the promise to be more intelligent.

But considering what Milton's pride was, the most significant fact to me is the terrible judgment that he passes upon those who unite in the flesh without being united in the spirit. There is no doubt that he was not united to his young wife in the spirit. Was it then his own condemnation he wrote down in 1643 in the following words?

Next he saith, " They must be one flesh "; which when all conjecturing is done, will be found to import no more but to make

legitimate and good the carnal act which else might seem to have
something of pollution in it; and infers thus much over, that the fit
union of their souls be such as may even incorporate them to love
and amity: but that can never be where no correspondence is of
the mind; nay, instead of being one flesh, they will be rather two
carcasses chained unnaturally together; or, as it may happen, a
living soul bound to a dead corpse; a punishment too like that inflicted by the tyrant Mezentius, so little worthy to be received as
that remedy of loneliness which God meant us: Since we know it is
not the joining of another body will remove loneliness, but the
uniting of another compliable mind; and that it is no blessing but
a torment, nay, a base and brutish condition to be one flesh, unless
where nature can in some measure fix a unity of disposition.[44]

And again:

   . . . I suppose it will be allowed us that marriage is a human
society, and that all human society must proceed from the mind
rather than the body, else it would be but a kind of animal or
beastish meeting: if the mind therefore cannot have that due company by marriage that it may reasonably and humanly desire, that
marriage can be no human society, but a certain formality; or
gilding over of little better than a brutish congress, and so in
very wisdom and pureness to be dissolved.[45]

   " A base and brutish condition," " two carcasses
chained unnaturally together," " a brutish congress ":
did Milton ever apply such words to anything he was in
the remotest way concerned in?   I think we can safely
answer: Never.

   He says himself that in marriage, whatever be the
higher aims in it, " that to him is greatest which is most
necessary; and marriage is then most broken to him when
he utterly wants the fruition of that which he sought
therein, whether it were religious, civil, or corporal society."   But let us have the whole passage, significant in
its hopeless attempt to cover the facts which " drive many
to transgress the conjugal bed ":

   [44] *Ibid.*, III, 249.          [45] *Ibid.*, III, 210.

. . . touching matrimony, there be three chief ends thereof agreed on: godly society; next, civil; and thirdly, that of the marriage bed. Of these the first in name to be the highest and most excellent, no baptized man can deny. . . . And out of question the cheerful help that may be in marriage towards sanctity of life, is the purest, and so the noblest end of that contract: but if the particular of each person be considered, then of those three ends which God appointed, that to him is greatest which is most necessary; and marriage is then most broken to him when he utterly wants the fruition of that which he most sought therein, whether it were religious, civil, or corporal society. . . . And having shewn that disproportion, contrariety, or numbness of mind may justly be divorced, by proving already the prohibition thereof opposes the express end of God's institution, suffers not marriage to satisfy that intellectual and innocent desire which God himself kindled in man to be the bond of wedlock, but only to remedy a sublunary and bestial burning, which frugal diet, without marriage, would easily chasten. Next, that it drives many to transgress the conjugal bed, while the soul wanders after that satisfaction which it had hope to find at home, but hath missed; or else it sits repining, even to atheism, finding itself hardly dealt with, but misdeeming the cause to be in God's law. . . .[46]

So, " when all conjecturing is done," I can see nothing but a plain avowal in this other perhaps decisive text:

Who doubts not but that it may be piously said, to him who would dismiss his frigidity, Bear your trial; take it as if God would have you live this life of continence? If he exhort this, I hear him as an angel, though he speak without warrant; but if he would compel me, I know him for Satan.[47]

I have somewhat labored the point because careful examination of the divorce pamphlets seems to me to prove that Milton had been wrecked in what Meredith calls " the sensual whirlpools "; and this fact became all important in his conception of life.

[46] *Ibid.*, III, 205.         [47] *Ibid.*, III, 261.

The whole of his character predestined him to this
catastrophe.  His temperament was ardent, his chastity
had been rigid.  He was rushed into marriage by irresistible impulse.  His high opinion of himself, his pride in
his strength and intellect, naturally made him believe that
he would master and elevate his wife, and allowed him
no consideration before he took the step his whole being
longed for.  And no doubt Milton would not have found
out his mistake had his wife's character been somewhat
malleable.  The illusion that made him marry would have
lasted some time at least, and his natural generosity would
probably have kept him thereafter from owning his wife's
intellectual inferiority,[48] even in his own mind.  He would
then have found in his first union the tranquil happiness
of his last marriages.

But the young woman's refusal gave Milton the first
great shock of his life.  He saw at once his irreparable
mistake.  He found himself placed in a dilemma intolerable both to his purity and to his pride.  Physical passion
had been roused in him, and then thwarted; he was not
really married, and he was now forbidden to get married.
His highest ideal, that of love as a harmony between body
and spirit, was at once shattered and soiled.  And the
cause of this painful degradation was the blind impulse
of the flesh.  Hence the anger against the mistrust of the
flesh which remained, under his more liberal general ideas,
all through his life.  The flesh will play an essential part
in the Fall.

No doubt all this remained half sentimental in him.
Intellectually, as ever, he generalized; he never owned

[48] I do not think that what Milton said in his rage ought to be reckoned
against Mary Powell.  She was very young at the time.  She said afterwards
her mother had urged her to do it; and we hear nothing further against
her after she came back to Milton.

completely even to himself that the flesh had carried
him away. He was too proud for that. Hence, in the
divorce treatises, the many rebellions against the flesh,
refusals to admit its power; passionate refusals which are
really proofs of the sensual force in him. What had lured
him became to him that " female charm " which lured
Adam in *Paradise Lost*.

Desire had urged him to union, when there was no
intellectual harmony between his wife and him (such is
the central point of his argumentation in the treatises).
Hence his larger conception of evil. Milton never quite
forgot his grudge against the flesh, but he placed higher
than that his great general idea. Evil will be to him
Passion triumphant over Reason, Sentiment blinding the
Intellect, or overruling it. This principle which he had
acquired in the bitterness of personal despair will become
for him a powerful instrument of philosophical explanation, which he will apply to politics and religion. For
here intervenes again another characteristic of Milton's,
his need of being not one single individual, but the norm,
the rule, the law to all. What he has learned out of personal experience, that will become to him the experience
of mankind. The lesson he has felt so deeply is valid
for man in general. Milton will preach to the whole
world the doctrine he has discovered in his own soul.[49] He
will bring salvation to all tortured men. He writes his
treatises on divorce so that all shall profit by his misfortune. His peculiar pride makes him unsatisfied at being
only one man, and naïvely and sincerely he carries his

---

[49] Let it be understood once for all that I am not speaking of intellectual
discovery, but of the intense realization of an idea, which made it in Milton
a passionate conviction. The theories about reason and passion, love and
lust, etc., were current at the Renaissance. What I investigate is how and
why Milton came to adopt them. This remark applies to most of Milton's
philosophy, which is at once original and current.

personal needs into the political world and into the City
of God.

His high idea of himself, in another direction, will not
let him admit that there is anything fundamentally bad
in him. The sensual powers he feels so deep in him cannot be damnable. His sanity of mind shows him quite
clearly that the normal instincts of human nature must
be satisfied. Consequently, whereas the flesh is an evil
power when it carries the mind away, when, on the contrary, its instincts are approved by reason, they are good
and legitimate and must be listened to. The distinction
appears in the divorce pamphlets. Milton's fundamentally sensual nature, on the one side, and his pride of
intellect, on the other, came naturally to this compromise:
sensual love is praiseworthy and sacred when it is made
legitimate by the approval of reason; it is execrable, it is
" the Fall," when it goes against reason; which means
that when the minds are not in harmony, the union in the
flesh is a degradation, even in marriage. Once again Milton generalized and formulated the rule, not only for
sensual passion, but for all passion whatsoever.

Probably there took place also at this time the further
development of another of Milton's great philosophical
ideas. We shall see that for him the body and the soul
came to be one. Was it not in the anguish of his first
unhappy marriage that this conviction first sank deeply
into him? Then it was that he conceived that degradation of the body was degradation of the soul, and that the
harmony to be established was not between two different
powers, but within the same power. Then he felt himself
wholly one, moved in his entirety, and suffering in his
entirety, body and soul together, from the same pain.
Then probably he acquired, sentimentally at least, the

conviction of the unity of soul and body, which later made him reject altogether all dualistic doctrines.

Thus Milton, through sentimental experience, came to a vision of several great conceptions, which we shall see shaping in the divorce treatises: the conception of sensuality, which is the triumph of the flesh over reason; the conception of the Fall, which is the triumph of passion over reason, sensuality being only one incident — howbeit the most important one — of the Fall; the conception of normal human nature — man's instinct is good in itself: only its aberrations are to be condemned; and reason is the criterion.

*The Doctrine and Discipline of Divorce*, written in 1643, was completely rearranged and much augmented in 1644. This second edition is far more readable and interesting. It is clearly divided into chapters and the author's ideas are more developed.

The central idea of the book is that marriage, or love, must be based on intellectual harmony between man and woman. Where such harmony of feelings and thoughts does not exist, the marriage is null, and divorce should be pronounced on the husband's petition.

Milton is much too dignified to bring his own case forward. He therefore puts himself in a false position from the beginning; and this brings a strong element of unconscious humor — for he is in such deadly earnest — into the treatise. What drives him to plead for divorce is in reality his wife's refusal. But he cannot own that. Therefore he launches into the abstract thesis, and feels the pride of legislating for the universe, without — he thinks — being influenced by his own case. But his personal situation is visible all the time, first by his preoccupation with writing down sensual passion, while in all his

other works he stands for the legitimacy of physical love
— and often in these treatises also; then by his evident
interest in the means of curbing the flesh; and most of
all by the intensely passionate nature of his argument,
which throws the glamor of poignant and intimate poetry
over splendid passages scattered here and there among
the waste of scholastic argument.   The lyrical accent
is unmistakable.   Milton was too much the poet to
keep it down, even had he suspected that it betrayed
him.

*The Doctrine and Discipline of Divorce* (if we join with
it *Tetrachordon*, which is but a sequel and a repetition)
is the most interesting, the most living work Milton produced in prose — if we are willing to skip over the waste
places.   The man, the thinker, the poet are visible and
active under the polemist.

Milton first addresses Parliament, with a hope of getting into civil law his ideas on divorce.   His repeated
appeals to Parliament, and their utter lack of any sort
of result, in the end led him to apply a destructive philosophy to that institution.   Milton insists on the mission
of England.   His ideas, once adopted by England, will
conquer the world:

Whatever else ye can enact, will scarce concern a third part of
the British name: but the benefit and good of this your magnanimous example, will easily spread far beyond the banks of Tweed
and the Norman isles.   It would not be the first or second time,
since our ancient druids, by whom this island was the cathedral of
philosophy to France, left off their pagan rights, that England hath
had this honour vouchsafed from heaven, to give out reformation
to the world.   Who was it but our English Constantine that baptized the Roman empire?   Who but the Northumbrian Willibrode,
and Winifride of Devon, with their followers, were the first apostles
of Germany?   Who but Alcuin and Wickliff, our countrymen,
opened the eyes of Europe, the one in arts, the other in religion?

Let not England forget her precedence of teaching nations how to live.[50]

> Then he vindicates the rights and necessities of nature:

It was for many ages that marriage lay in disgrace with most of the ancient doctors, as a work of the flesh, almost a defilement, wholly denied to priests, and the second time dissuaded to all, as he that reads Tertullian or Jerome may see at large. Afterwards it was thought so sacramental, that no adultery or desertion could dissolve it; and this is the sense of our canon courts in England to this day, but in no other reformed church else: yet there remains in them also a burden on it as heavy as the other two were disgraceful or superstitious, and of as much iniquity, crossing a law not only written by Moses, but charactered in us by nature, of more antiquity and deeper ground than marriage itself; which law is to force nothing against the faultless proprieties of nature. . . .[51]

Here is the ideal sought by Milton, fixed by God himself — with contempt for the body and means of curbing the flesh; but is not physical passion glowing in the page?

First, we know St. Paul saith, "It is better to marry than to burn." . . . but what might this burning mean? Certainly not the mere motion of carnal lust, not the mere goad of a sensitive desire: God does not principally take care for such cattle. What is it then but that desire which God put into Adam in Paradise, before he knew the sin of incontinence; that desire which God saw it was not good that man should be left alone to burn in; the desire and longing to put off an unkindly solitariness by uniting another body, but not without a fit soul to his, in the cheerful society of wedlock? . . . Whereof who misses, by chancing on a mute and spiritless mate, remains more alone than before, and in a burning less to be contained than that which is fleshly, and more to be considered; as being more deeply rooted even in the faultless innocence of nature. As for that other burning, which is but as it were the venom of a lusty and over-abounding concoction, strict life and labour, with the abatement of a full diet, may keep that low and obedient enough. . . . This is that rational burning that marriage is to remedy, not to be allayed with fasting, nor with any

[50] *Prose Works*, III, 178.    [51] *Ibid.*, III, 181–82.

penance to be subdued: which how can he assuage who by mishap hath met the most unmeet and unsuitable mind? Who hath the power to struggle with an intelligible flame, not in Paradise to be resisted, become now more ardent by being failed of what in reason, it looked for; and even then most unquenched, when the importunity of a provender burning is well enough appeased; and yet the soul hath obtained nothing of what it justly desires. Certainly such a one forbidden to divorce, is in effect forbidden to marry, and compelled to greater difficulties than in a single life; for if there be not a more humane burning which marriage must satisfy, or else may be dissolved, than that of copulation, marriage cannot be honourable for the meet reducing and terminating lust between two; seeing many beasts in voluntary and chosen couples live together as unadulterously, and are as truly married in that respect.[52]

And the following slur on poor Mary Powell is too well known to be omitted:

. . . when he shall find himself bound fast to an uncomplying discord of nature, or, as it oft happens, to an image of earth and phlegm, with whom he looked to be the copartner of a sweet and gladsome society, and sees withal that his bondage is now inevitable; though he be almost the strongest Christian, he will be ready to despair in virtue, and mutiny against Divine Providence. . . .[53]

Nor does he think humbly of his subject — and did he ever of anything he undertook?

. . . to be wise and skilful in these matters, men heretofore of greatest name in virtue have esteemed it one of the highest arcs, that human contemplation circling upwards can make from the globy sea whereon she stands. . . .[54]

The second part of the *Doctrine and Discipline* is made up of repetitions which have little interest. Milton launches into an endless — and baseless — criticism of innumerable Biblical texts. He brings at times undeniable ingenuity, but oftener mere lumbering awkwardness, to

[52] *Ibid.*, III, 191–92.   [53] *Ibid.*, III, 194.   [54] *Ibid.*, III, 195.

the attempt at turning to advantage even the texts which
tell most obviously against him.  The second book cannot therefore compare with the first, in which the question
had been considered from a human point of view.  Some
odd points, however, deserve attention.  Here is a passage
where the poet's genius stands revealed for a few lines:

> To banish for ever into a local hell, whether in the air or in
> the centre, or in that uttermost and bottomless gulf of chaos,
> deeper from holy bliss than the world's diameter multiplied; they
> thought not a punishing so proper and proportionate for God to
> inflict, as to punish sin with sin.[55]

In this same chapter III of Book II, we see Milton still
believing in predestination,[56] which he rejected so absolutely later.[57]  Chapter XXI contains in germ an idea that
is destined to grow:  that there is no law for the reasonable man.  Another familiar notion is that all the prerogatives of popes and clergy came by usurpation; even
the part of the civil magistrate must be reduced to a
minimum; Milton will think later that the best government is that which governs least:[58]

> Another act of papal encroachment it was to pluck the power and
> arbitrament of divorce from the master of the family, into whose
> hands God and the law of all nations had put it, and Christ so
> left it, preaching only to the conscience, and not authorizing a
> judicial court to toss about and divulge the unaccountable and
> secret reason of disaffection between man and wife, as a thing most
> improperly answerable to any such kind of trial.  But the popes
> of Rome, perceiving the great revenue and high authority it would
> give them even over princes, to have the judging and deciding of
> such a main consequence. . . .[59]

Milton seems to expect a complete adhesion on the
legislator's part, and describes thus the effects of the new
laws:

[55] *Ibid.*, III, 224.  [57] See below, pp. 123–31.  [59] *Prose Works,* III, 263–64.
[56] *Ibid.*, III, 223.  [58] See below, p. 188.

Many helpless Christians they [the legislators] shall raise from the depth of sadness and distress, utterly unfitted as they are to serve God or man: many they shall reclaim from obscure and giddy sects, many regain from dissolute and brutish licence, many from desperate hardness, if ever that were justly pleaded. They shall set free many daughters of Israel not wanting much of her sad plight whom " Satan had bound eighteen years." Man they shall restore to his just dignity and prerogative in nature, prefering the soul's free peace before the promiscuous draining of a carnal rage. Marriage, from a perilous hazard and snare, they shall reduce to be a more certain haven and retirement of happy society. . . .[60]

And he concludes in this masterly manner:

. . . which yet I shall not doubt to leave with them as a conclusion, that God the Son hath put all other things under his own feet, but his commandments he hath left all under the feet of charity.[61]

In July, 1644, Milton published *The Judgment of Martin Bucer concerning Divorce*. This treatise has no interest for us, being only a polemical weapon against the adversaries of the *Doctrine and Discipline*. For the Presbyterians had rebelled in a body against the new doctrine. Milton is henceforth among the sectaries and " in a world of discontent." They preach against him in the churches; the Westminster Assembly puts him on the Index and causes the printer's guild to instigate pursuits against him for an offence then very common and generally little thought of: his book had been printed without license. This came to nothing, as a taste for liberty was growing in England; Cromwell threw his sword into the scales on the side of toleration.

In March, 1645, *Tetrachordon* came out. This is less a sequel to, than a repetition of, the *Doctrine and Discipline*.

[60] *Ibid.*, III, 272.      [61] *Ibid.*, III, 273.

It has the same faults and the same qualities, to a greater
extent in both cases, so that at times it is of all Milton's
prose works that which rises nearest to the sublime, and
again for long passages, especially in the second part, it
is one of the dreariest and most puerile works ever written
by a great man.  Milton was trying to digest the Scriptures; an operation which he may be said never to have
carried through to a successful conclusion, even his long
life proving too short for that.  There are in him too
many ideas absolutely opposed to the orthodox interpretation of the Bible, and yet he will not abandon the Bible.
Hence endless dissertations, arguments, and subtleties to
conciliate what is not to be conciliated.

Milton examines first what God's aims were when he
instituted marriage.  He explains what woman's position
is relatively to man; his ideas on this point will not vary:
he tries to do woman full justice.  He sees in her an
inferior, who has qualities peculiarly her own, but never
a slave.

But St. Paul ends the controversy, by explaining, that the woman
is not primarily and immediately the image of God, but in reference
to the man: " The head of the woman," saith he, 1 Cor. xi., " is
the man "; " he the image and glory of God, she the glory of the
man "; he not for her, but she for him.[62]

Then Milton insists on the need for man of intercourse
with woman, from all points of view, physical, moral, intellectual.  In a language which at times reaches sublim-
ity, he develops his very high conception of the relationship between the sexes, which are necessary one to the
other and can reach only in union the fulness of their
powers, the sum of their humanity.  We shall have to

[62] *Ibid.*, III, 324.  *Cf.* below, p. 168, the end of this passage, in which
Milton fully safeguards woman's dignity.

refer to this passage again and again, as it is one of the most important in all Milton's work, and so we give it here in full:

And here "alone" is meant alone without woman; otherwise Adam had the company of God himself, and angels to converse with; all creatures to delight him seriously, or to make him sport. God could have created him out of the same mould a thousand friends and brother Adams to have been his consorts; yet for all this, till Eve was given him, God reckoned him to be alone. . . .

"For man to be alone."] Some would have the sense hereof to be in respect of procreation only; and Austin contests that manly friendship in all other regard had been a more becoming solace for Adam, than to spend so many secret years in an empty world with one woman. But our writers deservedly reject this crabbed opinion; and defend that there is a peculiar comfort in the married state beside the genial bed, which no other society affords. No mortal nature can endure, either in the actions of religion, or study of wisdom, without sometime slackening the cords of intense thought and labour, which, lest we should think faulty, God himself conceals us not his own recreations before the world was built: "I was," saith the Eternal Wisdom, "daily his delight, playing always before him." And to him, indeed, wisdom is as a high tower of pleasure, but to us a steep hill, and we toiling ever about the bottom. He executes with ease the exploits of his omnipotence, as easy as with us it is to will; but no worthy enterprise can be done by us without continual plodding and wearisomeness to our faint and sensitive abilities. We cannot, therefore, always be contemplative, or pragmatical abroad, but have need of some delightful intermissions, wherein the enlarged soul may leave off a while her severe schooling, and, like a glad youth in wandering vacancy, may keep her holidays to joy and harmless pastime; which as she cannot well do without company, so in no company so well as where the different sex in most resembling unlikeness, and most unlike resemblance, cannot but please best and be pleased in the aptitude of that variety. Whereof lest we should be too timorous, in the awe that our flat sages would form us and dress us, wisest Solomon among his gravest proverbs countenances a kind of ravishment and erring fondness in the entertainment of wedded leisures; and in the Song of Songs, which is generally believed, even in the jolliest expressions, to figure the spousals of the church with Christ, sings of a thousand raptures between those two lovely ones far on the hither side of carnal enjoyment. . . . We may conclude, therefore, seeing orthodoxal expositors confess to our hands, that by loneliness is not only meant the want of copulation, and that man is not less alone by turning in a body to him, unless there be in it a mind answerable; that it is a work more worthy the care and consultation of God to provide for the worthiest part of man, which is his mind, and not unnaturally to set it beneath the formalities and respects of the body, to make it a servant of its own vassal: I say, we may conclude that such a marriage, wherein the mind is so disgraced and vilified below the body's interest, and can have no just or tolerable contentment, is not of God's institution, and therefore no marriage.[63]

Then Milton insists again on the horror of lust, of physical union where no harmony of souls exists,[64] and again on his definition of marriage and his fundamental distinctions:

And although copulation be considered among the ends of marriage, yet the act thereof in a right esteem can no longer be matrimonial, than it is an effect of conjugal love. When love finds itself utterly unmatched, and justly vanishes, nay, rather, cannot but vanish, the fleshly act indeed may continue, but not holy, not pure, not beseeming the sacred bond of marriage; being at best but an animal excretion, but more truly worse and more ignoble than that mute kindliness among the herds and flocks: in that proceeding as it ought from intellective principles, it participates of nothing rational, but that which the field and the fold equals. For in human actions the soul is the agent, the body in a manner passive.[65]

Then Milton devotes many pages to discussing the question whether the law can in a certain measure countenance sin. But many pages may be forgiven him, when they bring an expression worthy of *Paradise Lost:* " Suppose it anyway possible to limit sin, to put a girdle about that chaos."

[63] *Prose Works*, III, 329–32.     [64] *Ibid.*, III, 333.     [65] *Ibid.*, III, 342.

Then, not having succeeded, unfortunately, in putting a girdle round the chaos of his explanations, he goes on in a quite different style. Let us note, however, that Milton's mind is ever dwelling on the origins. *Paradise Lost* was in him as in a sort of gestation, of which signs are in all his works. Always, at the thought of the dawn of the world his mind rises, poetry flows. The early days before the Fall will become for him the normal state of man, what he ought to be, what he gets to be when regenerated.[66] Thus, before the Fall, man and woman living in perfect union of soul and body, lust could not exist, since it is the separation of the two loves. Divorce could not therefore be necessary.[67] Where love is, there is no lust, even as where reason rules, there is no law.

It is interesting to see Milton discuss texts which are obviously against him, such as Christ's dictum: " Whoso shall put away his wife, except it be for fornication, and shall marry another, committeth adultery." Here are germs of ideas which shall grow, which we shall find again in the *Areopagitica* and in the *Treatise of Christian Doctrine*. First of all, divine truth, in revelation, has been accommodated to time and place and the Scripture must not be taken literally; then the text itself has often been corrupted. He is not yet bold enough to defend these theories openly, but he gives sufficient hints of his later ideas:

No other end therefore can be left imaginable of this excessive restraint, but to bridle those erroneous and licentious postillers the pharisees. . . . And as the physician cures him who hath taken down poison, not by the middling temper of nourishment, but by the other extreme of antidote; so Christ administers here a sharp

---

[66] See below, pp. 155 ff.      [67] *Prose Works*, III, 389.

and corrosive sentence against a foul and putrid licence; not to eat into the flesh, but into the sore.[68]

Then Milton, in his argumentative rage, forgets his most sacred principles, his contempt for all authorities, and goes through the Fathers, the Councils, and the Reformers, down to " Grotius, yet living, and of prime note among learned men," [69] and *Tetrachordon* ends on words of threatening and contempt, whereas the *Doctrine and Discipline* had ended on words of love.  Milton has parted from his people.  Threats and contempt are left:

Henceforth let them, who condemn the assertion of this book for new and licentious, be sorry; lest, while they think to be of the graver sort, and take on them to be teachers, they expose themselves rather to be pledged up and down by men who intimately know them, to the discovery and contempt of their ignorance and presumption.[70]

Contempt and insults fill the *Colasterion,* published along with *Tetrachordon.*  Milton goes through the tale of his adversaries, telling each one of them, in little varied language: " I mean not to dispute philosophy with this pork." [71]  However, he examines a few propositions of each opponent, in the following manner (it is true enough that little " philosophy " comes into it):

He passes to the third argument, like a boar in a vineyard, doing nought else, but still as he goes champing and chewing over what I could mean by this chimæra of a " fit conversing soul," notions and words never made for those chops; but like a generous wine, only by overworking the settled mud of his fancy, to make him drunk, and disgorge his vileness the more openly. . . .
Another thing troubles him, that marriage is called " the mystery of joy."  Let it still trouble him; for what hath he to do either with joy or with mystery? [72]

[68] *Ibid.,* III, 392.      [70] *Ibid.,* III, 433.      [72] *Ibid.,* III, 453-55.
[69] *Ibid.,* III, 431.      [71] *Ibid.,* III, 445.

Some remnants of grace and dignity are visible in a sort of apology to the reader, at the end:

> I have now done that which for many causes I might have thought could not likely have been my fortune, to be put to this underwork of scouring and unrubbishing the low and sordid ignorance of such a presumptuous losel. Yet Hercules had the labour once imposed upon him to carry dung out of the Augean stable. . . .
>
> But as for the subject itself . . . if any man equal to the matter shall think it appertains him to take in hand this controversy, . . . let him not, I entreat him, guess by the handling, which meritoriously hath been bestowed on this object of contempt and laughter, that I account it any displeasure done me to be contradicted in print, but as it leads to the attainment of anything more true, shall esteem it a benefit; and shall know how to return his civility and fair argument in such a sort, as he shall confess that to do so is my choice, and to have done thus was my chance.[73]

Thus did Milton suffer, and meditate upon the cause of his suffering. His ideas are no longer philosophical abstractions, but the hard and poignant lessons driven by despair into his very flesh. His conception of the Fall takes shape, and the notion that the Fall occurs generally, and most painfully, through woman. He is thus again predestined to the theme of *Paradise Lost:* the fall of man because of woman.

Meantime, however, he forgave his wife. Surely this pardon is a safe sign of his good sense, independence, and generosity. He had gone all lengths in favor of divorce; for so proud a man, the greatest obstacle to a reconciliation should have been his published words. A sect of " Divorcers " followed him; he was going to regenerate mankind. But Milton did not quake before the laughter his retraction indeed was sure to bring upon him; once again he defied public opinion, that of his few friends this time. He took back his wife.

[73] *Ibid.*, III, 460–61.

Milton had learnt that reality does not shape itself upon abstract ideas. His struggle and his little success had shown him that man is but little corrigible — and woman still less. He took back his wife and never tried to lift her to that degree of intellectual eminence that would have made her a fit mate. He thus accepted compromise. The cycle of his first disillusion was complete. His idea of human nature was lowered. He was prepared for the second and greater disillusion which came gradually from 1650 to 1660; even as in his marriage trials he had lost his faith in woman and probably a little of his faith in himself, in the political struggle he was to lose his faith in human nature in the masses. There will be left to him only his faith in God, but in that he will center all hopes lost on Earth, and take a glorious compensation for all his disillusions. For Milton in his pride and strength could never come to ultimate despair.

## IV. THE SECOND CRISIS: THE BREAK WITH THE PRESBYTERIANS

Another disillusion had come to Milton from this whole controversy. He had rather expected to be greeted as a great reformer; he thought he had but to write and Parliament would be convinced, the law changed and mankind saved. His whole character and career disposed him to this illusion: his natural and naïve pride, the full consciousness of his power, the high opinion all his acquaintances had of him; the very soul of the times, which was full of high dreams and seemed ripe for great changes — all that carried him away, all that deceived him. A storm of insult and reprobation greeted his divorce tracts, and the complete silence of Parliament was a severe blow.

He discovered then, in a personal adventure, what the history of the Commonwealth was going to confirm: men care little for abstract ideas; it is not sufficient to be in the right, or to believe one is, to be listened to.

Two sonnets in 1645 give vent to his anger:

### ON THE DETRACTION WHICH FOLLOWED UPON MY WRITING CERTAIN TREATISES

A book was writ of late called *Tetrachordon*,
  And woven close, both matter, form, and style;
  The subject new: it walked the town a while,
  Numb'ring good intellects; now seldom pored on.
Cries the stall-reader, " Bless us! what a word on
  A title-page is this! " and some in file
  Stand spelling false, while one might walk to Mile-
  End Green. Why, is it harder, Sirs, than Gordon,
Colkitto, or Macdonnel, or Galasp?
  Those rugged names to our like mouths grow sleek
  That would have made Quintilian stare and gasp.
Thy age, like ours, O Soul of Sir John Cheke,
  Hated not learning worse than toad or asp,
  When thou taught'st Cambridge, and King Edward, Greek.

### ON THE SAME

I did but prompt the age to quit their clogs
  By the known rules of ancient liberty,
  When straight a barbarous noise environs me
  Of owls and cuckoos, asses, apes, and dogs:
As when those hinds that were transformed to frogs
  Railed at Latona's twin-born progeny,
  Which after held the sun and moon in fee.
  But this is got by casting pearl to hogs;
That bawl for freedom in their senseless mood,
  And still revolt when truth would set them free.
  Licence they mean when they cry Liberty;
For who loves that, must first be wise and good;
  But from that mark how far they rove we see,
  For all this waste of wealth, and loss of blood.

Milton is looking for the cause of his failure. He finds it in the ambition and avarice of the Presbyterians. They, as well as the prelates, are " blind mouths." The political test of "passion triumphing over reason " is not yet formulated (it will be at the end of the *Defensio secunda* and will give him the light whereby to see and judge the failure of the Commonwealth), but it is clearly realized, and, in 1647, applied to the Presbyterians in another sonnet:

### ON THE NEW FORCERS OF CONSCIENCE UNDER THE LONG PARLIAMENT

Because you have thrown off your prelate lord,
  And with stiff vows renounced his liturgy,
  To seize the widowed whore Plurality
  From them whose sin ye envied, not abhorred,
Dare ye for this adjure the civil sword
  To force our consciences that Christ set free,
  And ride us with a classic hierarchy
  Taught ye by mere A. S. and Rutherford?
Men whose life, learning, faith, and pure intent
  Would have been held in high esteem with Paul,
  Must now be named and printed heretics
By shallow Edwards and Scotch what d'ye call:
  But we do hope to find out all your tricks,
  Your plots and packing worse than those of Trent,
      That so the Parliament
May, with their wholesome and preventive shears,
Clip your phylacteries, though balk your ears,
      And succour our just fears,
When they shall read this clearly in your charge,
New Presbyter is but Old Priest writ large.

Thus did Milton find out his friends the Presbyterians: they are no better than the Bishops; as he condemned the ones, he now condemns the others.

But not only will not men follow reason, they try to

muzzle her.  Milton is once more on the walls: he attacks censorship and publishes the *Areopagitica*, appealing again to Parliament, in 1644.  He is still young and full of hope.  He has received heavy blows, but he has not lost his trust that the Kingdom is coming and that the Saints will presently set things to rights.  Parliament, it is true, has taken no notice of the *Doctrine and Discipline*. But, on the other side, the House of Lords does not at all encourage the Presbyterian plans against the liberty of the press.  Milton has been left unmolested.  Therefore he has not yet given up hope.  *Tetrachordon* will again be addressed " To the Parliament."

The Presbyterians show themselves to be enemies of liberty, " Forcers of Conscience."  But what of that? They will not belong to the Kingdom.  The hope of England is no longer in them.  Cromwell's power is growing. His army is being organized, and he is beginning to speak firmly to the Presbyterians.  After Marston Moor, he has the right and the power to do so.  And his voice is in favor of liberty.  The Independents, all men who needed liberty, like Milton, are gathering round the new chief. The *Areopagitica* is therefore full of hope and ardor.  Milton opens fire upon the Presbyterians.

The *Areopagitica* is admittedly the best sustained of Milton's pamphlets.  But it is less interesting for us here than the last pamphlets against the Bishops, than the divorce treatises, than the *Defensio secunda*.  It teaches us less about the man Milton or his ideas; it is rather, as its name indicates, a fine piece of eloquence than a personal or even strictly polemical effort.  Also the most sublime passages in Milton's prose are not here; the tone is more sustained, but hardly rises to the greatest heights of Milton's power.  It is, however, for its general ideas, calculated to please the modern mind, and for its qualities of style, the most praised prose work of Milton's; and certainly we cannot grudge it its reputation.

Many points in it are of interest for the purposes of this study.  At the beginning, Milton complains of the English climate, a grumble that will be re-echoed in *Paradise Lost;* he speaks of

the industry of a life wholly dedicated to studious labours, and those natural endowments haply not the worst for two and fifty degrees of northern latitude; [74]

and later he will sing thus:

> Higher argument
> Remains, sufficient of itself to raise
> That name, unless an age too late, or cold
> Climate, or years, damp my intended wing.

The praise of books is famous:

. . . for books are not absolutely dead things, but do contain a progeny of life in them to be as active as that soul was whose progeny they are; nay, they do preserve as in a vial the purest efficacy and extraction of that living intellect that bred them.  I know they are as lively, and as vigorously productive, as those fabulous dragon's teeth: and being sown up and down, may chance to spring up armed men.  And yet, on the other hand, unless wariness be used, as good almost kill a man as kill a good book: who kills a man kills a reasonable creature, God's image; but he who destroys a good book, kills reason itself, kills the image of God, as it were, in the eye.  Many a man lives a burden to the earth; but a good book is the precious life-blood of a master-spirit, embalmed and treasured up on purpose to a life beyond life.  It is true, no age can restore a life, whereof, perhaps, there is no great loss; and revolutions of ages do not oft recover the loss of a rejected truth, for the want of which whole nations fare the worse. [75]

Thus highly does Milton think of his trade.

[74] *Prose Works,* II, 53.        [75] *Ibid.,* II, 55.

Again a principle is expressed which will become one of his chief ideas:

"To the pure, all things are pure"; not only meats and drinks, but all kind of knowledge, whether of good or evil: the knowledge cannot defile, nor consequently the books, if the will and conscience be not defiled.[76]

Another celebrated formula sets Spenser above Aquinas: "our sage and serious poet Spenser, (whom I dare be known to think a better teacher than Scotus and Aquinas)."[77] Milton is not yet an Arminian, but Arminius already is "the acute and distinct Arminius,"[78] and Milton insists on the idea of free will, which is now deeply fixed in him in its definite form.[79] A few months before, in his treatise on divorce Milton stood for predestination and against free will.[80] We find here, therefore, in the very year 1644, a new departure in his thought. Milton frees himself at one blow from both Presbyterian discipline and creed. Plato's *Republic* is treated slightingly,[81] Milton little realizing that most of his ideas were just as baseless as Plato's. Then comes a formal attack against the repressive principles of the Puritans, and a vindication of the rights of nature; here again Milton goes further than ever before, as far as he will ever go:

Wherefore did he [God] create passions within us, pleasures round about us, but that these rightly tempered are the very ingredients of virtue? [82]

Here is his opinion of contemporary Italy:

. . . when I have sat among their learned men, (for that honour I had,) and been counted happy to be born in such a place of

---

[76] *Ibid.*, II, 65.
[77] *Ibid.*, II, 68.
[78] *Ibid.*, II, 70.
[79] *Ibid.*, II, 74. See below, pp. 123–31.
[80] *Prose Works*, III, 223–25.
[81] *Ibid.*, II, 71–72.
[82] *Ibid.*, II, 74.

philosophic freedom, as they supposed England was, while themselves did nothing but bemoan the servile condition into which learning amongst them was brought; that this was it which had damped the glory of Italian wits; that nothing had been there written now these many years but flattery and fustian.[83]

## But here is his opinion of England:

Lords and commons of England! consider what nation it is whereof ye are, and whereof ye are the governors: a nation not slow and dull, but of a quick, ingenious, and piercing spirit; acute to invent, subtile and sinewy to discourse, not beneath the reach of any point the highest that human capacity can soar to.   Therefore the studies of learning in her deepest sciences have been so ancient, and so eminent among us, that writers of good antiquity and able judgment have been persuaded, that even the school of Pythagoras, and the Persian wisdom, took beginning from the old philosophy of this island. . . .

Yet that which is above all this, the favour and the love of Heaven, we have great argument to think in a peculiar manner propitious and propending towards us.   Why else was this nation chosen before any other, that out of her, as out of Sion, should be proclaimed and sounded forth the first tidings and trumpet of reformation to all Europe?   And had it not been the obstinate perverseness of our prelates against the divine and admirable spirit of Wickliffe, to suppress him as a schismatic and innovator, perhaps neither the Bohemian Husse and Jerome, no, nor the name of Luther or of Calvin, had been ever known: the glory of reforming all our neighbours had been completely ours. . . .

Now once again by all concurrence of signs, and by the general instinct of holy and devout men, as they daily and solemnly express their thoughts, God is decreeing to begin some new and great period in his church, even to the reforming of reformation itself; what does he then but reveal himself to his servants, and as his manner is, first to his Englishmen? [84]

Such were the hopes of the time; here is the reason why Milton had left literature, to help to found the coming Kingdom:

[83] *Ibid.*, II, 82.          [84] *Ibid.*, II, 90-91.

Methinks I see in my mind a noble and puissant nation rousing herself like a strong man after sleep, and shaking her invincible locks: methinks I see her as an eagle mewing her mighty youth, and kindling her undazzled eyes at the full midday beam; purging and unscaling her long-abused sight at the fountain itself of heavenly radiance; while the whole noise of timorous and flocking birds, with those also that love the twilight, flutter about, amazed at what she means, and in her envious gabble would prognosticate a year of sects and schisms.[85]

Milton's former violence against the prelates has turned against the pastors of Presbyterianism; he has scented hypocrisy and greed, and he hits straight out:

There be, who knows not that there be? of protestants and professors, who live and die in as errant and implicit faith, as any lay papist of Loretto.

A wealthy man, addicted to his pleasure and to his profits, finds religion to be a traffic so entangled, and of so many piddling accounts, that of all mysteries he cannot skill to keep a stock going upon that trade. What should he do? Fain he would have the name to be religious, fain he would bear up with his neighbours in that. What does he therefore, but resolves to give over toiling, and to find himself out some factor, to whose care and credit he may commit the whole managing of his religious affairs; some divine of note and estimation that must be. To him he adheres, resigns the whole warehouse of his religion, with all the locks and keys, into his custody; and indeed makes the very person of that man his religion: esteems his associating with him a sufficient evidence and commendatory of his own piety. So that a man may say his religion is now no more within himself, but is become a dividual movable, and goes and comes near him according as that good man frequents the house. He entertains him, gives him gifts, feasts him, lodges him; his religion comes home at night, prays, is liberally supped, and sumptuously laid to sleep; rises, is saluted, and after the malmsey, or some well-spiced bruage, and better breakfasted, than He whose morning appetite would have gladly fed on green figs between Bethany and Jerusalem, his religion walks abroad at eight, and leaves his kind entertainer in the shop trading all day without his religion.[86]

[85] *Ibid.*, II, 94.     [86] *Ibid.*, II, 85–86.

Henceforth the very idea of a priesthood will be repugnant to Milton. Priests will be to him the enemies of intellectual liberty.[87]   Kings will soon go the same way; Milton will soon come to a point of view best expressed by Diderot, in the following century, in his vulgar but forcible lines (Milton was afraid neither of vulgarity nor of forcibleness):

> Des boyaux du dernier des prêtres
> Étranglons le dernier des rois.

Priest and king alike will be enemies to Milton.

In June, 1644, Milton dedicated to Hartlib his treatise *On Education.* Little need be said of this production, so easily accessible to all. The most remarkable thing about it — and that which has been oftenest remarked upon — is that Milton is setting their task to colleges of Miltons. He puts upon youths much too heavy a burden, because he himself had carried it lightly. We find here again, therefore, a striking example of that tendency of Milton's, made up of pride, of naïveté, and of a sort of monstrous modesty, to take himself as a normal specimen of human beings, to set down as the rule what fits his case.

Besides, in this whole evolution of his thought, from 1641 to 1645, we must needs notice how complete and absolutely dominant is Milton's egotism. He always follows the most advanced minds of his time; occasionally he precedes them. But it is always for personal motives, on private occasions, in safeguard of his own rights. He attacks the prelates from love of liberty, no doubt, but most of all from love of his own liberty, for he has been " church-outed by the prelates "; " hence may appear the right I have to meddle in these matters," as he puts it.[88]

[87] See below, p. 182 i.    [88] *Prose Works*, II, 482.

He discovers the necessity of new laws on divorce — when his own marriage goes wrong. He finds out how narrow-minded the Presbyterians are — when they won't allow him to settle his private affairs as he likes; and the necessity of the freedom of the press — when they want to prevent him from publishing his tracts. And he writes *On Education* because, owing to entirely fortuitous circumstances, he has been brought to act as preceptor to a few friends' children. All this might be thought petty? But we may as well think, on the contrary, what a powerful personality was here, a personality which, in the exercise of its normal needs, was brought up against everything that was arbitrary in the laws and customs of his time! This man was under no necessity to think in order to discover the abuses of the social order; all he had to do was to live, and he naturally came to stumble against every prejudice and to trip against every error. He was naïvely surprised, and wondered why everyone did not feel as he did. His egotism and his pride were so deep that they acted as hardly conscious natural forces, as though human nature, trammelled, bound, and imprisoned in all other men, had held to its free course in Milton alone.

For the most remarkable thing of all is that, in our eyes, Milton was each time in the right — against bishops, against Presbyters, against censors, against royalists. It is true that he did represent human nature; he was essentially " representative "; he was a specimen of humanity as it ought to be — if only it were up to sample.

V.  The Political Struggle and The Conception
of Evil

From 1645 to 1649, Milton remained a silent witness
to the Civil War.  Probably none of the contending parties satisfied him any longer.  Probably also there was
then taking place in his thought that revolution which
made him give up religious orthodoxy, and embrace practically every heresy man ever went in for.

Milton ever retained an extremely intense religious feeling, exemplified chiefly by an active and constant faith
in God.  But he went farther and farther away from all
religious formulas.  His idea of God himself became
vaguer and larger than that of the orthodox.  The one
deep feeling he never lost was the certainty of the inevitable justice of God.  There was nothing of the mystic
about Milton, and very little sentimentality.  His was a
cold, reasonable, precise mind — I mean, of course, when
his own immediate personal concerns were not at stake.
The work of his thought under the obscure influence of
his character, brought him, by ways we have pointed out,
to believe in the unity of God and man, of God and the
world.  Therefore, he saw in history and in the doings of
man the motions of God: an incomprehensible and all-
powerful God, of whom men — free beings — were infinitely small parts; a God of whom Milton knew only
one thing precisely, that he was just, and that destiny was
only his will and the manifestation of his justice.  This
was the postulate on which Milton lived.  With that God
of Justice he had identified his own self, so deeply did he
feel that his own essence was that spirit of eternal justice.

From this point of view Milton was to watch the Revolution, then the Commonwealth and the Restoration. His conception of God was but a deep conviction of the justice of destiny; justice that does not work from the outside, however, that is not put upon man by an external God, but which works inside man himself, comes out of his deeds. For God works in man. He is in man, and as man — a free being — accepts or rejects that presence in his actions and his will, he succeeds or fails. Milton saw that a country given over to passions and private greed, with no care for justice and right, inevitably rushes to perdition. Thus he judged first the King, then the Protector, then the people. Whatever course events may take, Milton will never doubt the justice of God; he will be more and more convinced that man's greed and perversity is the sufficient cause of man's misfortunes. Man is ever responsible for his fate.

Milton reentered the lists in January, 1649, at the time of the execution of the King, probably because he did not see till then what could be the use of pamphleteering. But now there was in power a group of men of whom he approved, whom he admired, and by whom the Kingdom might after all be established. For the same reasons as in 1641, a maturer Milton took up his weapons again. From before the King's trial, he was at work on a treatise to prove that the people had the right to judge and condemn kings; a few days before the execution, in the midst of the terror of the majority, his voice rose — it was the first to rise — to proclaim what seemed to him the justice of God, and he published *The Tenure of Kings and Magistrates* in January, 1649.

This is one of the most important and most interesting of Milton's pamphlets. His political doctrine is now

fixed; political evil is the triumph of passion over reason.
Milton begins as follows:

> If men within themselves would be governed by reason, and not
> generally give up their understanding to a double tyranny, of
> custom from without, and blind affections within, they would dis-
> cern better what it is to favour and uphold the tyrant of a nation.
> But, being slaves within doors, no wonder that they strive so much
> to have the public state conformably governed to the inward vicious
> rule by which they govern themselves. For, indeed, none can love
> freedom heartily but good men; the rest love not freedom but
> licence, which never hath more scope, or more indulgence than under
> tyrants. Hence is it that tyrants are not oft offended, nor stand
> much in doubt of bad men, as being all naturally servile. . . .[89]

Man is free by nature, being the image of God; soon Milton will say: being part of God. The just man is not
subject to law. It is the corruption of man, the Fall,
that made government necessary. And government comes
from the people, who entrusted kings and magistrates with
the prerogative of power in the public interest:

> No man, who knows aught, can be so stupid to deny that all men
> were born naturally free, being the image and resemblance of God
> himself, and were, by privilege above all the creatures, born to
> command, and not to obey: and that they lived so, till from the
> root of Adam's transgression falling among themselves to do wrong
> and violence, and foreseeing that such courses must needs tend to the
> destruction of them all, they agreed by common league to bind
> each other from mutual injury, and jointly to defend themselves
> against any that gave disturbance or opposition to such agreement.
> Hence came cities, towns, and commonwealths. And because no
> faith in all was found sufficiently binding, they saw it needful to
> ordain some authority that might restrain by force and punishment
> what was violated against peace and common right.
> This authority and power of self-defence and preservation being
> originally and naturally in every one of them, and unitedly in them
> all; for ease, for order, and lest each man should be his own partial

[89] *Prose Works*, II, 2.

judge, they communicated and derived either to one, whom for the eminence of his wisdom and integrity they chose above the rest, or to more than one, whom they thought of equal deserving: the first was called a king; the other, magistrates: not to be their lords and masters, (though afterward those names in some places were given voluntarily to such as had been authors of inestimable good to the people,) but to be their deputies and commissioners, to execute, by virtue of their intrusted power, that justice, which else every man by the bond of nature and of covenant must have executed for himself. . . .[90]

A tyrant is therefore the prince who thinks this power vested in himself, and given for his own uses:

And surely no Christian prince, not drunk with high mind, and prouder than those pagan Cæsars that deified themselves, would arrogate so unreasonably above human condition, or derogate so basely from a whole nation of men, his brethren, as if for him only subsisting, and to serve his glory, valuing them in comparison of his own brute will and pleasure no more than so many beasts, or vermin under his feet, not to be reasoned with, but to be trod on; among whom there might be found so many thousand men for wisdom, virtue, nobleness of mind, and all other respects but the fortune of his dignity, far above him.[91]

The source of evil is here in the king's passions. They are inspired by Satan, the root of all evil passions, and it is a duty to resist such a king.

So that if the power be not such, or the person execute not such power, neither the one nor the other is of God, but of the devil, and by consequence to be resisted. . . .
. . . A tyrant, whether by wrong or by right coming to the crown, is he who, regarding neither law nor the common good, reigns only for himself and his faction. . . .[92]

And Milton runs through history looking for proofs and examples. Then he turns to the Presbyterians and their priests, and declares that the source of evil in priests is

[90] *Ibid.*, II, 8-10.    [91] *Ibid.*, II, 13.    [92] *Ibid.*, II, 17.

ever " covetousness, which, worse than heresy, is idolatry ":

As for the party called presbyterian, of whom I believe very many
to be good and faithful Christians, though misled by some of turbulent spirit, I wish them, earnestly and calmly, not to fall off from
their first principles, nor to affect rigour and superiority over men
not under them; not to compel unforcible things, in religion
especially, which, if not voluntary, becomes a sin. . . .
I have something also to the divines, though brief to what were
needful; not to be disturbers of the civil affairs, being in hands
better able and more belonging to manage them; but to study harder,
and to attend the office of good pastors, knowing that he, whose
flock is least among them, hath a dreadful charge, not performed by
mounting twice into the chair with a formal preachment huddled up
at the odd hours of a whole lazy week. . . . It would be good
also they lived so as might persuade the people they hated covetousness, which, worse than heresy, is idolatry; hated pluralities, and
all kind of simony; left rambling from benefice to benefice, like
ravenous wolves seeking where they may devour the biggest. . . .
But if they be the ministers of mammon instead of Christ, and
scandalize his church with the filthy love of gain, aspiring also to
sit the closest and the heaviest of all tyrants upon the conscience,
and fall notoriously into the same sins, whereof so lately and so
loud they accused the prelates; as God rooted out those wicked ones
immediately before, so will he root out them, their imitators; and,
to vindicate his own glory and religion, will uncover their hypocrisy
to the open world. . . .[93]

Bad priests are the best supports of tyranny; and, following the natural bent of Milton's mind, the pamphlet
begun against the King ends against priests — divines
generally, not even particularly evil ones:

For divines if we observe them have their postures, and their
motions no less expertly, and with no less variety, than they that
practise feats in the Artillery-ground. Sometimes they seem furi-
ously to march on, and presently march counter; by and by they
stand, and then retreat; or if need be, can face about, or wheel in a

[93] *Ibid.*, II, 35-37.

whole body, with that cunning and dexterity as is almost unper-
ceivable, to wind themselves by shifting ground into places of more
advantage.  And providence only must be the drum, providence the
word of command, that calls them from above, but always to some
larger benefice, or acts them into such or such figures and pro-
motions.  At their turns and doublings no men readier, to the right,
or to the left; for it is their turns which they serve chiefly; herein
only singular, that with them there is no certain hand right or left,
but as their own commodity thinks best to call it.  But if there
come a truth to be defended, which to them and their interest of
this world seems not so profitable, straight these nimble motionists
can find not even legs to stand upon. . . .[94]

Poor creatures after all, these; and Milton mostly despises them; but as for those among them who dare stand
against his ideas, here they be:

> . . . a pack of hungry churchwolves, who in the steps of Simon
Magus their father, following the hot scent of double livings and
pluralities, advowsons, donatives, inductions, and augmentations,
though uncalled to the flock of Christ, but by the mere suggestion of
their bellies, like those priests of Bel, whose pranks Daniel found
out; have got possession, or rather seized upon the pulpit, as the
stronghold and fortress of their sedition and rebellion against the
civil magistrate.  Whose friendly and victorious hand having rescued
them from the bishops, their insulting lords, fed them plenteously,
both in public and in private, raised them to be high and rich of
poor and base; only suffered not their covetousness and fierce ambition (which as the pit that sent out their fellow-locusts hath been
ever bottomless and boundless) to interpose in all things, and over
all persons, their impetous ignorance and importunity? [95]

Thus Milton stood by his own side.  He was soon recognized as a useful ally by the heads of the government,
and in March, 1649, became " Secretary for foreign
tongues " to the Republic.  This title, and the modest
functions appertaining thereto, soon became a mere pre-
text.  Milton became, in the natural course of things, the

[94] *Ibid.*, II, 45.        [95] *Ibid.*, II, 47.

" Intellectual " on the side of the Republic, and directed
the defence of the party in power against all attacks that
came under the heading of letters.

The first attack was the *Eikon Basilike* in August.   Milton was officially given the task to answer it.   The importance of Milton's work for the Commonwealth can
only be fully appreciated if we remember the fact that,
in the reality of things, the republican government represented only a minority, that it ruled by force, and had
against it the whole of European opinion.   It was therefore essential for Cromwell and his collaborators to try to
bring back public opinion to their side, at least in England; all the more essential since in theory they were
republican and supposed to rule by the will of the people.
Milton's task really was to educate the poor ignorant
people of England, and impress favorably public opinion
in Europe.

His *Eikonoklastes* came out in October, 1649.   The
book takes up and examines one by one the arguments
and the facts of the *Eikon Basilike*.   It teaches us but
little that is new about Milton's thought and is really fit
subject only for the historian.   Milton's general ideas,
however, are expressed with energy, particularly towards
the end.   We feel his anger — the republican anger — at
the immense popularity of the *Eikon Basilike,* and mistrust of the people is already in Milton's mind.   In 1649
already he feels that the masses are against him:

He bids his son " keep to the true principles of piety, virtue, and
honour, and he shall never want a kingdom."   And I say, people
of England! keep ye to those principles, and ye shall never want
a king.   Nay, after such a fair deliverance as this, with so much
fortitude and valour shewn against a tyrant, that people that should
seek a king claiming what this man claims, would show themselves

to be by nature slaves and arrant beasts; not fit for that liberty which they cried out and bellowed for, but fitter to be led back again into their old servitude, like a sort of clamouring and fighting brutes, broke loose from their copyholds, that know not how to use or possess the liberty which they fought for but with the fair words and promises of an old exasperated foe, are ready to be stroked and tamed again, into the wonted and well-pleasing state of their true Norman villanage to them best agreeable.[96]

And a curious passage follows, in which we cannot but see a sort of personal apology. Milton had given up the search for truth to devote himself to the search for justice, and he seems occasionally to have willingly sacrificed one goddess to the other: [97]

It happened once . . . to be a great and solemn debate in the court of Darius what thing was to be counted strongest of all other. He that could resolve this, in reward of his excellent wisdom, should be clad in purple, drink in gold, sleep on a bed of gold, and sit next Darius. None but they, doubtless, who were reputed wise, had the question propounded to them; who after some respite given them by the king to consider, in full assembly of all his lords and gravest counsellors, returned severally what they thought. The first held that wine was strongest; another, that the king was strongest; but Zorobabel, prince of the captive Jews, and heir to the crown of Judah, being one of them, proved women to be stronger than the king, for that he himself had seen a concubine take his crown from off his head to set it upon her own; and others beside him have likewise seen the like feat done, and not in jest. Yet he proved on, and it was so yielded by the king himself, and all his sages, that neither wine, nor women, nor the king, but truth of all other things was the strongest.

For me, though neither asked, nor in a nation that gives such rewards to wisdom, I shall pronounce my sentence somewhat different from Zorobabel; and shall defend that either truth and justice are all one, (for truth is but justice in our knowledge, and justice is but truth in our practice); and he indeed so explains himself, in saying that with truth is no accepting of persons, which is the

[96] *Prose Works*, I, 482–83.
[97] See Appendix B (p. 348) on Professor S. B. Liljegren's researches.

property of justice, or else if there be any odds, that justice, though not stronger than truth, yet by her office, is to put forth and exhibit more strength in the affairs of mankind. For truth is properly no more than contemplation; and her utmost efficiency is but teaching: but justice in her very essence is all strength and activity; and hath a sword put into her hand, to use against all violence and oppression on the earth.[98]

God himself brings about the triumph of justice, and fate is favorable to just causes; " What I will is Fate," as God shall be made to say in *Paradise Lost:*

He would fain bring us out of conceit with the good success, which God vouchsafed us. We measure not our cause by our success, but our success by our cause. Yet certainly in a good cause success is a good confirmation; for God hath promised it to good men almost in every leaf of scripture. If it argue not for us, we are sure it argues not against us; but as much or more for us, than ill success argues for them; for to the wicked God hath denounced ill success in all they take in hand.[99]

Hence the problem in Milton's mind when his own cause will be lost.

A few weeks after the *Eikonoklastes,* Salmasius published in Holland his *Defensio Regia pro Carolo I.* This book, written in Latin, was meant for Europe. Milton was asked to appear at that court and present the defence for England. He sacrificed his eyesight to the undertaking;[100] but in December, 1650, his *Pro populo Anglicano defensio* appeared, and made him a celebrated man throughout Europe. The book itself is of little interest, being mostly made up of quotations and discussion of authorities. But interspersed here and there all through it, we find important hints as to Milton's state of thought at the time.

<hr>

[98] *Prose Works,* I, 484.    [99] *Ibid.,* I, 494.
[100] On this see Appendix A.

Milton naturally opposes the theory of the divine right of kings. For the whole people are " of God," and supreme power is vested in the people.

> . . . for so all of us are of God, we are all his offspring. So that this universal right of Almighty God's, and the interests that he has in princes, and their thrones, and all that belongs to them, does not at all derogate from the people's right; but that notwithstanding all this, all other kings, not particularly and by name appointed by God, owe their sovereignty to the people only, and consequently are accountable to them for the management of it.[101]

The general thesis of the book is that God is in favor of liberty, and that Christ came to confirm our liberties.[102] God takes a direct part in that spirit in the whole of history:

> Or do you think that God takes no care at all of civil affairs? . . . God has not so modelled the government of the world as to make it the duty of any civil community to submit to the cruelties of tyrants. . . .[103]

And God leads the people, being in them:

> . . . you say, that all kings are of God, and that therefore the people ought not to resist them, be they never such tyrants. I answer you, the convention of the people, their votes, their acts, are likewise of God . . . so certain is it, that free assemblies of the body of the people are of God, and that naturally affords the same argument for their right of restraining princes from going beyond their bounds, and rejecting them if there be occasion. . . .[104]

The assembly of the commons is essentially the organ of the people's will:

> . . . by the very same reason the commons apart must have the sovereign power without the king, and a power of judging the

---

[101] *Prose Works,* I, 47.
[102] *Ibid.,* I, 61.
[103] *Ibid.,* I, 86.
[104] *Ibid.,* I, 94.

king himself; because before there ever was a king, they, in the
name of the whole body of the nation, held councils and parliaments, had the power of judicature, made laws, and made the
kings themselves. . . .[105]

The end is an exhortation to the English people: liberty
is grounded on virtue, and God watches over the fulfilment of that pact:

After the performing so glorious an action as this, you ought to
do nothing that is mean and little, not so much as to think of,
much less to do, anything but what is great and sublime.  Which
to attain to, this is your only way: as you have subdued your
enemies in the field, so to make appear, that unarmed, and in the
highest outward peace and tranquility, you of all mankind are
best able to subdue ambition, avarice, the love of riches. . . . But
if it should fall out otherwise (which God forbid), if as you have
been valiant in war, you should grow debauched in peace, you that
have had such visible demonstrations of the goodness of God to
yourselves, and his wrath against your enemies; . . . you will find
in a little time, that God's displeasure against you will be greater
than it has been against your adversaries, greater than his grace
and favour has been to yourselves, which you have had larger
experience of than any other nation under heaven.[106]

Milton is no longer so sure of the people as he would
like to be; he knows his party is in the minority; although that minority is in power, Milton is somewhat
anxious about the future.  The first *Defence* ends on a
little disguised threat to the people.  The *Second Defence* will end on advice to Cromwell which proves that
Milton was no longer sure even of the governing minority.
Thus, even at the moment when the Kingdom was nearest,
it seemed to be receding from the vision of the poet and
prophet.

It is interesting to give some specimens of his insults
to Salmasius, which make up a fair part of the book.

[105] *Ibid.*, I, 176.        [106] *Ibid.*, I, 212.

The art of insult was certainly not yet a lost art in the seventeenth century:

You say, it is a maxim of the English, " That enemies are rather to be spared than friends "; and that therefore, " we conceived we ought not to spare our king's life, because he had been our friend." You impudent liar, what mortal ever heard this whimsy before you invented it? But we will excuse it. You could not bring in that threadbare flourish, of our being more fierce than our own mastiffs, (which now comes in the fifth time, and will as oft again before we come to the end of your book,) without some such introduction. We are not so much more fierce than our own mastiffs, as you are more hungry than any dog whatsoever, who return so greedily to what you have vomited up so often.[107]

Some are princes' secretaries, some their cup-bearers, some masters of the revels; I think you had best be master of the perjuries to some of them. You shall not be master of the ceremonies, you are too much a clown for that; but their treachery and perfidiousness shall be under your care.[108]

And I pray by whom were you desired [to write]? By your wife, I suppose who, they say, exercises a kingly right and jurisdiction over you; and whenever she has a mind to it . . . cries: " Either write, or let us fight "; that made you write perhaps, lest the signal should be given. Or were you asked by Charles the younger, and that profligate gang of vagabond courtiers, and like a second Balaam called upon by another Balak to restore a desperate cause by ill writing, that was lost by ill fighting? That may be; but there is this difference, for he was a wise understanding man, and rid upon an ass that could speak, to curse the people of God: thou art a very talkative ass thyself, and rid by a woman. . . . But they say, that a little after you had written this book you repented of what you had done. It is well, if it be so; and to make your repentance public, I think the best course that you can take will be, for this long book that you have writ, to take a halter, and make one long letter of yourself. So Judas Iscariot repented. . . . Christ delivered all men from bondage, and you endeavour to enslave all mankind. Never question, since you have been such a villain to God himself, his church, and all mankind in general, but that the same fate attends you that befell your equal, out of despair rather than

107 *Ibid.*, I, 92.          108 *Ibid.*, I, 152.

repentance, to be weary of your life, and hang yourself, and burst
asunder as he did; and to send beforehand that faithless and treach-
erous conscience . . . to that place of torment that is prepared for
you.[109]

In 1652, the royalist party opposed to Milton the *Regii
sanguinis clamor ad cœlum,* which consisted mostly of a
personal attack upon him.  In June, 1654, Milton replied
in his *Defensio secunda pro populo Anglicano.*  This is
perhaps the best of all Milton's prose works; it can be
read through with pleasure.  Fine passages are numerous; an important part of the work is autobiographical;
another part is made up of portraits of the best known
characters of the republican party; and the end develops
Milton's fundamental principles in political theory.  This
we shall have to use in our study of Milton's ideas (in
Part II); for the rest, it is impossible to quote here even
a small part of the many beautiful pages of the *Defensio
secunda;* they are so well known and so easily accessible
that it is needless to draw attention to them.

Let us note only Milton's warning to Cromwell and
again to the English people.

Milton was not pleased with Cromwell's religious
policy.  His pamphlets written in 1659 abundantly show
why: he wanted the Church to be disestablished, and he
wanted the suppression of all paid clergy.  But Cromwell, for his own ends, went the opposite way.  Milton
warns him in the *Second Defence:*

Then, if you leave the church to its own government, and relieve
yourself and the other public functionaries from a charge so oner-
ous, and so incompatible with your functions; and will no longer

───────

[109] *Ibid.,* I, 210–11.  " Beforehand," probably because the body will only
be sent to hell at the Last Judgment.  It may seem that Milton was still a
dualist in 1651; but perhaps little weight can be allowed to such a rhetorical
passage.

suffer two powers, so different as the civil and the ecclesiastical, to commit fornication together, and by their mutual and delusive aids in appearance to strengthen, but in reality to weaken and finally to subvert, each other; if you shall remove all power of persecution out of the church, (but persecution will never cease, so long as men are bribed to preach the gospel by a mercenary salary, which is forcibly extorted, rather than gratuitously bestowed, which serves only to poison religion and to strangle truth,) you will then effectually have cast those money-changers out of the temple, who do not merely truckle with doves but with the Dove itself, with the Spirit of the Most High.[110]

Besides, Milton was suspicious of the coming tyranny. He asked Cromwell to surround himself with the old republicans, the faithful companions of his wars; and Cromwell was successively to cause to be arrested — on some ground or other — Bradshaw, Vane, for whom Milton had a great regard, and Colonel Overton, who was a private friend of Milton's. In 1654, things had not yet gone so far. Cromwell was still the hero; but already too many things are being asked of him in that *Defensio secunda;* Milton surely has his doubts, only too amply confirmed later. He has his doubts also of the people's steadfastness, and in his conclusion very neatly " washes his hands " of it, and claims that, anyhow, " whatever turn things take " he has done his duty. He openly tells his fellow-countrymen: " If the conclusion do not answer to the beginning, that is their concern. I have delivered my testimony." No great signs of trust in this conclusion:

With respect to myself, whatever turn things may take, I thought that my exertions on the present occasion would be serviceable to my country; and as they have been cheerfully bestowed, I hope that they have not been bestowed in vain. And I have not circum-

110 *Ibid.,* I, 293.

scribed my defence of liberty within any petty circle around me, but have made it so general and comprehensive, that the justice and the reasonableness of such uncommon occurrences, explained and defended, both among my countrymen and among foreigners, and which all good men cannot but approve, may serve to exalt the glory of my country, and to excite the imitation of posterity. If the conclusion do not answer to the beginning, that is their concern; I have delivered my testimony, I would almost say, have erected a monument, that will not readily be destroyed, to the reality of those singular and mighty achievements which were above all praise. As the epic poet, who adheres at all to the rules of that species of composition, does not profess to describe the whole life of the hero whom he celebrates, but only some particular action of his life, as the resentment of Achilles at Troy, the return of Ulysses, or the coming of Æneas into Italy; so it will be sufficient, either for my justification or apology, that I have heroically celebrated at least one exploit of my countrymen; I pass by the rest, for who could recite the achievements of a whole people? If after such a display of courage and of vigour, you basely relinquish the path of virtue, if you do anything unworthy of yourselves, posterity will sit in judgment on your conduct. They will see that the foundations were well laid; that the beginning (nay, it was more than a beginning) was glorious; but with deep emotions of concern will they regret, that those were wanting who might have completed the structure. They will lament that perseverence was not conjoined with such exertions and such virtues. They will see that there was a rich harvest of glory, and an opportunity afforded for the greatest achievements, but that men only were wanting for the execution; while they were not wanting who could rightly counsel, exhort, inspire, and bind an unfading wreath of praise round the brows of the illustrious actors in so glorious a scene.[111]

## VI. FAILURE

So Milton's thoughts turned to literature again. After the *Defensio tertio*, which calls for no special comment, he wrote no more under Cromwell. Things were not going well. But Milton obviously did not see what he

[111] *Ibid.*, I, 299–300.

could do. He kept up his rather loose connection with the government; but his heart was no longer in it. In 1658, he began work again on *Paradise Lost,* evidently thinking his political rôle was over.

Cromwell died in September, 1658. Milton once again interrupted the holy work, now begun, and tried to bring light and reason into the troubled time. He first of all attempted to prove whether the new leaders would be wiser than Cromwell. The two pamphlets published in 1659 are directed against Cromwell's ecclesiastical policy and ask for the disestablishment of the Church and, in fact, the suppression of the clergy.

In February, 1659, he submitted to Parliament again (alas, poor Milton!) his *Treatise of Civil Power in Ecclesiastical causes, showing that it is not lawful for any Power on Earth to compel in matters of Religion.* He comes back to his old idea that Christ established liberty. Neither blasphemies nor heresies much frighten him:

> But some are ready to cry out, what shall then be done to blasphemy? Them I would first exhort, not thus to terrify and pose the people with a Greek word; but to teach them better what it is, being a most usual and common word in that language to signify any slander, any malicious or evil speaking, whether against God or man. . . . But we shall not carry it thus; another Greek apparition stands in our way, Heresy and Heretic; in like manner also railed at to the people as in a tongue unknown. They should first interpret to them that heresy, by what it signifies in that language, is no word of evil note, meaning only the choice or following of any opinion, good or bad, in religion, or any other learning. . . .[112]

He vigorously condemns all persecutors, especially Protestant ones; and then develops a curious theory that Catholicism is no religion but a survival of the Roman government:

[112] *Ibid.,* II, 526-27.

How many persecutions, then, imprisonments, banishments, pen-
alties, and stripes; how much bloodshed have the forcers of conscience to answer for, and protestants rather than papists! . . . But
as for popery and idolatry, why they also may not hence plead
to be tolerated, I have much less to say. Their religion the more
considered, the less can be acknowledged a religion; but a Roman
principality rather, endeavouring to keep up her old universal
dominion under a new name and mere shadow of a catholic
religion. . . .[113]

He then explains how Christ governs the church himself [114] and ends by apologizing for having been too short:

The brevity I use, not exceeding a small manual, will not
therefore, I suppose, be thought the less considerable, unless with
them, perhaps, who think that great books only can determine
great matters. I rather choose the common rule, not to make much
ado, where less may serve; which in controversies, and those
especially of religion, would make them less tedious and by consequence read oftener by many more, and with more benefit.[115]

In August of the same year, he went on with his *Considerations touching the likeliest means to remove Hirelings out of the Church.* " The likeliest means " fall but
little short of suppressing the clergy entirely. Tithes are
to be done away with; priests can be fed by their flocks,
or preferably they can have some other profession. His
real thought is that any of the flock can play the part of
the pastor. Priests are not necessary to the Church.
This is Milton's ultimate revenge for having been
" church-outed by the prelates." He is here " church-
outing " not only the prelates, but all varieties of priests
whatsoever.

Temples and churches are also declared to be unneces-
sary; houses and barns are much preferable.

. . . they may be trusted to meet and edify one another, whether
in church or chapel, or, to save them the trudging of many miles

---

[113] *Ibid.,* II, 532.    [114] See below, pp. 174 ff.    [115] *Prose Works,* II, 548.

thither, nearer home, though in a house or barn. For notwithstanding the gaudy superstition of some devoted still ignorantly to temples, we may be well assured, that he who disdained not to be laid in a manger, disdains not to be preached in a barn; and that by such meetings as these, being indeed most apostolical and primitive, they will in a short time advance more in Christian knowledge and reformation of life, than by the many years' preaching of such an incumbent, I may say, such an incubus ofttimes, as will be meanly hired to abide long in those places.[116]

## The money given to the Church would find a better use in other ways:

. . . to erect in greater number, all over the land, schools, and competent libraries to those schools, where languages and arts may be taught free together, without the needless, unprofitable, and inconvenient removing to another place. So all the land would be soon better civilized, and they who are taught freely at the public cost might have their education given them on this condition, that therewith content, they should not gad for preferment out of their own country, but continue there thankful for what they received freely, bestowing it as freely on their country, without soaring above the meanness wherein they were born. But how they shall live when they are thus bred and dismissed, will be still the sluggish objection. To which is answered, that those public foundations may be so instituted, as the youth therein may be at once brought up to a competence of learning and to an honest trade; and the hours of teaching so ordered, as their study may be no hinderance to their labour or other calling.[117]

## Priests need not go to the universities, where their influence has always been for evil:

I answer, that what learning, either human or divine, can be necessary to a minister, may as easily and less chargeably be had in any private house . . . though, to say truth, logic also may much better be wanting in disputes of divinity, than in the subtile debates of lawyers, and statesmen, who yet seldom or never deal with syllogisms. And those theological disputations there held by professors and graduates are such, as tend least of all to the edifica-

116 *Ibid.*, III, 26.          117 *Ibid.*, III, 27.

tion or capacity of the people, but rather perplex and leaven pure doctrine with scholastical trash . . . and to speak freely, it were much better there were not one divine in the universities, no school-divinity known, the idle sophistry of monks, the canker of religion. . . .[118]

## And here is the conclusion, surely decisive enough:

This is that which makes atheists in the land, whom they so much complain of: not the want of maintenance, or preachers, as they allege, but the many hirelings and cheaters that have the gospel in their hands; hands that still crave, and are never satisfied. Likely ministers indeed, to proclaim the faith, or to exhort our trust in God, when they themselves will not trust him to provide for them in the message whereon, they say, he sent them; but threaten, for want of temporal means, to desert it; calling that want of means, which is nothing else but the want of their own faith; and would force us to pay the hire of building our faith to their covetous incredulity! . . . Heretofore in the first evangelic times, (and it were happy for Christendom if it were so again,) ministers of the gospel were by nothing else distinguished from other Christians, but by their spiritual knowledge and sanctity of life, for which the church elected them to be her teachers and overseers, though not thereby to separate them from whatever calling she then found them following besides; as the example of St. Paul declares, and the first times of Christianity. When once they affected to be called a clergy, and became, as it were, a peculiar tribe of Levites, a party, a distinct order in the commonwealth, bred up for divines in babbling schools, and fed at the public cost, good for nothing else but what was good for nothing, they soon grew idle: that idleness, with fulness of bread, begat pride and perpetual contention with their feeders, the despised laity, through all ages ever since; to the perverting of religion, and the disturbance of all Christendom. . . . Under this pretence, exempt from all other employment, and enriching themselves on the public, they last of all prove common incendiaries, and exalt their horns against the magistrate himself that maintains them, as the priest of Rome did soon after against his benefactor the emperor, and the presbyters of late in Scotland. Of which hireling crew, together with all the mischiefs, dissensions, troubles, wars merely of their kin-

[118] *Ibid.*, III, 37–38.

dling, Christendom might soon rid herself and be happy, if
Christians would but know their own dignity, their liberty, their
adoption, and let it not be wondered if I say, their spiritual priesthood, whereby they have all equally access to any ministerial
function. . . .[119]

Milton rather suspects he is shouting in a desert, but
he will do his duty:

If I be not heard nor believed, the event will bear me witness
to have spoken truth: and I in the meanwhile have borne my witness, not out of season, to the church and to my country.[120]

But he was not quite done yet; in March, 1660, he published his last political work, of which the mere title, at
the time, is a deed of great courage and naïveté. Milton
was the last soldier on the breach; the city of the Saints
— what there had been of it — was tumbling down about
him. He knew it, but pride and anger upheld him to
the last. His last effort was *The Ready and Easy Way
to establish a free Commonwealth, and the Excellence
thereof, compared with the inconveniences and dangers
of readmitting Kingship in this Nation.*

Whoever doubts Milton's courage, has but to meditate
upon these words, published a few months before the
arrival of Charles II:

Certainly then that people must needs be mad or strangely in-
fatuated, that build the chief hope of their common happiness or
safety on a single person; who, if he happen to be good, can do
no more than another man; if to be bad, hath in his hands to do
more evil without check, than millions of other men. The happiness of a nation must needs be firmest and certainest in full and
free council of their own electing, where no single person, but
reason only, sways. And what madness is it for them who might
manage nobly their own affairs themselves, sluggishly and weakly
to devolve all on a single person; and, more like boys under age

[119] *Ibid.*, III, 39-40.     [120] *Ibid.*, III, 41.

than men, to commit all to his patronage and disposal, who neither can perform what he undertakes; and yet for undertaking it, though royally paid, will not be their servant, but their lord! How unmanly must it needs be, to count such a one the breath of our nostrils, to hang all our felicity on him, all our safety, our well-being, for which if we were aught else but sluggards or babies, we need depend on none but God and our own counsels, our own active virtue and industry! [121]

## He proposes his new plan: he wants a Council chosen for life; he has had enough of Parliaments:

And, although it may seem strange at first hearing, by reason that men's minds are prepossessed with the notion of successive parliaments, I affirm, that the grand or general council, being well chosen, should be perpetual: for so their business is or may be, and ofttimes urgent; the opportunity of affairs gained or lost in a moment. The day of council cannot be set as the day of a festival; but must be ready always to prevent or answer all occasions. By this continuance they will become every way skilfullest, best provided of intelligence from abroad, best acquainted with the people at home, and the people with them. The ship of the commonwealth is always under sail; they sit at the stern, and if they steer well, what need is there to change them, it being rather dangerous? Add to this, that the grand council is both foundation and main pillar of the whole state; and to move pillars and foundations, not faulty, cannot be safe for the building.

I see not, therefore, how we can be advantaged by successive and transitory parliaments; but that they are much likelier continually to unsettle rather than to settle a free government, to breed commotions, changes, novelties, and uncertainties, to bring neglect upon present affairs and opportunities, while all minds are in suspense with expectation of a new assembly, and the assembly, for a good space, taken up with the new settling of itself. After which, if they find no great work to do, they will make it, by altering or repealing former acts, or making and multiplying new; that they may seem to see what their predecessors saw not, and not to have assembled for nothing; till all law be lost in the multitude of clashing statutes.[122]

[121] *Ibid.*, II, 118.          [122] *Ibid.*, II, 121-22.

He examines possible variations of the system, but insists that the chief point must be a good education of the people:

To make the people fittest to choose, and the chosen fittest to govern, will be to mend our corrupt and faulty education, to teach the people faith, not without virtue, temperance, modesty, sobriety, parsimony, justice; not to admire wealth or honour; to hate turbulence and ambition; to place every one his private welfare and happiness in the public peace, liberty, and safety.[123]

They should have here also schools and academies at their own choice, wherein their children may be bred up in their own sight to all learning and noble education; not in grammar only, but in all liberal arts and exercises. This would soon spread much more knowledge and civility, yea, religion, through all parts of the land, by communicating the natural heat of government and culture more distributively to all extreme parts, which now lie numb and neglected; would soon make the whole nation more industrious, more ingenious at home, more potent, more honourable abroad. To this a free commonwealth will easily assent; (nay, the parliament hath had already some such thing in design;) for of all governments a commonwealth aims most to make the people flourishing, virtuous, noble, and high-spirited. Monarchs will never permit; whose aim is to make people wealthy indeed perhaps, and well fleeced, for their own shearing, and the supply of regal prodigality; but otherwise softest, basest, viciousest, servilest, easiest to be kept under. And not only in fleece, but in mind also sheepishest.[124]

To balance the power of his Central Council, Milton wishes to set up in each county a Provincial Council and give such Councils the largest prerogatives, so that in practice the real business of the Central Council will be the directing of foreign affairs:

Both which, in my opinion, may be best and soonest obtained, if every county in the land were made a kind of subordinate commonalty or commonwealth, and one chief town or more, according as the shire is in circuit, made cities, if they be not so called already;

[123] *Ibid.*, II, 126.     [124] *Ibid.*, II, 136.

where the nobility and chief gentry, from a proportionable compass of territory annexed to each city, may build houses or palaces befitting their quality; may bear part in the government, make their own judicial laws, or use those that are, and execute them by their own elected judicatures and judges without appeal, in all things of civil government between man and man.  So they shall have justice in their own hands, law executed fully and finally in their own counties and precincts, long wished and spoken of, but never yet obtained.  They shall have none then to blame but themselves, if it be not well administered; and fewer laws to expect or fear from the supreme authority. . . .[125]

They shall not then need to be much mistrustful of their chosen patriots in the grand council; who will be then rightly called the true keepers of our liberty, though the most of their business will be in foreign affairs.[126]

It is a sort of provincial oligarchy that Milton wishes to establish.  Perhaps he longed, his whole life through, for the peace of the Horton period, when he frequented " the nobility and chief gentry."  Anyhow, he has lost his last illusion: his faith in the people.  Nothing remains but despair on the Earth — for the present — and trust in God, who will set things right, no doubt; but at the time Milton lifts up his voice in ultimate bitterness of spirit, and delivers judgment on the people of England:

I have no more to say at present: few words will save us, well considered; few and easy things, now seasonably done.  But if the people be so affected as to prostitute religion and liberty to the vain and groundless apprehension, that nothing but kingship can restore trade, not remembering the frequent plagues and pestilences that then wasted this city, such as through God's mercy we never have felt since; and that trade flourishes nowhere more than in the free commonwealths of Italy, Germany, and the Low Countries, before their eyes at this day; yet if trade be grown so craving and importunate through the profuse living of tradesmen, that nothing can support it but the luxurious expenses of a nation upon trifles or superfluities; so as if the people generally should betake themselves to frugality, it might prove a dangerous matter, lest tradesmen should mutiny for want of trading; and that therefore we must forego and set to sale religion, liberty, honour, safety, all concernments divine or human, to keep up trading: if, lastly, after all this light among us, the same reason shall pass for current, to put our necks again under kingship, as was made use of by the Jews to return back to Egypt, and to the worship of their idol queen, because they falsely imagined that they then lived in more plenty and prosperity; our condition is not sound, but rotten, both in religion and all civil prudence; and will bring us soon, the way we are marching, to those calamities, which attend always and unavoidably on luxury, all national judgments under foreign and domestic tyranny. . . .[127]

What I have spoken, is the language of that which is not called amiss " The good old Cause " : if it seem strange to any, it will not seem more strange, I hope, than convincing to backsliders. Thus much I should perhaps have said, though I was sure I should have spoken only to trees and stones; and had none to cry to, but with the prophet, " O earth, earth, earth! " to tell the very soil itself, what her perverse inhabitants are deaf to. Nay, though what I have spoke should happen (which thou suffer not, who didst create mankind free! nor thou next, who didst redeem us from being servants of men!) to be the last words of our expiring liberty. But I trust I shall have spoken persuasion to abundance of sensible and ingenuous men; to some, perhaps, whom God may raise from these stones to become children of reviving liberty; and may reclaim, though they seem now choosing then a captain back for Egypt, to bethink themselves a little, and consider whither they are rushing; to exhort this torrent also of the people, not to be so impetuous, but to keep their due channel; and at length recovering and uniting their better resolutions, now that they see already how open and unbounded the insolence and rage is of our common enemies, to stay these ruinous proceedings, justly and timely fearing to what a precipice of destruction the deluge of this epidemic madness would hurry us, through the general defection of a misguided and abused multitude.[128]

---

[127] It is curious to see Milton making such short work of economic factors, which we set such store by nowadays. [128] *Prose Works*, II, 137-38.

### VII. The Problem

The Cause is lost. The sons of Belial hold the world, and lead it to ruin and chastisement. The Saints have disappeared: killed, in prison, in exile, in misery. Milton is in hiding, perhaps in peril of his life.

How is such a world to be explained? Can the triumph of crime be understood, if there be such things as justice, liberty, God? Such was the problem for Milton at the Restoration, and for several years he had seen it looming on his thought's horizon. Had God then forsaken his own elect? If Cromwell had succeeded in organizing a true Kingdom of God, Milton would have again become a literary man in search of a subject, as in 1640, instead of being an Apostle preaching the Faith. Perhaps a *Paradise Lost* would have been written, but the poem would have been essentially different. It would have been a splendid song of triumph, no doubt, but somewhat superfluous. The failure of all the terrestrial hopes of the Puritans made something more of *Paradise Lost*. Disaster gave to the poem that vital and impassioned interest which makes of it more than a work of art, the ultimate question of man interrogating destiny. This it is that places *Paradise Lost* so high in human consciousness: it is an attempt to give a precise answer to a metaphysical question which arises both from personal anguish and universal suffering. It is a voice singing of mankind at a loss to understand its repeated failures in its struggle against Fate.

The long series of disillusions that had set the problem had also provided Milton with the elements of the answer. Milton finds in human nature all the causes of its failures, and consequently he thinks that man holds in his power the means to shape the future. The workings of Milton's thought and his own private experience, as we have seen, go together.

Very early in his life, at a time when his doctrine was still orthodox, he reached the idea that desire was legitimate. This was in his troubles and trials of 1643. This central conception, based essentially on his high idea of himself that could not regard as evil what he felt to be normal in his heart, is probably what ruined his orthodoxy. He probably passed from the idea of the legitimacy of desire to that of the goodness of matter, and then to that of the divinity of matter. His own desires could not be vile; his intellect, working on this basis, found in the end that his desires came from God, the source of all good, and consequently that the body, the instrument of desire, the flesh contemned by the Puritans, came from God, was part of God. Thus disappeared the distinction between body and soul — a useless distinction if the body be as divine as the soul. So Milton felt God in the desire of the flesh and the material laws of nature. He identified God with the Creation; he felt God in himself, not by a mystical feeling of union, but through intense consciousness of the " goodness " of the flesh, of matter.

But God was necessarily much more than that. Rising to the rank of member of God, Milton could not but feel his limitations. God is the Creation, but he is much more; he is the infinite, he is justice, he is the incomprehensible. This ruined in Milton's mind the idea of the Trinity; above the created world, which he called the Son, he set incomprehensible Destiny, which he called the Father.

It is no doubt impossible to trace in detail the evolu-

tion of a man's thought; but details are of little importance; the essential thing here is to seize the harmony
between Milton's ideas and Milton's character. The central point of his cosmology, the God-all, and divine matter as a source of all good, seems to coincide thus with
his high conception of himself and his tendency to vindicate the legitimacy of his desires. The same coincidence
exists in his ethics. He set down as a principle that his
desires could not be evil, since his reason approved of
them. Hence what is peculiarly his religion: regeneration
through Reason, Christ being the incarnation of divine
Reason coming to tame passion. From that same pride
comes all his need of liberty, which is the basis of his
politics. The regenerated man, in whom reason rules,
cannot but be free; and politics merge into theology
through the idea that man is a part of God and that regenerated man is a member of Christ, is the very reason
of God:

What have we, Sons of God, to do with law?

On this monumental pride, in all its close organization,
disaster after disaster came down, from Milton's first
marriage to the Restoration. But Milton, who did not
look upon himself as a being apart, applied to the body
politic the notions derived from his own sentimental experience. Thus he discovered the causes of the failure of
the Puritans: in the greed of the Presbyterians, in Cromwell's self-interested policy, in the blindness of the people,
whom he accuses explicitly of not having got rid of
" avarice, ambition, and sensuality." [129]  These passions
necessarily brought back the tyrant. Yet all hope is not

[129] *Defensio secunda*, in *Prose Works*, I, 295. See below, pp. 185 ff.

over for the Saints; in them at least let divine reason rule, and the same law of destiny will bring deliverance.

On these lines Milton undertook to " justify the ways of God to men." What he says to mankind is substantially this: " Your misfortunes come from your passions; do not accuse God; the consequences of your follies are on you; Destiny justly registers your mistakes and your crimes and deals them out again unto you as disasters and calamities. Your destiny is consequently in your own hands: amend yourselves and you will mend your fortunes." Very old, very sensible, very commonplace advice, no doubt; but surely that enhances its value. And there is a light in it by which to understand history and to build for the future.

Milton devoted the rest of his life to this last great work; the literary ambition of his youth united with the thirst for reality that had ruled his manhood. His great literary work is a great Act: a deed wrought in hope and power not only for the glory of the doer but for the comfort of mankind. Milton, once again, comes to the rescue of Man in his struggle against the Fates.

# PART II

# THE SYSTEM

MILTON has written a systematic treatise *De doctrina Christiana;*[1] he has also scattered his ideas in numerous prose writings produced as circumstances called for them; and lastly, in accordance with his own conception of poetics, he has expressed his ideas in his poems, either plainly, or allegorically, or in the very construction of them.

In order to study what there is of lasting originality in Milton's thought, and especially to disentangle from theological rubbish the permanent and human interest of that thought, these different expressions must be unified, compared, and made to tally. The best way seems to be to adopt the abstract plans of nineteenth-century metaphysics, which can be applied with necessary adaptations to any organized system of thought. Consequently, in Milton's ideas, there may be studied (1) an *Ontology,* or a doctrine of the conditions of general being and of separate beings; (2) a *Cosmology,* or a doctrine of the formation of this world, and its laws; (3) a *Psychology,* or a doctrine of man and his fundamental tendencies and powers, from which will come naturally a system of ethics based on it. In order to compass a complete study of Milton's ideas, we must add (4) *Religion,* or the doctrine of the salvation of man, whom psychology shows to be fallen; and (5)

---

[1] Mr. J. H. Hanford, in a careful study of "The Date of Milton's *De Doctrina Christiana*" (*Studies in Philology,* 1920, XVII, 309–19) comes to the conclusion that the work was written between 1655 and 1660. This date is in harmony with the analysis given below (Part IV, Sect. II, chapter III) of the resemblances between the *De doctrina* and the 1655 edition of *Man's Mortality,* and seems to me quite acceptable.

*Politics,* the crowning doctrine of Milton's thought, which is for him the study of man's destiny on earth.

In politics lies the great problem of Milton's thought, the aim of which is essentially " To justify the ways of God to men "; that is to say, to show that destiny is not blind, but just. Through his passionate study of destiny, Milton takes his place among the great searchers of mankind, who, from Æschylus to Hugo, have looked the problem of evil in the face, have asked the question which all religions and all philosophies try to answer: what is destiny? This is the very revolt of that thinking reed of Pascal's, knowing that the universe is crushing him, and calling the universe to account. Milton has tried to answer that question. In the measure in which the solution he proposes is human and universal, and not merely peculiar to one time or one sect, but grounded on elements that are truly alive in all men, Milton's philosophy is valid for mankind in general.

The classification I propose follows in a general way the course of the *De doctrina,* in which Milton deals first with God and his decree (Chapters I to IV), which is his *ontology;* then with creation through the Son (V to X), which is his *cosmology;* then with the Fall and its consequences (XI to XIII), which is his *psychology;* then with regeneration (XIV and following), which is his *religion.*

This last part gets entangled in interminable theology, of little interest. Milton's theory of politics, which applies the foregoing to the events of this world, is found in all his works, peeping through at any moment in the *De doctrina,* and forming the very basis of the poems and whatever substance there is in the polemical tracts.

# CHAPTER I

## ONTOLOGY

### I. THE ABSOLUTE

MILTON'S God is far from the God of popular belief or even orthodox theology. He is, properly speaking, identical with the Absolute of nineteenth-century philosophy. He is no Creator external to his Creation, but Total and Perfect Being, which includes in himself the whole of space and the whole of time. Therefore Milton's doctrine of God is rather to be called an Ontology than a Theology.

Milton, in order to express his ideas, makes use here of ordinary expressions to which he gives — as the rest of his system shows — a larger meaning than theologians. God includes the whole of space. Among his attributes are " immensity and infinity," [1] and consequently " omnipresence." [2] This commonplace idea of omnipresence will become for Milton a basis for pantheism. God is everywhere because God is everything.

Running through the whole of the *De doctrina* — and in this it is still a poet's work — there is the fierce joy of the iconoclast, a well-nigh juvenile jubilation, under the stiff sentences and accumulated texts, in the destruction

---

[1] *Treatise of Christian Doctrine,* in *Prose Works,* IV, 22. I use Bishop Sumner's translation and adopt most of his interpretations. Sumner's work has been done in a most competent manner. His poor opinion of Milton as a theologian — which is perfectly justified, and which Milton would have taken as a compliment — has never prevented him from seeing Milton's meaning, and his adverse commentaries make Milton's position extremely clear.

[2] *Ibid.,* IV, 24.

of orthodox ideas, in the ardor of turning on the theologians the tables of their own definitions.  This work, which seems theological and frigid, is in reality a passionate attack against the whole line of theology, an attack in which Milton puts the whole concentrated fire of the personal pamphlets.  We must remember, as we labor through this work, Milton's hatred of the clergy and all " clerical " work: " school divinity, the idle sophistry of monks, the canker of religion," as he calls it.  The contrast between these passionate feelings and the passionless geometrical style he has forced himself to adopt, puts a sort of jubilant hypocrisy in the most apparently anodyne remarks.

Like Blake, Milton might say to his adversary:

> Both read the Bible day and night
> But thou read'st black when I read white.

Thus Milton adds to his definition of omnipresence: " Our thoughts of the omnipresence of God, whatever may be the nature of the attributes, should be such as appear most suitable to the reverence due to the Deity." [3] Who dares deny it?  But here is the chief of the attributes, and here is a thought " most suitable to the reverence due ": Matter is a part of God, and the qualities of matter are so wonderful that therein lies one of the chief glories of God.  " It is an argument of supreme power and goodness that such diversified, multiform, and inexhaustible virtue should exist and be *substantially* inherent in God. . . .  For the original matter of which we speak is . . . intrinsically good and the chief productive stock of every subsequent good." [4]  Thus " reverence due

[3] *Ibid.*, IV, 24.
[4] *Ibid.*, IV, 179.  See below (pp. 136–37) for the whole important passage.

to the Deity " is made into a weapon against orthodoxy, and in favor of pantheism.

*Paradise Lost* identifies God with the primitive infinite abyss from which the world is to rise.  God addresses the Son-Creator:

> Ride forth and bid the deep
> Within appointed bounds be heav'n and earth;
> Boundless the deep, because I am who fill
> Infinitude; nor vacuous the space — [5]

because God fills it at all points.  And even as God comprehends the whole of space, so the whole of time is in Him; from all eternity, he has willed the whole of Being, has it completely present in Himself:

. . . he knows beforehand the thoughts and actions of free agents as yet unborn, and many ages before those thoughts or actions have their origin. . . .

God's general decree is that whereby he has decreed from all eternity of his own most free and wise and holy purpose, whatever he himself willed, or was about to do. . . .

. . . according to his perfect foreknowledge of all things that were to be created. . . .

. . . For the foreknowledge of God is nothing but the wisdom of God, under another name, or that idea of every thing which he had in his mind, to use the language of men, before he decreed anything.[6]

Hence these curious passages in *Paradise Lost:*

> . . . in a moment will create
> Another world, out of one man a race
> Of men innumerable.[7]

> Immediate are the acts of God, more swift
> Than time or motion, but to human ears
> Cannot without process of speech be told,
> So told as earthly notion can receive.[8]

---

[5] *Paradise Lost*, VII, 166–69.          [7] *P. L.*, VII, 154–56.
[6] *Treatise*, in *Prose Works*, IV, 27–31.   [8] *Ibid.*, VII, 176–79.

Bishop Newton, the best qualified and the most precise of Milton's critics from the theological point of view (leaving Sumner aside), thus comments upon this passage, and he is fully borne out by the *De doctrina,* which was unknown to him:

> Milton seems to favor the opinion of some divines, that God's creation was instantaneous, but the effects of it were made visible and appeared in six days, in condescension to the capacities of angels, and is so narrated by Moses, in condescension to the capacities of men. The world exists potentially in God, from all Eternity, and God only reveals it gradually to his creatures.

God, being the Absolute, is necessarily immutable. " The immutability of God has an immediate connection with the last attribute [eternity]." [9]  A Being infinitely wise and good would neither wish to change an infinitely " good state for another, nor would be able to change it without contradicting his own attributes." [10]   The only principle which allows human reason to venture into the study of God is this same principle of non-contradiction: " It must be remembered, . . . that the power of God is not exerted in things which imply a contradiction." [11] " He can do nothing which involves a contradiction." [12] Milton uses this idea frequently; for instance, to prove that " God is not able to annihilate anything altogether, because by creating nothing he would create and not create at the same time, which involves contradiction." [13] The same principle proves the Unity of God, which is incompatible with plurality, and therefore with Trinity. [14] There is no room for " mysteries " in Milton's philosophy.

[9] *Treatise,* IV, 24.
[10] *Ibid.,* IV, 28.
[11] *Ibid.,* IV, 25.
[12] *Ibid.,* IV, 26.
[13] *Ibid.,* IV, 182.
[14] *Ibid.,* IV, 26.

## II. God Non-manifested

The Absolute can neither change nor desire change. It cannot be manifested without becoming relative. Therefore, God, Perfect and Total being, is utterly non-manifested. As soon as action appears in the world, Milton speaks of the Son and no longer of God. The difference is essential, for the Son is not infinite, he is limited; he is not eternal, he has had a beginning. God is the Absolute, the Son is the Relative, the Real.

What has been called, in too narrow an expression, Milton's Arianism is an important part of his ontology. The Absolute can only be One.[15] Milton throws back on the Son all the notions that generally attach to God, and, above this God-Creator and His Creation, sets an infinitely greater, more incomprehensible, more inaccessible being, Total Being, of which the whole Creation, Creator included, is only an infinitely small part. For Milton, God is the Uncreated, the Infinite, Potential Being, Unlimited, Unknowable. The Son is the Created, the Finite Being manifest, limited, what is known of God. " In pursuance of his decree, . . . [God] has begotten his only Son "[16] " Only," and yet all beings are " sons of God " for Milton, but as parts of this, the " only Son." God has done nothing else,[17] and even his title, " God,"

---

[15] *Treatise*, IV, 25–26.

[16] *Ibid.*, IV, 79.

[17] This is naturally the weak point of the system, as of all systems of the Absolute; why has the Absolute become relative? Why has God created the Son? Even that was a creation, hence a limitation, and calls for all the objections that make Milton put the Creation to the Son's account and not God's. Milton has done his best to lessen this unavoidable contradiction by setting an abyss between God and the Son. See below, pp. 118–20, on the " how " of this creation of the Son.

as implying a sort of activity and manifestation, has been passed on to the Son.  In the creation book, *Paradise Lost,* VII, the Son is called " God."

Milton devotes the longest chapter of the *De doctrina* [18] to this all-important distinction.  Through the Son everything was created.  " The Son existed in the beginning, under the name of the logos or word, and was the first of the whole creation, by whom afterwards all other things were made." [19] . . . Yet " he who is properly the Son is not coeval with the Father; . . . nor did the Father beget him from any natural necessity, but of his own free will. . . ." [20]   For Milton insists that Creation was in no way necessary:  " For questionless, it was in God's power consistently with the perfection of his own essence not to have begotten the Son, inasmuch as generation does not pertain to the nature of the Deity, who stands in no need of propagation; but whatever does not pertain to his own essence or nature, he does not effect like a natural agent from any physical necessity." [21]

The Son is in Time: " . . . the Son was begotten of the Father in consequence of his decree, and therefore within the limits of time." [22]   The Son is limited and not infinite, and God gave him only a part of his substance; otherwise " there would be two infinite Gods . . . which no man in his senses will admit. . . . God imparted to the Son as much as he pleased of the divine nature, nay of the divine substance itself. . . ." [23]   The Son is therefore " the secondary and instrumental Cause," " a secondary and delegated power." [24]   The Son is manifested, the Father cannot be so:

---

[18] Chapter V, 73 pages, whereas the 33 chapters amount only to 500.
[19] *Treatise,* IV, 80–81.       [21] *Ibid.,* IV, 83.       [23] *Ibid.,* IV, 85.
[20] *Ibid.,* IV, 83.            [22] *Ibid.,* IV, 84.       [24] *Ibid.,* IV, 91.

". . . in the beginning was the Word." . . . It was not said, from everlasting, but *in the beginning*. *The Word,* — therefore the word was audible. But God, as he cannot be seen, so neither can he be heard. . . .[25]

*God was manifest in the flesh* — namely, in the Son, his own image; in any other way he is invisible. . . .[26]

. . . the nature of the Son is indeed divine, but distinct from and clearly inferior to the nature of the Father . . . to be the one invisible God, and to be the only begotten and visible, are things so different that they cannot be predicated of one and the same essence.[27]

Therefore also, God cannot create — which is to manifest one's self. Hence the Son, creating, takes the name of God:

. . . it is not unusual among the prophets for God to declare that he would work himself, what afterwards he wrought by means of his Son . . . the name of Jehovah was in Him [Christ].[28]

. . . the Son, . . . in his capacity of creator.[29]

The following gifts . . . were received by him from the Father. . . . Secondly, creation — but with this peculiarity, that it is always said to have taken place *per eum*, through him, not by him, but by the Father.[30]

Those distinctions are perhaps even more clearly marked in *Paradise Lost*. The Father was not obliged to create the Son:

No need that thou
Shouldst propagate, already infinite;
And through all numbers absolute, though one.[31]

The creation of the Son took place on one particular day:

This day I have begot whom I declare
My only Son.[32]

The Son is the Father's Creative Power:

Son, who art alone
My word, my wisdom, and effectual might.[33]

[25] *Ibid.*, IV, 109.   [28] *Ibid.*, IV, 127.   [31] *P. L.*, VIII, 419–21.
[26] *Ibid.*, IV, 115.   [29] *Ibid.*, IV, 131.   [32] *Ibid.*, V, 603–04.
[27] *Ibid.*, IV, 142–43.   [30] *Ibid.*, IV, 137.   [33] *Ibid.*, III, 169–70.

> Father eternal, thine is to decree,
> Mine, both in Heav'n and Earth, to do thy will.[34]

## The Son is the sole manifestation of the Father:

> Thee next they sang of all creation first,
> Begotten Son, Divine Similitude,
> In whose conspicuous count'nance, without cloud
> Made visible, th' Almighty Father shines,
> Whom else no creature can behold; on thee
> Imprest the effulgence of his glory abides,
> Transfused on thee his ample Spirit rests.
> He Heav'n of Heavens and all the powers therein
> By thee created. . . .[35]

## And the Father says:

> Effulgence of my glory, Son belov'd,
> Son in whose face invisible is beheld
> Visibly, what by Deity I am,
> And in whose hand what by decree I do,
> Second Omnipotence. . . .[36]

Omnipotence, since He alone makes everything; but Second, because he is only the expression of the Supreme Will.  Thus, in Book VII, the Son is the Demiurge:

> And thou my word, begotten Son, by thee
> This I perform; speak thou, and be it done.[37]

And from line 232 onwards, the Son, creating, assumes the name " God."  He speaks, and yet God — " neither can be heard."  He comes and goes, and God had not moved, and yet had been with him:

> The Filial Power arrived, and sate him down
> With his great Father; for he also went
> Invisible, yet stay'd (such privilege
> Hath Omnipresence).[38]

## A privilege not shared in by the Son.

[34] *Ibid.*, X, 68–69.
[35] *Ibid.*, III, 383–91.
[36] *Ibid.*, VI, 680–84.
[37] *Ibid.*, VII, 163–64.
[38] *Ibid.*, VII, 587–90.

Not only does God not act, but he cannot be said to think — he knows: " the phrases *he did not think it* . . . appear inapplicable to the supreme God. For *to think* is nothing else than to entertain an opinion, which cannot be said properly of God." [39]  The direct consequence of all this is that God is absolutely unknowable. This throws a light on Milton's way of believing in the Old Testament, in which God constantly speaks and acts and reveals himself: " He is invisible, neither can he be heard," says Milton.

Milton accepts the Scripture as a representation of God in harmony with our feeble powers. Since we cannot know God as he is, let us humbly accept the figures of speech that enable us somewhat to understand him; let us remember they are but figures of speech, but let us not presume on going further:

It follows, finally, that God must be styled by us WONDERFUL, and INCOMPREHENSIBLE. . . . Some description of this divine glory has been revealed, as far as it falls within the scope of human comprehension.[40]

. . . Our safest way is to form in our minds such a conception of God, as shall correspond with his own delineation and representation of himself in the sacred writings. . . . For it is on this very account that he has lowered himself to our level, lest in our flights above the reach of human understanding, and beyond the written word of Scripture, we should be tempted to indulge in vague cogitations and subtleties.[41]

This is in no way, as Masson would have it,[42] a proof of literal belief. Milton insists on the incapacity of the human understanding to grasp the absolute, and is really directing a hit at theologians, since he continues:

[39] *Treatise*, IV, 145.
[40] *Ibid.*, IV, 29.
[41] *Ibid.*, IV, 16–17.
[42] *Life*, vol. VI, end.

There is no need then that theologians should have recourse here to what they call anthropopathy. . . .

If " it repented Jehovah that he had made man " . . . let us believe that it did repent him, only taking care to remember that what is called repentence when applied to God, does not arise from inadvertency, as in men. . . ." [43]

Milton means that anyhow we cannot understand God; so we may as well use Bible figures about him; whatever higher efforts we may make we shall understand no better: " For however we may attempt to soften down such expressions by a latitude of interpretation, when applied to the Deity, it comes in the end to precisely the same." [44] This same high conception of the Divine Absolute, and not mistrust of human reason in itself, will cause Raphael to say:

> Commission, from above
> I have received, to answer the desire
> Of knowledge within bounds; beyond abstain
> To ask, nor let thine own inventions hope
> Things not revealed, which th' invisible King,
> Only omniscient, hath supprest in night,
> To none communicable in earth or heaven.[45]

Milton is generally charged with not having given a sufficiently " living " idea of God in *Paradise Lost*. But he never tried; truly humble before his conception of Unknowable Being, Milton put into His mouth the words that were necessary to make us understand the poem, and never attempted to describe God. Every time he touches that subject he notes his incompetence and remains silent before Him of whom all that is known is that He is incomprehensible.

> Thee Father first they sung, Omnipotent,
> Immutable, Immortal, Infinite,

---

[43] *Treatise*, IV, 17–18.    [44] *Ibid.*, IV, 18.    [45] *Paradise Lost*, VII, 118–24.

> Eternal King! Thee Author of all Being,
> Fountain of Light, Thy self invisible
> Amidst the glorious brightness where thou sit'st
> Thron'd inaccessible, but when thou shad'st
> The full blaze of thy beams, and thro' a cloud
> Drawn round about thee like a radiant shrine,
> Dark with excessive bright thy skirts appear;
> Yet dazzle heav'n, that brightest Seraphim
> Approach not, but with both wings veil their eyes.[46]

In this voluntary abdication of the poet, there is more true philosophy and therefore, perhaps, at bottom more true poetry than in the most impressive descriptions, necessarily the most precise, and thus the most misleading.

### III. INDIVIDUAL BEINGS: THE " RETRACTION "

From the Absolute nothing can proceed. As Milton says, He has neither reason nor power to change into a less perfect state. How is it possible, then, to derive from the Absolute, the only necessary cause of all that is, the existence of limited individual beings? This is the most important problem for all philosophies of the Absolute; on this all the systems issuing from Kant have been wrecked. Neither Fichte nor Hegel ever could explain why and how the Absolute, God, made himself into the relative, the finite, the many. Schelling put the question unavoidably to his great predecessors, and finding no answer in them, gave up his own early systems and founded the metaphysics of the Irrational. This system is an avowal of the failure of German philosophy: it sets down as a principle that there exists an unexplainable, an irrational abyss, between God and his creatures, between the Absolute and Nature. At the foundation of the world

[46] *Ibid.*, III, 372–82.

there comes into play an illogical power, which has no common measure with Reason. After or alongside of Schelling, Schopenhauer enlarged the breach and founded his whole system on that notion.[47]

Milton saw the problem. He found no solution that could be drawn from Scripture or theology. So he boldly took a passage out of the *Zohar*[48] and made it the very centre of his metaphysics:

> . . . I uncircumscribed myself retire,
> And put not forth my goodness, which is free
> To act or not. . . .[49]

According to his eternal plans, God withdraws his will from certain parts of Himself, and delivers them up, so to speak, to obscure latent impulsions that remain in them. Through this "retraction," matter is created; through this retraction, individual beings are created. The parts of God thus freed from his will become persons.[50]

The question of free will thus becomes with Milton ontological. Being is Freedom. Milton has precise and powerful arguments on this point. For him, the most essential character of a human being is his reason (we should now say "consciousness"). Reason is essentially a choice between different courses of action, or between different ideas. Choice implies liberty. A being not free would be a mere machine moved from outside and not a person: it could have no consciousness, no reason. We read in the *Areopagitica*:

[47] *Cf.* Windelband, *History of Philosophy* (New York, 1901), pp. 615–22.
[48] See below, pp. 286–89.
[49] *Paradise Lost*, VII, 170–72.
[50] This is the answer to the "how?"; of the answer to the "why?" we shall get a hint later (see Section V of this chapter).

. . . when God gave him [Adam] reason, he gave him freedom to choose, for reason is but choosing; he had been else a mere artificial Adam, such an Adam as he is in the motions.[51]

And in *Paradise Lost:*

> Reason also is choice [52]

and

> whence the soul
> Reason receives, and reason is her being.[53]

The *De doctrina* devotes two chapters [54] to the support of the notion of free will because free will has no place in Calvinism, the reigning doctrine of the time in England.

God of his wisdom determined to create men and angels reasonable beings, and therefore free agents. . . .[55]

. . . when the efficient is compelled by some extraneous force to operate the effect, . . . whatever effect the efficient produces, it produces *per accidens.*[56]

Had therefore God not withdrawn from beings, there would have been in the Universe nothing but God.

This is the central point of Milton's doctrine, the instrument of his justification of God, for man's responsibility is derived from it. Therefore Milton has carried as high upwards as he can that principle of liberty, implanting it in God himself, " which is free to act or not," and of all creation he has made a liberation.

IV. THE TOTAL PLAN OF BEING: THE DECREE OF GOD

Thus God has shaped from all eternity his total plan of the world, taking into account the freedom of individuals. His decree is not absolute, but contingent,[57]

[51] *Prose Works*, II, 74.
[52] III, 108.
[53] V, 486–87.
[54] III and IV.

[55] *Treatise*, IV, 39.
[56] *Ibid.*, IV, 34.
[57] *Ibid.*, IV, 31.

that is to say, based on the liberty of created beings.
Thus is destiny established:

> Though I uncircumscribed myself retire
> And put not forth my goodness, which is free
> To act or not, Necessity and Chance
> Approach not me, and what I will is fate.[58]

The plan of being is made up of two elements. First,
it is a tabulation of all the wills of the created beings, in
all their spontaneous and free manifestations, foreseen
and known by God from all eternity; those wills are, so
to speak, the materials at the disposal of the Great Ar-
chitect. Then it is the expression of the Total Will, God,
who has taken measures to see that his own aims shall
be reached, by organizing the interplay of free wills, and
the course of the world which is beyond them: historical
events, accidents, and so on. The whole, material and
disposition, represents the Will of the Total Being, God,
who has willed even the material of free wills, necessary
to the execution of his plans. God's statement therefore
means: " Although I freed from myself all separate beings, I did so willing and knowing fully what the results
would be, and I remain the master of their destiny and
the World's: "

> Necessity and Chance
> Approach not me, and what I will is fate.

Satan himself, the great Rebel, the free Will that opposes the Creator, is only an instrument in the carrying

---

[58] *Paradise Lost*, VII, 170–73. The punctuation of this all important passage is frequently bungled, the meaning then being left to take care of itself.
Beeching, in the Oxford edition, gives the only acceptable punctuation: a
full stop after " nor vacuous the space," and a comma after " to act or not."
These four lines, and the two preceding ones quoted above (p. 115) give the
very essence of Milton's system. They are placed at the crucial moment in
*Paradise Lost* when the revolt of the Angels seems to have compromised the
fulfilment of God's will.

out of the ultimate plan.  God speaks of his rebellion as

My damage fondly deemed.[59]

What Satan foolishly thinks he has done against God, has been done, of Satan's own free will, in fulfilment of God's decree.

The *De doctrina* develops these ideas systematically:

God's general decree is that whereby he has decreed from all eternity of his own most free and wise and holy purpose, whatever he himself willed, or was about to do.[60]

We must conclude, therefore, that God decreed nothing absolutely, which he left in the power of free agents. . . .[61]

. . . the Deity purposely framed his own decrees with reference to particular circumstances, in order that he might permit free causes to act conformably to that liberty with which he had endued them . . . he perfectly foreknew . . . from the beginning what would be the nature and event of every future occurrence when its appointed season should arrive.[62]

. . . that idea of every thing, which he had in his mind, to use the language of men, before he decreed anything.[63]

He would indeed be mutable, neither would his *counsel stand,* if he were to obstruct by another decree that liberty which he had already decreed, or were to darken it with the least shadow of necessity.

. . . the liberty of man must be considered entirely independent of necessity. . . . If . . . it [necessity] constrain them [free agents] against their will, man being subject to this compulsory decree, becomes the cause of sins only *per accidens,* God being the cause of sins *per se.*[64]

Nor does it follow from hence, that what is temporal becomes the cause of, or a restriction upon what is eternal, for it was not any thing temporal, but the wisdom of the eternal mind that gave occasion for framing the divine counsel.[65]

---

[59] *Paradise Lost,* VII, 152.  Hence God's irony, a feeling which dominates all his statements about the Rebel Angels.  See below, pp. 229–32.
[60] *Prose Works,* IV, 30.
[61] *Ibid.,* IV, 31.
[62] *Ibid.,* IV, 36.
[63] *Ibid.,* IV, 31.
[64] *Ibid.,* IV, 37.
[65] *Ibid.,* IV, 38.

The same doctrine is developed in *Paradise Lost* and forms the substance of the longest of those theological speeches Milton has so often been reproached for.  But these ideas are the very framework of the poem, which without them would only be a repetition of an absurd legend.  Indeed, the same people who object to them are wont to charge Milton with being antiquated in his beliefs.  We cannot therefore object to Milton's bringing in such explanations; the only fair criticism attaches to the form of these disquisitions, which is cold and often pedantic.  But, even in these contemned passages, beautiful lines are frequent, and they express subtle and solid ideas.  The reader who cares to understand Milton's thought, and does not read for mere romantic reasons, is grateful to the poet for his attempt at clearness and simplicity.  Who could have obscured, under splendid rhetoric, ideas sufficiently hard to follow when stated nakedly, better than Milton himself, had he cared to?

God explains himself thus about Adam's case:

I made him just and right,
Sufficient to have stood, though free to fall.
Such I created all th' ethereal Powers,
And spirits, both them who stood, and them who fail'd;
Freely they stood who stood, and fell who fell.
Not free, what proof could they have giv'n sincere
Of true allegiance, constant faith or love,
Where only what they needs must do, appear'd;
Not what they would?  What praise could they receive?
What pleasure I from such obedience paid,
When will and reason (reason also is choice)
Useless and vain, of freedom both despoil'd,
Made passive both, and serv'd necessity,
Not Me?  They therefore, as to right belong'd,
So were created, nor can justly accuse
Their Maker, or their making, or their fate;

As if predestination over-rul'd
Their will, dispos'd by absolute decree,
Or high fore-knowledge.  They themselves decreed
Their own revolt, not I: if I fore-knew,
Fore-knowledge had no influence on their fault,
Which had no less prov'd certain unforeknown.
So without least impulse, or shadow of fate,
Or ought by Me immutably foreseen,
They trespass; authors to themselves in all,
Both what they judge, and what they choose; for so
I form'd them free, and free they must remain,
Till they enthrall themselves; I else must change
Their nature, and revoke the high decree,
Unchangeable, eternal, which ordain'd
Their freedom; they themselves ordain'd their fall.[66]

This theory, set down early in the poem, is repeated as often as is necessary.  Thus God reminds Raphael of it so that he shall instruct man:

. . . such discourse bring on
As may advise him of his happy state,
Happiness in his power left free to will,
Left to his own free will, his will though free,
Yet mutable.[67]

Satan owns that he alone is responsible for his fall:

Hadst thou the same free will and power to stand?
Thou hadst: whom hast thou then or what to accuse? [68]

The angels are subject to the same law:

. . . freely we serve,
Because we freely love, as in our will
To love or not; in this we stand or fall,
And some are fall'n,[69]

says Raphael to Adam.  And God repeats, after the Fall:

[66] *P. L.*, III, 98–128.
[67] *Ibid.*, V, 233–37.
[68] *Ibid.*, IV., 66–67.
[69] *Ibid.*, V, 538–41.

> No decree of mine
> Concurring to necessitate his fall,
> Or touch with lightest moment of impulse
> His free will, to her own inclining left
> In even scale.  But fall'n he is. . . .[70]

But the power of God goes beyond all free wills: he
directs the laws which move events and destiny which is
over all; in reality, no law binds God whose will is
always done:

> Yet more there be who doubt His ways not just,
> And to His own edicts found contradicting,
> Then give the reins to wand'ring thought,
> Regardless of His glory's diminution;
> Till, by their own perplexities involved,
> They ravel more, still less resolved,
> But never find self-satisfying solution.
> As if they would confine th' interminable,
> And tie Him to His own prescript,
> Who made our laws to bind us, not Himself.[71]

Thus God has used evil, has used even Satan:

> . . . for what can scape the eye
> Of God all-seeing, or deceive His heart
> Omniscient, Who, in all things wise and just,
> Hinder'd not Satan to attempt the mind
> Of man.[72]

Thus does God deal justice on earth, through the course
of history, to men and nations.  Therefore Blake was
able to say: " . . . in Milton, the Father is Destiny." [73]

That is why Adam, when the plans of God are revealed
to him in the end, after having seen all the evil, crime,

[70] *Ibid.*, X, 43–47.  *Cf.* Sumner's notes (*Prose Works*, IV, 33–70), in
which he has gathered all the passages from the poems where traces of the
doctrine are found.

[71] *Samson Agonistes*, ll. 300–09.

[72] *P. L.*, X, 5–9.

[73] *The Marriage of Heaven and Hell*, in *Poetical Works*, ed. Sampson
(Oxford, 1914), p. 249.

and suffering that are to be, understands the will of
God, and cries:

> O goodness infinite! goodness immense!
> That all this good of evil shall produce,
> And evil turn to good! more wonderful
> Than that which by creation first brought forth
> Light out of darkness! Full of doubt I stand,
> Whether I should repent me now of sin,
> By me done and occasion'd; or rejoice
> Much more, that much more good thereof shall spring,
> To God more glory.[74]

This is one of the most important passages of *Paradise
Lost*, the conclusion of the twelve books, the answer to
the first problem:

> To justify the ways of God to men.

And this leads us to the problem which takes us from
ontology to cosmology, to the boldest question of the
human mind: what were the aims of creation?  We have
seen how God created the world by withdrawing from
beings and giving them freedom.  But why did He
create it?

### V. THE AIMS OF CREATION

Milton, as is fit, is very reserved on this subject, and
expresses himself in terms carefully vague and general.
He always thought that some things are beyond the
human mind, and this is one of them.

He is sure that God had aims.  Here is the conclusion
of the *De doctrina*, where the ultimate results of the epic
adventure of Creation are thus summed up:

I reply, there shall be no end of his kingdom, *for ages of ages,*
. . . until *time* itself *shall be no longer,* . . . until every thing
which his kingdom was intended to effect shall have been accom-

[74] *P. L.*, XII, 469–77.

plished; . . . [it] will not *pass away* as insufficient for its purpose; it will not be *destroyed*, nor will its period be a period of
dissolution, but rather of perfection and consummation, like the
end of the law. . . .[75]

There were, therefore, plans to be fulfilled, plans that
were shaped before the Creation, by Eternal Wisdom
playing before the Supreme. Milton devotes sublime
passages to the state of the Deity before Creation:

> God himself conceals us not his own recreations before the world
> was built: " I was," saith the Eternal Wisdom, " daily his delight,
> playing always before him." And to him, indeed, wisdom is as
> a high tower of pleasure, but to us a steep hill, and we toiling
> ever about the bottom. He executes with ease the exploits of his
> omnipotence. . . .[76]

> Before the hills appear'd, or fountain flowed,
> Thou [Urania] with eternal Wisdom didst converse,
> Wisdom thy sister, and with her didst play
> In presence of th' Almighty Father, pleased
> With thy celestial song.[77]

It was during this divine play that the plans of the world
were made. We shall see later the connotations of the
two passages, and what direction of Milton's thought
towards the more abstruse secrets of occultism they
reveal.[78]

More precise ideas can be obtained if we consider the
results of creation: the perfect and harmonious life of
the Communion of the Saints in God.[79] God has drawn
from himself a perfectly organized society of free spirits,
an expression of and a witness to his glory (" To God more
glory," says Adam). Evil, Sin, Suffering, end in this.

[75] *Treatise*, IV, 488.
[76] *Tetrachordon*, in *Prose Works*, III, 331.
[77] *P. L.*, VII, 8–12.
[78] See below, pp. 291–92.
[79] See below, Part II, Ch. IV.

There existed in the Infinite a sort of latent life which God has liberated, given over to its own forces, and which developed and expressed itself, in the good towards joy eternal, in the evil towards pain eternal.  God has intensified his own existence, raising to glory the good parts of himself, casting outside of himself the evil parts of himself too, because

> Evil into the mind of God or man
> May come and go. . . .[80]

Terrible words, applied to God; and Satan confirms them with his " The Son of God I also am." [81]  For God is the One Being, and all is in him.

This is as near as we can get to Milton's idea of God's aims: to drive away the evil latent in the Infinite, to exalt the good latent also.

Nor was Milton alone in such thoughts.  The Kabbalists give dark hints of an evil side to their unfathomable God, and we shall see that Milton had drunk, and possibly drunk deeply, of the Kabbalah.

[80] *P. L.*, V, 117–18.          [81] *P. R.*, IV, 518.

## CHAPTER II

### COSMOLOGY

## I. THE SON

GOD being the Unmanifest Absolute, the Son is the Real, the Relative, the First Creature, the Creator of the World. It will be evident from Milton's conception of matter that this First Creature comprehends all others. The Son is the Spirit of God manifested in the Cosmos. He has created all things, but by drawing them from himself; matter is " of him." So he is not only the Creator but also the Creation: all that is, is a part of Him, vivified by his divine force, a free fragment of the Total Being, remaining Him by its quality and its destiny.

Such is the essential idea of Milton's cosmology.

## II. THE HOLY SPIRIT

The Holy Spirit is somewhat of a supernumerary in Milton's system. Milton dare not deny his existence, but he has no precise place to give him; so he more or less tolerates him, although he has no great belief in him. He seems in a hesitating mood as he begins his Chapter VI of the *De doctrina* and sees the unavoidable question looming up:

Having concluded what relates to the Father and the Son, the next subject to be discussed is that of the Holy Spirit . . . With regard to the nature of the Spirit, in what manner it exists, or whence it arose, Scripture is silent; which is a caution to us not to be too hasty in our conclusions on the subject.[1]

---

[1] *Prose Works*, IV, 150-51.

He might (and we might) as well leave it at that. Yet he goes on, in some perplexity:

The name of Spirit is also frequently applied to God and angels, and to the human mind. When the phrase, the Spirit of God, or the Holy Spirit, occurs in the Old Testament, it is to be variously interpreted; sometimes it signifies God the Father himself . . . ; sometimes the power and virtue of the Father, and particularly that divine breath or influence by which every thing is created and nourished . . . " the Spirit of God moved upon the face of the waters." Here however, it appears to be used with reference to the Son. . . .[2] Sometimes it means an angel. . . . Sometimes it means Christ. . . . Sometimes it means that impulse or voice of God by which the prophets were inspired . . . the spiritual gifts conferred by God on individuals. . . .[3]

And Milton concludes, somewhat dispiritedly:

Lest, however, we should be altogether ignorant who or what the Holy Spirit is, . . . it may be collected from the passages quoted above, that the Holy Spirit . . . was created or produced of the substance of God . . . probably [4] before the foundations of the world were laid, but later than the Son, and far inferior to him.[5]

God is first described as creating the heaven and the earth; the Spirit is only represented as moving upon the face of the waters already created.[6]

On the whole then, the Holy Spirit may, or may not, have been a being created and used by God (*i.e.* the Son, the Creator) to shape the Earth, this world. Milton shows little interest in this hypothetical being. In his thought, the Son is essentially the Spirit of Creation; and the first aspect of creation is matter.

[2] This sufficiently accounts for *P. L.*, VII, 235: " The Spirit of God."
[3] *Treatise*, IV, 151–53.
[4] Milton is not sure, because the " Holy Spirit " might be Christ. *Cf.* also *Treatise*, IV, 175.
[5] *Ibid.*, IV, 169.
[6] *Ibid.*, IV, 175.

### III. MATTER

God has created all beings, not out of nothing, but out of himself. Since God is entirely non-manifested, this applies to the Son. The Son is thus both Creator and Creation — the spirit or essence that resides in things and is their being, and not a Creator that shapes from outside an independent matter. All things or beings are thus parts of God. Matter is part of the substance of God, and from this matter, divine in its essence, all things have come. Milton develops these ideas at full length, and draws from them their boldest consequences:

In the first place . . . neither the Hebrew verb . . . , nor the Greek κτίζειν, nor the Latin *creare*, can signify to create out of nothing. . . . On the contrary, these words uniformly signify to create out of matter. . . .

It is clear then that the world was framed out of matter of some kind or other. For, since action and passion are relative terms, and since, consequently, no agent can act externally unless there be some patient, such as matter, it appears impossible that God should have created this world out of nothing; not from any defect of power on his part, but because it was necessary that something should have previously existed capable of receiving passively the exertion of the divine efficacy . . . it necessarily follows, that matter must either have always existed independently of God, or have originated from God at some particular point of time. That matter should have been always independent of God, (seeing that it is only a passive principle, dependent on the Deity, and subservient to him; and seeing, moreover, that, as in number, considered abstractedly, so also in time or eternity there is no inherent force or efficacy), that matter, I say, should have existed of itself from all eternity, is inconceivable. If on the contrary it did not exist from all eternity, it is difficult to understand from whence it derives its origin. There remains, therefore, but one solution of the difficulty, for which moreover we have the authority of Scripture, namely, that all things are of God. . . .

In the first place, there are, as is well known to all, four kinds

of causes, — *efficient, material, formal,* and *final.*  Inasmuch as
God is the primary, and absolute, and sole cause of all things,
there can be no doubt but that he comprehends and embraces
within himself all the causes above mentioned.    Therefore the
material cause must be either God or nothing.    Now, nothing is
no cause at all; and yet it is contended that forms, and, above all,
that human forms, were created out of nothing.    But matter and
form, considered as internal causes, constitute the thing itself; so
that either all things must have had two causes only and those
external, or God will not have been the perfect and absolute cause
of every thing.    Secondly, it is an argument of supreme power and
goodness, that such diversified multiform and inexhaustible virtue
should exist and be *substantially* inherent in God (for that virtue
cannot be *accidental* which admits of degrees, and of augmentation
or remission, according to his pleasure) and that this diversified
and substantial virtue should not remain dormant within the Deity,
but should be diffused and propagated and extended as far and
in such manner as he himself may will.    For the original matter
of which we speak, is not to be looked upon as an evil or trivial
thing, but as intrinsically good, and the chief productive stock of
every subsequent good.    It was a substance, and derivable from no
other source than from the fountain of every substance, though at
first confused and formless, being afterwards adorned and digested
into order by the hand of God.[7]

Milton here defines in unmistakable terms the essential principle of his thought: " all things are of God:
*omnia ex Deo.*"   This principle is the basis of his politics
as well as of his cosmology.   It is the basis of his ethics
also: since matter is divine in essence nothing that comes
normally from matter can be anathema; the desires of
the flesh, for instance, are in themselves divine.

This divine matter is incorruptible:

Matter . . . proceeded incorruptible from God; and . . . it remains incorruptible as far as concerns its essence.[8]

Consequently, nothing can ever perish finally:

[7] *Treatise,* IV, 176–79.        [8] *Ibid.,* IV, 180.

. . . if all things are not only from God, but of God, no created thing can be finally annihilated.[9]

And man's immortality is based on the very nature of things; but therefore all things and beings are normally immortal, like man.

This matter, "productive stock of every subsequent good," contains in itself, in its divine essence, all the possibilities of life and intelligence. All beings come from it, so that there is no essential difference between inanimate things and animals, between animals and men; the whole of Being is one great scale, with gaps, going from matter to God; the whole of Being is God, made of his substance, organized by his will. This scale Raphael explains thus to Adam:

> O Adam! One Almighty is, from Whom
> All things proceed, and up to him return,
> If not deprav'd from good, created all
> Such to perfection, one first matter all,
> Indu'd with various forms, various degrees
> Of substance, and in things that live, of life;
> But more refin'd, more spiritous, and pure,
> As nearer to Him plac'd, or nearer tending,
> Each in their several active spheres assign'd:
> Till body up to spirit work, in bounds
> Proportion'd to each kind. So, from the root
> Springs lighter the green stalks; from thence the leaves
> More aery; last, the bright consummate flow'r
> Spirits odorous breathes; flow'rs, and their fruit,
> Man's nourishment, by gradual scale sublim'd
> To vital spirits aspire, to animal,
> To intellectual; give both life and sense,
> Fancy and understanding; whence the soul
> Reason receives; and reason is her being,
> Discursive or intuitive; discourse,
> Is oftest yours, the latter most is ours;
> Diff'ring but in degree, of kinds the same.[10]

[9] *Ibid.*, IV, 181.          [10] *P. L.*, V, 469-90.

It is owing to this identity of essence that food can be assimilated by beings, and that inert matter may feed intelligence. This nutritious matter circulates through the scale of beings:

> Therefore what He gives
> (Whose praise be ever sung!) to man, in part
> Spiritual, may of purest spirits be found
> No ingrateful food: and food alike those pure
> Intelligential substances require,
> As doth your rational; and both contain
> Within them ev'ry lower faculty
> Of sense, whereby they hear, see, smell, touch, taste;
> Tasting concoct, digest, assimilate,
> And corporeal to incorporeal turn.
> For know, whatever was created, needs
> To be sustain'd and fed: of elements,
> The grosser feeds the purer; earth the sea;
> Earth, and the sea feed air; the air, those fires
> Ethereal; and as lowest, first the moon;
> Whence, in her visage round, those spots, unpurg'd
> Vapors, not yet into her substance turn'd.
> Nor doth the moon no nourishment exhale
> From her moist continent, to higher orbs.
> The sun, that light imparts to all, receives
> From all his alimental recompense
> In humid exhalations; and at ev'n
> Sups with the Ocean.[11]

Everything then has come out of divine matter. But Milton goes further. Everything has come out of matter by a normal development of its latent powers without any intervention of God. Matter is the " productive stock of every subsequent good." Milton's thought is clearly expressed when he speaks of the reproduction of man, the point at which the intervention of God might the most easily be admitted:

[11] *Ibid.*, V, 404–26. We shall come back to this curious passage when studying Milton's sources. See below, pp. 305–06.

. . . the propagation and production of the human form were analogous to those of other forms, and were the proper effect of that power which had been communicated to matter by the Deity.[12]

Being is thus organized from God to matter, by the retraction of God, and from matter to God by the evolution of the latent divine powers of matter. Milton has a conception of natural laws, which he calls " natural necessity " (he has been careful to point out that God is not subject to it [13]) and which work in the reproduction of species. Thus Adam meditates:

> what if thy son
> Prove disobedient, and reprov'd, retort,
> Wherefore didst thou beget me? I sought it not;
> Wouldst thou admit for his contempt of thee
> That proud excuse? Yet him not thy election
> But natural necessity begot.[14]

Different names may be given to this Miltonic system: it is pantheism, it is materialism, and yet it can be called spiritualism; for Milton, the spirit contains matter, and matter is only a part of that Spirit who is God. The origin of matter is thus explained:

For spirit being the more excellent substance, virtually and essentially contains within itself the inferior one; as the spiritual and rational faculty contains the corporal, that is, the sentient and vegetative faculty. For not even divine virtue and efficiency could produce bodies out of nothing, . . . unless there had been some bodily power in the substance of God; since no one can give to another what he does not himself possess.[15]

And both (intelligence and reason) contain

> Within them ev'ry lower faculty
> Of sense, whereby they hear, see, smell, touch, taste.[16]

[12] *Treatise*, IV, 195.
[13] See above, p. 118.
[14] *P. L.*, X, 760–65.
[15] *Treatise*, IV, 181.
[16] *P. L.*, V, 410–11.

In reality, however, Milton is neither materialist nor spiritualist: he acknowledges no distinction between spirit and matter, the only difference being from the lesser to the greater degree. The body is for him the agglomeration of sensorial faculties, and the spirit that of the higher; and the two orders shade into each other, " till body up to spirit works." Therefore for Milton the question of the existence of the soul is suppressed. Or, to put it in a negative form, Milton does not believe in the existence of the soul. Body and soul are for him one and the same thing. The word " soul " is merely an abstract expression which separates arbitrarily the higher from the lower faculties and corresponds to no separate reality:

> . . . *man became a living soul;* whence it may be inferred . . . that man is a living being, intrinsically and properly one and individual, not compound or separable, not, according to the common opinion, made up and framed of two distinct and different natures, as of soul and body, — but the whole man is soul, and the soul man, that is to say, a body, or substance individual, animated, sensitive and rational. . . .[17]

And again:

> . . . that the spirit of man should be separate from the body, so as to have a perfect and intelligent existence independently of it, . . . the doctrine is evidently at variance both with nature and reason. . . . For the word *soul* is applied to every kind of living being, . . . yet it is never inferred from these expressions that the soul exists separate from the body in any of the brute creation.[18]

Man has been created similar to animals, and Milton insists on the point:

> There seems therefore no reason why the soul of man should be made an exception to the general law of creation. For . . . God

[17] *Treatise*, IV, 188.          [18] *Ibid.*, IV, 189.

breathed the breath of life into other living beings, and blended it
. . . intimately with matter. . . .[19]

. . . he infused the breath of life into other living beings also;
. . . every living thing receives animation from one and the same
source of life and breath. . . . Nor has the word *spirit* any other
meaning in the sacred writings, but that breath of life which we
inspire, or the vital, or sensitive, or rational faculty, or some action
or affection belonging to those faculties.[20]

For Milton knows that the Hebrews did not believe in
the existence of the soul, in our sense: " . . . in the
Scripture idiom, the soul is generally often put for the
whole animate body. . . ."[21] So we have in *Paradise
Lost:*

> And God said: let the waters generate
> Reptile with spawn abundant, living soul.[22]

And

> Let th' Earth bring forth fowl living in her kind,
> Cattle and creeping things, and beast of the earth,
> Each in their kind.[23]

What is called " soul " is propagated naturally in the
course of generation:

It would seem, therefore, that the human soul is not created
daily by the immediate act of God, but propagated from father to
son in natural order. . . .[24]

If the soul be equally diffused throughout any given whole, and
throughout every part of that whole, how can the human seed, the
noblest and most intimate part of all the body, be imagined destitute and devoid of the soul of the parents, or at least of the
father, when communicated to the son by the laws of generation?[25]

For matter produces life and all forms, including the
soul: " It is acknowledged by the common consent of

---

[19] *Ibid.,* IV, 195.
[20] *Ibid.,* IV, 188.
[21] *Ibid.,* IV, 281, and the foregoing quotations.
[22] *P. L.,* VII, 387–88.

[23] *P. L.,* VII, 451–53.
[24] *Treatise,* IV, 189.
[25] *Ibid.,* IV, 192–93.

almost all philosophers, that every *form,* to which class the human soul must be considered as belonging, is produced by the power of matter." [26] All this is only the normal development of the idea contained in Milton's phrase about matter being the "productive stock of every subsequent good."

### IV. DEATH AND RESURRECTION — BODY AND SPIRIT

In this cosmology, there is no place for death. Immortality is a direct consequence of the way the world is built, since "no created thing can be finally annihilated." Matter is divine and indestructible, and man has no soul that can be separated from his body. Therefore, every being is naturally and normally immortal.

Milton has adopted the view that death is merely a sort of cosmological incident of no particular importance, more or less equivalent to a sleep of matter. Death was brought into the world as a punishment of and a cleansing from sin. But for sin, death would not have existed; Adam and his children would have been transformed into "spirits" in the natural course of their evolution. The angel tells Adam:

> And from these corporal nutriments, perhaps,
> Your bodies may at last turn all to spirit,
> Improv'd by tract of time; and wing'd ascend
> Ethereal, as we; or may, at choice,
> Here or in heav'nly Paradises, dwell;
> If ye be found obedient.[27]

The body is destined to become spirit; that is, a substance similar to matter but more subtle, more lasting and better. Pure spirit exists no more for Milton than

[26] *Ibid.,* IV, 193.   [27] *P. L.,* V, 496–501.

" soul." A spirit is a being superior to man in its higher faculties, but essentially made of a more subtle body than man's. It seems evident that in Milton's mind, God himself — the manifest God, that is, the Creating Son — is a spirit of this kind, so that all he had to do was to " retire " his higher faculties from a part of that substance of his to create matter, made up of his lower faculties, with latent possibilities left of the higher ones.

This conception of "spirit" is best illustrated by the passage on love among the angels:

> To whom the angel, with a smile that glowed
> Celestial rosy red, love's proper hue,
> Answered, Let it suffice thee that thou know'st
> Us happy, and without love no happiness.
> Whatever pure thou in the body enjoy'st
> (And pure thou wert created) we enjoy
> In eminence, and obstacle find none
> Of membrane, joint or limb, exclusive bars.
> Easier than air with air, if spirits embrace
> Total they mix, union of pure with pure
> Desiring; nor restrain'd conveyance need
> As flesh to mix with flesh, or soul with soul.[28]

Death was then brought into the world by Sin. " The death of the body is to be considered in the light of a punishment for sin." [29]   Therefore, in the allegory of the second book of *Paradise Lost*, Death is born of Sin, and in the tenth book Sin introduces Death into the Earth. Even Nature would have been immortal had not man sinned: " All nature is likewise subject to mortality and a curse on account of man." [30]   That is why when Eve fell,

[28] *Ibid.*, VIII, 618–29.  Milton's conception of love might be by many thought as " material " as his conception of " spirit " or " soul."
[29] *Treatise*, IV, 269.
[30] *Ibid.*, IV, 260.

> Earth felt the wound, and Nature from her seat
> Sighing through all her works gave signs of woe,
> That all was lost.[31]

And when Adam yields,

> Earth trembled from her entrails, as again
> In pangs, and Nature gave a second groan.[32]

Disorder and death come into the whole of Nature: disorder of inanimate things, death of animate. This is one of the grandest passages in Milton. Death and Sin begin their work:

> . . . they both betook them several ways,
> Both to destroy or unimmortal make
> All kinds, and for destruction to mature
> Sooner or later.[33]

Then God gives orders and his ministers change the natural order of things:

> The sun
> Had first his precept so to move, so shine,
> As might affect the earth with cold and heat
> Scarce tolerable; and from the north to call
> Decrepit winter; from the south to bring
> Solstitial summer's heat; . . .
>
> .　.　.　.　.　.　.　.
>
> 　　　　. . . to bring in change
> Of seasons to each clime; else had the spring
> Perpetual smil'd on earth with vernant flow'rs,
> Equal in days and nights, except to those
> Beyond the polar circles; to them day
> Had unbenighted shone, while the low sun
> To recompense his distance, in their sight
> Had rounded still th' horizon, and not known
> Or east or west; which had forbid the snow
> From cold Estotiland; and south as far
> Beneath Magellan. . . .
>
> .　.　.　.　.　.　.　.

---

[31] *P. L.*, IX, 782–84.　　[32] *Ibid.*, IX, 1000–01.　　[33] *Ibid.*, X, 610–13.

> . . . Thus began
> Outrage from lifeless things; but Discord first
> (Daughter of Sin) among th' irrational,
> Death introduc'd through fierce antipathy:
> Beast now with beast gan war, and fowl with fowl,
> And fish with fish; to graze the herb all leaving,
> Devour'd each other; nor stood much in awe
> Of man, but fled him; or with count'nance grim
> Glar'd on him passing.[34]

But once matter was submitted to the curse, man had to die wholly; he had no soul to survive.

. . . the whole man dies. . . . For . . . what could be more absurd, than that the mind, which is the part principally offending, should escape the threatened death; and that the body alone, to which immortality was equally allotted, before death came into the world by sin, should pay the penalty of sin by undergoing death, though not implicated in the transgression?

It is evident that the saints and believers of old, the patriarchs, prophets and apostles, without exception, held this doctrine.[35]

. . . the soul (whether we understand by this term the whole human composition, or whether it is to be considered as synonymous with the spirit) is subject to death, natural as well as violent.[36]

The . . . text . . . "the spirit shall return unto God . . ." must be understood with considerable latitude. . . . Euripides . . . has, without being aware of it, given a far better interpretation of this passage than the commentators. . . . That is, every constituent part returns at dissolution to its elementary principle. This is confirmed by Ezek. xxxvii. 9: "come from the four winds, O breath"; it is certain therefore that the spirit of man must have previously departed thither from whence it is now summoned to return.[37]

Thus the soul, like the body — since there is no difference — returns to the elements at death. But "no

---

[34] *Ibid.*, X, 651–714.
[35] *Treatise*, IV, 271.
[36] *Ibid.*, IV, 275.
[37] *Ibid.*, IV, 278–79. *Cf.* the *Suppliants*, 532.

created thing can be finally annihilated." [38]   God's plans would be frustrated by the destruction of his work:

God is neither willing, nor, properly speaking, able to annihilate anything altogether.   He is not willing, because he does everything with a view to some end, — but nothing can be the end neither of God nor of anything whatever. . . . Again, God is not able . . . because by creating nothing he would create and not create at the same time, which involves a contradiction.[39]
. . . the covenant with God is not dissolved by death.[40]

And Milton adds the (to be) Kantian argument of practical reason:

. . . were there no resurrection, the righteous would be of all men the most miserable, and the wicked who have a better portion in this life, most happy; which would be altogether inconsistent with the . . . justice of God.[41]

Resurrection is indeed the only hypothesis left.   Death is a sleep.   And Milton adds the further consolation that, in the state of death, time does not exist, because time " is the measure of motion " [42] and in death there is no motion.   Therefore the interval between death and resurrection, however long the living may consider it, does not exist for the dead:

If . . . it be true that there is no time without motion, which Aristotle illustrates by the example of those who were fabled to have slept in the temple of the heroes, and who, on awaking, imagined that the moment in which they awoke had succeeded without an interval to that in which they fell asleep; how much more must intervening time be annihilated to the departed, so that to them to die and to be with Christ will seem to take place at the same moment? [43]

Therefore, at the end of the world there will take place the resurrection of the dead, proved by "testi-

[38] *Treatise*, IV, 181.
[39] *Ibid.*, IV, 181–82.
[40] *Ibid.*, IV, 480–81.

[41] *Ibid.*
[42] *Ibid.*, IV, 185.
[43] *Ibid.*, IV, 280.

monies from Scripture " and " several arguments from reason." [44]

Thus the plans of God and the destiny of individual beings will be accomplished — beings formed of divine matter and rising gradually by a progressive scale, reaching a consciousness of their Unity with God,[45] of their communion with the whole of Being. Thus will be realized fully those possibilities that were latent in the Infinite before creation, and which God made conscious by making them free. Those possibilities first formed matter, then all things and beings made of it, rising to life and intelligence, reaching perfection " in their kind " in this mortal life, and disappearing, washed of all their faults and failings, in death; but the covenant was not broken, God had created them in order to add them to himself; in the day of final glorification, he rouses them from that sleep of death into which each being had fallen in his turn and unites them all, in the total, perfect, and endless life which replaces the solitary and latent life of the Pre-Creation.

[44] *Ibid.*, IV, 480.
[45] *Ibid.* See also IV, 276, and the whole of Chapter XXXIII.

## CHAPTER III

## PSYCHOLOGY AND ETHICS

THE conception of the Fall comes into Milton's cosmology as disturbing the order established by God. In Milton's psychology, the Fall is the dominant conception, and this part of our study will be an analysis of the state of Fall and of the normal or regenerated state opposed to it. Milton's conception of man — and his consequent conception of ethics — are organized around these two ideas.

### I. THE ORIGIN OF EVIL AND THE DUALITY OF MAN

The origin of evil is a redoubtable problem for the deist, and still more for the pantheistic deist, Milton. For everything comes from God. Therefore Milton dared to say:

> Evil into the mind of God or man
> May come and go, so unapproved, and leave
> No spot or blame behind.[1]

Evil exists as a possibility in God himself. This allows us to understand that when God " retires," abandons certain parts of himself to their latent impulses, evil is expressed, owing to free will.

What does this " evil " consist in?

The study of the Fall teaches us that for Milton man is a double being, in whom co-exist desire and intelligence or passion and reason. The two powers ought to be in

[1] *P. L.*, V, 117-19.

harmonious equilibrium, desire being normally expressed, but remaining under the leadership of reason. Evil appears, the Fall takes place, when passion triumphs over reason.

## II. The Fall

### A. *The Fall in general: the triumph of passion over reason*

Michael explains thus to Adam what the Fall consists in:

> Since thy original lapse, true liberty
> Is lost, which always with right reason dwells
> Twinned, and from her hath no dividual being:
> Reason in man obscured, or not obeyed,
> Immediately inordinate desires
> And upstart passions catch the government
> From reason, and to servitude reduce
> Man till then free.[2]

Passion triumphant over reason — such is the source of all evil: moral evil, physical evil (the consequence of moral evil), and political evil. That is what Milton calls "evil concupiscence."[3] The state of Fall is thus analyzed:

> They sat them down to weep; nor only tears
> Rained at their eyes, but high winds worse within
> Began to rise — high passions, anger, hate,
> Mistrust, suspicion, discord — and shook sore
> Their inward state of mind, calm region once
> And full of peace, now tost and turbulent:
> For understanding ruled not, and the will
> Heard not her lore, both in subjection now
> To sensual appetite, who from beneath
> Usurping over sov'reign reason claimed
> Superior sway.[4]

Before the Fall, Raphael had warned Adam:

[2] *P. L.*, XII, 83-90.    [3] *Treatise*, IV, 259.    [4] *P. L.*, IX, 21-31.

. . . take heed lest passion sway
Thy judgment to do ought which else free will
Would not admit.[5]

The dualism so clearly marked in the poems, of which it constitutes the symbolic basis (the Son being Reason, and Satan Passion), plays an equally important part in the prose works, in which Milton applies it to politics. It is a principle which had slowly crystallized through his private and public experience [6] into the very essence of his thought. From it endless consequences extend into all the regions of his philosophy.

Milton thus addresses his contemporaries:

Unless you will subjugate the propensity to avarice, to ambition, and sensuality, and expel all luxury from yourselves and your families, you will find that you have cherished a more stubborn and intractable despot at home, than you ever encountered in the field. . . . You, therefore, who wish to remain free, either instantly be wise, or, as soon as possible, cease to be fools; if you think slavery an intolerable evil, learn obedience to reason and the government of yourselves. . . .[7]

And the first pamphlet against monarchy begins as follows:

If men within themselves would be governed by reason, and not generally give up their understanding to a double tyranny, of custom from without, and blind affections within, they would discern better what it is to favour and uphold the tyrant of a nation. But, being slaves within doors, no wonder that they strive so much to have the public state conformably governed to the inward vicious rule by which they govern themselves. For, indeed, none

---

[5] *Ibid.,* VIII, 635–37.

[6] This, I must repeat, is in no way in contradiction with the fact that the idea existed outside him, before it came to him, in authors whom he knew perfectly well. Every thinker has to rediscover for himself truths which belong to all, and there is all the difference between an idea thus adopted through personal experience, and one borrowed merely to fill up a gap in mental equipment.

[7] *Second Defence,* in *Prose Works,* I, 295, 299.

can love freedom heartily but good men; the rest love not freedom but licence, which never hath more scope, or more indulgence
than under tyrants.  Hence is it that tyrants are not oft offended,
nor stand much in doubt of bad men, as being all naturally
servile. . . .[8]

In the story of the Fall, the theory applies to Adam.
Adam has been carried away, against his reason, by his
passion for Eve:

> Against his better knowledge, not deceived,
> But fondly overcome with female charm.[9]

But with this " female charm," we come to a group of
ideas which played a capital part in Milton's thought,
because they came to him from the most painful experience of his own life.[10]

### B. *The Fall in particular: sensuality*

The first consequence of the Fall is sensuality, which
becomes, so to speak, the characteristic trait of the state
of Fall.  Milton in this follows Augustine:

They felt a new motion in their flesh, which had become rebellious as a consequence of their own rebellion. . . . Then it was
that the flesh began to covet against the spirit. . . . The motion
of concupiscence is the consequence of Sin.[11]

So Milton describes the first effect of the forbidden fruit,
which he looks upon as an aphrodisiac:

> They swim in mirth, and fancy that they feel
> Divinity within them breeding wings
> Wherewith to scorn the earth.  But that false fruit
> Far other operation first display'd,

[8] *Ibid.*, II, 2.
[9] *P. L.*, IX, 998–99.  Eve's case is quite as plain.  See below, pp. 159 ff.
[10] See above, pp. 49 ff.
[11] *De civitate Dei*, XIII–XIV.

Carnal desire inflaming: he on Eve
Began to cast lascivious eyes; she him
As wantonly repaid; in lust they burn:

. . . . . . . . . . . .

But come! so well refresh'd, now let us play,
As meet is, after such delicious fare;
For never did thy beauty, since the day
I saw thee first, and wedded thee, adorn'd
With all perfections, so inflame my sense
With ardor to enjoy thee; fairer now
Than ever; bounty of this virtuous tree!
   So said he, and forbore not glance or toy
Of amorous intent, well understood
Of Eve, whose eye darted contagious fire.
Her hand he seiz'd; and to a shady bank,
Thick overhead with verdant roof imbowr'd,
He led her nothing loth; flow'rs were the couch,
Pansies, and violets, and asphodel,
And hyacinth, earth's freshest softest lap.
There they their fill of love and love's disport
Took largely; of their mutual guilt the seal,
The solace of their sin; till dewy sleep
Oppress'd them, weary'd with their amorous play.[12]

This is the very perfection of the Fall. The proof is that
their knowledge of good and evil does not come to them
after the eating of the apple, but after the sensual crisis.
The first knowledge is sexual shame:

                        . . . up they rose
As from unrest, and each the other viewing,
Soon found their eyes how open'd, and their minds
How darken'd.[13]

Adam tells Eve that he sees

            . . . in our faces evident the signs
            Of foul concupiscence,[14]

and proposes to

[12] *P. L.*, IX, 1009–45.    [13] *Ibid.*, IX, 1051–54.    [14] *Ibid.*, IX, 1077–78.

cover round
Those middle parts, that this new comer, Shame,
There sit not, and reproach us as unclean.[15]

It was against sensuality that Raphael had warned Adam,
in scarcely veiled terms, at the end of their talk:

But if the sense of Touch, whereby mankind
Is propagated, seem such dear delight
Beyond all other, think the same vouchsaf'd
To cattle and each beast; which would not be
To them made common and divulg'd if ought
Therein enjoy'd were worthy to subdue
The soul of man, or passion in him move.[16]

And Raphael was mainly referring to this passion when
he cautioned Adam to

take heed lest passion sway
Thy judgment. . . .

Because, although the Fall is the triumph of passion in
general, the principal passion and the most powerful
desire lie in sexual inclination, through which the race
is perpetuated and life transmitted. Sexual desire is, so
to speak, essentially " desire." It is most capable of
obliterating reason completely and of leading man to the
worst folly. And in such obliteration is the abstract typical trait of the Fall. Therefore there will ever remain in
Milton a deep mistrust of woman, the witness of the
degradation:

Thy mate, who sees when thou art seen least wise.[17]

Milton, to mark the essential part of sensuality in the
Fall, brings the same motive into the fall of Satan. Satan
fell through pride. But during the first night of rebellion,
sensuality was born in him and his fall was consummated

---

[15] *Ibid.*, IX, 1096–98.    [16] *Ibid.*, VIII, 579–85.    [17] *Ibid.*, VIII, 578.

in incest. Milton paraphrases James: " Then when Lust hath conceived it bringeth forth Sin; and Sin, when it is finished, bringeth forth Death."

This makes of Satan Lust, since he " bringeth forth Sin," his daughter. The study of *Paradise Lost* shows us Satan as a general symbol of evil desire, opposed to the Son, who is Reason.[18] But Milton insists on the trait, which is peculiarly Lust, in the narrow sense: sensuality. Satan's daughter, Sin, speaks to him:

> . . . familiar grown,
> I pleased, and with attractive graces won
> The most averse, thee chiefly, who full oft
> Thyself in me thy perfect image viewing
> Becam'st enamoured, and such joy thou took'st
> With me in secret, that my womb conceived
> A growing burden.[19]

And Satan remembers, in his infernal and horrible tenderness,

> . . . dalliance had with thee in Heav'n and joys
> Then sweet, now sad to mention . . .[20]

## III. The Normal State

### A. *Legitimate sensuality*

For Milton, however, desire is not evil in itself. Desire is normal, necessary, good; it is divine in its origin like matter itself. Evil appears only when desire obliterates intellect. Therefore the regeneration of man will be, not the suppression of desire, but the triumph of reason over passion. When desire is approved of by reason, not only is it allowed, but it is good, necessary, " commanded."

---

[18] See Part III.   [19] *P. L.*, II, 761-67.   [20] *Ibid.*, II, 819-20.

We must be careful to note that evil is not the normal state of man. Primitive nature was good. Regenerated human nature is good. In it, desire, fully in harmony with reason, is legitimate. Milton, looking upon himself as a type of normal man, faces his own desires not only without shame, but with pride. Therefore, there exists a sensuality which is good.

Raphael explains clearly the essential differences:

> What higher in her society thou find'st
> Attractive, humane, rational, love still;
> In loving thou dost well, in passion not;
> Wherein true love consists not. Love refines
> The thoughts, and heart enlarges; hath his seat
> In reason, and is judicious; is the scale
> By which to heav'nly love thou may'st ascend;
> Not sunk in carnal pleasure, for which cause,
> Among the beasts no mate for thee was found.[21]

Love has his seat in reason. This means that physical love is legitimate when man and woman are united by the common interests of reason, affection, religion, all the higher inclinations.

For Milton, man is one; the soul has no separate existence. The whole being then participates in love, even physical love; the angels themselves love physically. Hence the abomination when man's inferior needs are satisfied without the participation of the higher desires. That is binding " the living soul to the dead corpse." That is prostituting the highest part of man to the vilest, that is man divided against himself. Such is, as we have seen, the theory that underlies the divorce treatises. But when, on the contrary, the physical inclination, far from " subduing the soul of man," is only the realization on

[21] *Ibid.*, VIII, 586–94.

the material plane of the whole soul, the material union
of two beings already united morally and intellectually,
then sex is the mysterious consecration of the whole of
man, and becomes sacred: it is the instrument of God
for the transmission of life.    Thus Adam answers the
suspicious angel:

> . . . procreation common to all kinds
> (Though higher in the genial bed by far
> And with mysterious reverence I deem).[22]

Therefore Milton places *before the Fall* his magnificent
hymn to connubial love:

> Nor turn'd, I ween,
> Adam from his fair spouse, nor Eve the rites
> Mysterious of connubial love refus'd:
> Whatever hypocrites austerely talk
> Of purity and place and innocence,
> Defaming as impure what God declares
> Pure, and commands to some, leaves free to all.
> Our Maker bids increase; who bids abstain,
> But our destroyer, foe to God, and man?
> Hail wedded love! mysterious law, true source
> Of human offspring, sole propriety,
> In Paradise of all things common else.
> By thee adult'rous lust was driv'n from men
> Among the bestial herds to range; by thee,
> (Founded in reason, loyal, just, and pure)
> Relations dear, and all the charities
> Of father, son, and brother first were known.
> Far be it that I should write thee sin or blame,
> Or think thee unbefitting holiest place,
> Perpetual fountain of domestic sweets,
> Whose bed is undefil'd and chaste pronounc'd,
> Present, or past; as saints and patriarchs us'd.
> Here, Love his golden shafts employs; here lights
> His constant lamp; and waves his purple wings;
> Reigns here and revels: not in the bought smile

[22] *Ibid.*, VIII, 597–99.

Of harlots, loveless, joyless, unendear'd;
Casual fruition, nor in Court amours,
Mix'd dance, or wanton mask, or midnight ball,
Or serenade, which the starv'd lover sings
To his proud Fair, best quitted with disdain.
These, lull'd by nightingales, embracing slept;
And on their naked limbs the flow'ry roof
Shower'd roses, which the morn repair'd.[23]

Milton feels a religious respect before this mystery of the springs of life, pure and noble, even in its physical instruments. The *De doctrina* speaks of " the human seed, the noblest and most intimate part of all the body." [24] Desire is then an essential element of man's nature. It is not to be eliminated without evil results, and we have heard Milton speaking of nature's current being stopped, when " the suffocation and upward forcing of some lower part affects the head and inward sense with dotage and idle fancies." [25] But the desires must be sanctioned by reason, " founded in reason " ; " the act thereof in a right esteem can no longer be matrimonial, than it is an effect of conjugal love . . . proceeding as it ought from intellective principles " ; it is to " participate of the rational." [26] And this satisfaction given to legitimate sensuality preserves man from evil passion:

By thee adult'rous lust was driven from men,
Among the bestial herds to range.

But this can only be attained, even in marriage, when the souls are in harmony: " for if there be not a more humane burning which marriage must satisfy, marriage

---

[23] *Ibid.*, IV, 741–73.
[24] *Prose Works*, IV, 193.
[25] See above, Part I, on the divorce tracts.
[26] *Tetrachordon*, in *Prose Works*, III, 341–42.

cannot be honorable for the meet reducing and terminating lust between two." [27]

The normal state is then in the union of the soul's desire and the body's. Therefore Milton placed sexual life in Paradise before the Fall, at a time when lust did not exist, since the harmony between mind and passion had not been broken. As the *De doctrina* has it, " since Adam's fall, the provision of a remedy against incontinence has become in some degree a secondary end " [28] of marriage, which existed before.

Milton goes further and higher, according to his habit, and justifies his ideas by what he considers in a measure as the example of God himself.[29] That is because this conception goes beyond psychology and reaches even into ontology. God is the all; God is matter; all the instincts of matter are therefore good, and normal man, who is matter, fulfils God's aims as he satisfies his own desires:

> Our Maker bids increase, who bids abstain,
> But our destroyer, foe to God and man!

## B. *The conception of woman*

From these ideas, Milton derives two conclusions: the necessity of woman, for the satisfaction of normal desire, for the regularisation of passion, which conjugal love submits to reason, and for a special sort of intellectual intercourse, not to be had between men; and then the inferiority of woman, who remains, after all, the instrument of desire. The two principles remain essential when Milton deals with the higher aspects of the problem of woman.

---

[27] See the full quotations in our chapter on the divorce pamphlets (above, pp. 64 ff.).

[28] *Prose Works,* IV, 239.

[29] I have quoted the texts out of *Tetrachordon,* and shall come back to them in discussing Milton's sources. See below, pp. 291-92.

Because of her passionate rôle, woman cannot participate fully in intelligence.  She can only participate in it through submission to it, even as desire is legitimate when it submits to reason.  And man is the representative of reason:

> He for God only, she for God in him.[30]

Therefore woman, who represents desire, must be submitted to man, who represents reason.  When the reverse happens, catastrophe follows.  So in the story of the fall in the IXth book of *Paradise Lost*, Eve carried away by her feelings, which rule her only too easily, is blinded in her intellect, because her intellect is of an inferior quality.  But Adam is not blinded.  His fall comes because he, clear intelligence, allows Eve, blind passion, to lead:

> Against his better knowledge, not deceived,
> But fondly overcome by female charm.

All Milton's ideas of woman and her part in life are derived then from his two principles: desire neither can, nor ought to be rejected, but desire must be in harmony with, subject to, reason.  On this basis, Milton reaches a very high conception of marriage and of woman.

> Though both
> Not equal, as their sex not equal seem'd:
> For contemplation he, and valor form'd;
> For softness she, and sweet attractive grace;
> He for God only, she for God in him.
> His fair large front and eye sublime declar'd
> Absolute rule; and hyacinthine locks
> Round from his parted forelock manly hung
> Clustring, but not beneath his shoulders broad.
> She, as a veil, down to the slender waist
> Her unadornèd golden tresses wore
> Dishevel'd, but in wanton ringlets wav'd,

[30] *P. L.*, IV, 299.

> As the vine curls her tendrils, which imply'd
> Subjection, but requir'd with gentle sway,
> And by her yielded, by him best receiv'd;
> Yielded with coy submission, modest pride,
> And sweet reluctant amorous delay.[31]

Adam knows she is his inferior:

> [God] at least on her bestow'd
> Too much of ornament; in outward show
> Elaborate; of inward, less exact.
> For well I understand in the prime end
> Of nature, her th' inferior, in the mind,
> And outward faculties, which most excel;
> In outward also her resembling less
> His image who made both, and less expressing
> The character of that dominion given
> O'er other creatures.[32]

And Eve accepts her inferiority, not as a degradation, but as a privilege the more, since thus she has more to receive, more to admire, more to possess — a typically feminine solution to the whole problem; she says to Adam:

> O thou! for whom,
> And from whom I was form'd, flesh of thy flesh,
> And without whom am to no end, my guide
> And head! what thou hast said is just and right.
> For we to Him indeed all praises owe,
> And daily thanks; I chiefly who enjoy
> So far the happier lot, enjoying thee
> Pre-eminent by so much odds; while thou
> Like consort to thyself canst nowhere find.[33]

She acknowledges, with a modesty which is mostly coquetry, and certainty of her own power,

> How beauty is excell'd by manly grace
> And wisdom, which alone is truly fair.

. . . . . . . . . . .

[31] *Ibid.*, IV., 295–311.    [32] *Ibid.*, VIII, 537–46.    [33] *Ibid.*, IV, 440–48.

> My author and my disposer, what thou bid'st
> Unargued I obey; so God ordains,
> God is thy law, thou mine.[34]

But woman is necessary to man, fills an otherwise irreme-
diable gap in his being:

> Bone of my bone, flesh of my flesh, myself
> Before me; woman is her name, of man
> Extracted. . . .
> And they shall be one flesh, one heart, one soul.[35]

And again:

> . . . to give thee being I lent
> Out of my side to thee nearest my heart
> Substantial life, to have thee by my side
> Henceforth; an individual solace dear;
> Part of my soul I see thee and thee claim
> My other half.[36]

Therefore woman has power over man, who needs her.
First through passion, which through woman alone takes
complete hold of him:

> . . . I . . . must confess to find
> In all things else delight indeed, but such
> As us'd or not, works in the mind no change,
> Nor vehement desire: these delicacies
> I mean of taste, sight, smell, herbs, fruits, and flow'rs,
> Walks, and the melody of birds; but here
> Far otherwise! transported I behold,
> Transported touch; here passion first I felt,
> Commotion strange, in all enjoyments else
> Superior and unmov'd; here only weak
> Against the charm of beauty's pow'rful glance.
> Or Nature fail'd in me, and left some part
> Not proof enough such object to sustain;
> Or from my side subducting, took perhaps
> More than enough.[37]

34 *Ibid.*, IV, 490–91, 635–37.      36 *Ibid.*, IV, 483–88.
35 *Ibid.*, VIII, 495–99.            37 *Ibid.*, VIII, 523–37.

For passion is founded on a need, on a failing in the very constitution of man. But woman has power also through the greater delicacy of her feelings:

> Neither her outside form'd so fair, nor aught
> In procreation common to all kinds
> (Though higher of the genial bed by far,
> And with mysterious reverence I deem)
> So much delights me, as those graceful acts,
> Those thousand decencies that daily flow
> From all her words and actions, mix'd with love
> And sweet compliance.[38]

This double power of woman, over man's higher, as over his lower inclinations, makes her dangerous in the extreme to him. He has only, as a refuge, God, and it is lucky for him that he is

> He, for God only; she for God in him:

His care for the impersonal is his only escape from, his only weapon over, woman. For otherwise, his whole being, from top to bottom, is liable to be

> Fondly overcome by female charm.

The angel severely reminds Adam of the tremendous fact:

> To whom the angel with contracted brow:
>   Accuse not Nature, she hath done her part;
> Do thou but thine, and be not diffident
> Of Wisdom; she deserts thee not, if thou
> Dismiss not her, when most thou need'st her nigh,

---

[38] *Ibid.*, VIII, 596–603. Let me hide here in a footnote a sentiment that will be considered by many as blasphemy. In the abstract (leaving aside a perhaps greater power of expression on Shakespeare's part) Milton is a greater poet than Shakespeare on this theme of human nature. For Shakepeare gets his effects at times of crisis and tragedy, when effects grow cheap, whereas Milton reaches his on ordinary themes, common to the whole of mankind in ordinary circumstances not peculiar to haughty aristocrats of the spirit.

By attributing overmuch to things
Less excellent, as thou thyself perceivest.
For what admir'st thou, what transports thee so?
An outside? fair no doubt, and worthy well
Thy cherishing, thy honouring, and thy love,
Not thy subjection: weigh with her thyself;
Then value: oft times nothing profits more
Than self-esteem, grounded on just and right,
Well managed; of that skill the more thou know'st,
The more she will acknowledge thee her head,
And to realities yield all her shows;
Made so adorn for thy delight the more,
So awful, that with honour thou may'st love
Thy mate, who sees when thou art seen least wise.[39]

## And God tells Adam, after the Fall:

Was she thy God, that her thou didst obey,
Before His voice?  Or was she made thy guide,
Superior, or but equal, that to her
Thou didst resign thy manhood, and the place
Wherein God set thee above her, made of thee
And for thee; whose perfection far excell'd
Hers, in all real dignity?  Adorn'd
She was indeed, and lovely to attract
Thy love, not thy subjection; and her gifts
Were such as under government well-seem'd;
Unseemly to bear rule, which was thy part.[40]

When woman is not properly under the rule of reason,
she becomes the principal source of evil, and causes

innumerable
Disturbances on earth through female snares
And strait conjunction with this sex . . .
Which infinite calamity shall cause
To human life, and household peace confound.[41]

And Adam is tempted to throw on woman the causes of
evil itself:

[39] *P. L.*, VIII, 560–78.    [40] *Ibid.*, X, 145–55.    [41] *Ibid.*, X, 896–908.

But still I see the tenor of man's woe
Hold on the same, from woman to begin.
　From man's effeminate slackness it begins,
Said the angel; who should better hold his place
By wisdom, and superior gifts receiv'd.[42]

For man is responsible for woman, and if she became the instrument of evil, the fault is his.

We find in the *Samson Agonistes* Milton's last word on the subject, fantastically put; and we can see that the problem was far from being solved in his mind:

It is not virtue, wisdom, valour, wit,
Strength, comeliness of shape, or amplest merit
That woman's love can win or long inherit;
But what it is, hard is to say,
Harder to hit,
Which way soever men refer it,
Much like thy riddle, Samson, in one day
Or seven, though one should musing sit.

.　.　.　.　.　.　.　.　.　.　.

Is it for that such outward ornament
Was lavished on their sex, that inward gifts
Were left for haste unfinished, judgment scant,
Capacity not raised to apprehend
Or value what is best
In choice, but oftest to affect the wrong?
Or was too much of self-love mixed,
Of constancy no root infixed,
That either they love nothing, or not long?
　Whate'er it be, to wisest men and best
Seeming at first all heav'nly under virgin veil,
Soft, modest, meek, demure,
Once joined, the contrary she proves, a thorn
Intestine, far within defensive arms
A cleaving mischief, in his way to virtue
Adverse and turbulent, or by her charms
Draws him awry enslaved

[42] *Ibid.*, XI, 628–32.

With dotage, and his sense depraved
To folly and shameful deeds which ruin ends.
What pilot so expert but needs must wreck,
Imbarked with such a steersmate at the helm?
    Favour'd of heav'n who finds
One virtuous, rarely found,
That in domestic good combines:
Happy that house! his way to peace is smooth;
But virtue, which breaks through all opposition,
And all temptation can remove,
Most shines and most is acceptable above.
    Therefore God's universal law
Gave to the man despotic power
Over his female in due awe,
Nor from that right to part an hour,
Smile she or lour:
So shall he least confusion draw
On his whole life, not swayed
By female usurpation, or dismayed.[43]

In this astonishing invective, in which a rich humor
mixes with fierceness, there is the bitterness of the man
who has suffered, and the resentment of the philosopher
who has not understood.  Even here, four lines remain
on the " favour'd of heaven," as a geological survival of
a lost continent, traces of an ideal " rarely found."

In the prose works, the ideal of the union of man and
woman is most precisely expressed.  A very high idea of
the possibilities of woman underlies the divorce tracts.
Woman must be the companion of man in all that is
highest in him.  "It is not good that man should be
alone," says Scripture; and Milton comments: "And
here ' alone ' is meant alone without woman; otherwise
Adam had the company of God himself, and angels to
converse with. . . ."  But there is in the *mind* of woman
something peculiar that makes it specially adequate to

[43] *Samson,* ll. 1010–60.

conversation with man; and from intellectual intercourse between the sexes, there arise feelings and ideas which are not reached by conversation between men only; hence the attack on Augustine's " crabbed opinion." " Some would have the sense hereof to be in respect of procreation only; and Austin contests that manly friendship in all other regard had been a more becoming solace for Adam, than to spend so many secret years in an empty world with one woman. But our writers deservedly reject this crabbed opinion," because woman's mind is different from man's, and in the interplay of these differences " the different sex in most resembling unlikeness, and most unlike resemblance, cannot but please best, and be best pleased in the aptitude of that variety." [44]

And Milton, setting his ideal in the existence of God himself, assimilates the rôle of woman in man's intellectual life to that of Wisdom playing before God. Milton evinces here the deepest psychological insight. Like God himself, man has need of recreation (the word takes on its other meaning here) in communion with an appropriate being who gives him rest, comfort, and strength; intellectually also, in the harmony of common interests and ideas, in a region where man is understood without effort, without the strenuous battle of ideas which conversation between men nearly always is; where man is understood, and finds not only passive acceptance of his notions, but improvement upon them through the greater delicacy of woman's perception of feeling; improvement

---

[44] *Tetrachordon,* in *Prose Works,* III, 329–31. The whole passage, whose every word deserves a commentary, is given above, pp. 65–66. It probably is the most important passage in Milton's prose for an understanding of his whole scheme of ideas; and we shall have to refer to it again.

not in contest, but in harmony.  Woman plays intellectually a different part from man's, one which is, in
Milton's idea, inferior; but which is not repetition, or
passiveness.  Woman's intellect has a quality peculiarly
her own, which is necessary to the intellectual life: " conjugal love arising from a mutual fitness to the final causes
of wedlock, help and society in religious, civil and
domestic conversation." [45]   Note that Milton says *help*.
He can therefore scarcely be accused of diminishing
woman.  In particular cases, he took pleasure in acknowl-
edging the superiority of certain feminine personalities.
We know this from his own intercourse with women, [46]
and from his written statement: woman may be the more
intelligent; then she should lead:

> Not but that particular exceptions may have place, if she exceed
> her husband in prudence and dexterity, and he contentedly yield:
> for then a superior and more natural law comes in, that the wiser
> should govern the less wise, whether male or female. [47]

This, in practical life, remains an exception; generally
man is to be the leader; but even then woman's dignity
is fully recognized:

> Nevertheless man is not to hold her as a servant, but receives
> her into a part of that empire which God proclaims him to, though
> not equally, yet largely, as his own image and glory: for it is
> no small glory to him, that a creature so like him should be made
> subject to him. [48]

Even in the explosion of his anger in the divorce tracts,
Milton never blasphemed against his high faith in a
feminine ideal.  And in the *De doctrina*, the final doctrine
remains the same as in the youthful writings:

[45] *Tetrachordon*, in *Prose Works*, III, 342.
[46] For example, his friendship with Lady Ranelagh.
[47] *Tetrachordon*, in *Prose Works*, III, 325.     [48] *Ibid.*

. . . marriage consists in the mutual exercise of benevolence, love, help, and solace between the espoused parties . . . the pleasures of society . . . conjugal assistance, which is afforded by love alone.[49]

Thus, for Milton, woman is essentially and necessarily different from man. It is only by their union in spirit, by woman's participation in man's intellectual occupations as well as in man's physical life, that both reach their perfection as human beings. But in this final harmony, woman remains under man, not as a slave under a master, but as a queen under a king.

Let us add one chivalrous trait to the picture. The element of chivalry is not lacking in Milton. What greater instance in the whole world than that of Adam deliberately and clear-headedly joining Eve in her transgression, not to be parted from her in the punishment?

Milton has felt that the subtle charm of woman is higher than intellect and man. The psychologist and the artist in him have seen that the most exquisite charm of life is given when intellect after all lets itself go, gives up its ceaseless watch, abdicates before living beauty. There is the ultimate triumph of woman. Women have much to forgive Milton. They even have to forgive him for being in the right about them — a difficult task, but they can do so, in consideration of this one speech of Adam's:

> Yet when I approach
> Her loveliness, so absolute she seems
> And in herself complete, so well to know
> Her own, that what she wills to do or say
> Seems wisest, virtuousest, discreetest, best;
> All higher knowledge in her presence falls
> Degraded, wisdom in discourse with her

[49] *Prose Works*, IV, 239, 252.

> Loses discountenanced, and like folly shows;
> Authority and reason on her wait,
> As one intended first, not after made
> Occasionally; and, to consummate all,
> Greatness of mind and nobleness their seat
> Build in her loveliest, and create an awe
> About her, as a guard angelic placed.[50]

It is true that the angel answers with " contracted brow "
and Adam, " half abashed," has to reply, in order to re-
assert his dignity, about her love and sweet compliance,

> . . . which declare unfeign'd
> Union of mind, or in us both one soul;
> Harmony to behold in wedded pair
> More grateful than harmonious sound to the ear.
> Yet these subject not; I to thee disclose
> What inward thence I feel; not therefore foil'd,
> Who meet with various objects, from the sense
> Variously representing; yet still free,
> Approve the best, and follow what I approve.[51]

But then Adam, who is not deficient in the better kind of
slyness, certainly scores off the surly angel when asking
him, immediately after

> Love not the heav'nly spirits, and how their love
> Express they . . . ?

Whereupon Raphael himself has to take refuge in blushes
and extremely candid admissions.[52]

### C. *Reason triumphant*

It was an intellectual error — brought about by Satan's
keen sophistry — that caused the Fall. " Deceived " is
the term Milton uses about our first parents, deceived by

---

[50] *P. L.*, VIII, 546–59.
[51] *Ibid.*, VIII, 603–11.
[52] *Ibid.*, VIII, 620 ff.  See above, p. 65.

the argument that passions bring forward to circumvent reason when it opposes them. Even thus, in Dante, the damned,

Charmo perduto il ben dell' intelletto.

Such is the state of damnation, the Fall. Reason restores man when it triumphs over both the sophistry and the charms of passion:

to vanquish *by wisdom* hellish wiles.

Redemption is the return of reason. The triumph is won, not on the cross, but in the desert, where Satan tries to deceive Christ by appealing to his passions, his physical needs, his ambition, his pride. The whole of *Paradise Regained* is a struggle between intellect and passion, not on the plane of action, but on the purely intellectual plane of discussion. Reason triumphs, regenerated man is free, for " what obeys reason is free." [53]

But in order to bring about this triumph of reason, to reëstablish man in his natural state, a new intervention of the Creator is necessary. This " second creation " constitutes properly the religion peculiar to Milton.

[53] *P. L.,* IX, 351–52.

## CHAPTER IV

### RELIGION

### I. The Second Creation

IN order to reach His ends, God causes a second creation to concentrate in the first one: within the Son,
who had created, and out of whom had been created,
the World, is formed Christ, who creates and out of whom
are created, the elect: He creates them out of himself;
they are " members of Christ " ; he is incarnated in them,
as the Son had materialized into a World. And as the
Son is the Created World, Christ is the Elect, the
" Greater Man," the assembly of all men who alone
deserve the name " man."

A diagram of Being may be constructed thus:

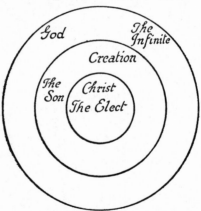

Christ, for Milton, is Intelligence coming down into
man to dominate the passions, by incarnation into a group
of men who are the elect.

## II. Christ: Intelligence Triumphant Over Passion

Milton first reminds us that regeneration comes from God, and that through it God's plans are being carried out:

> . . . the Father is often called *our Saviour,* inasmuch as it is by his eternal counsel and grace alone that we are saved.[1]

God himself has taken in hand the work of salvation — the manifested God, that is the Son:

> . . . he by whom all things were made . . . he who in the beginning was the Word, and God with God, and although not supreme, yet the first born of every creature, must necessarily have existed previous to his incarnation. . . .[2]

But Milton is careful to use the word " Christ " throughout the chapters on Regeneration: " Christ " is the Savior of Men; the Son was the creator of the World. Christ is in the Son, the two are one, only the Son is greater than Christ, who is only a part of Him.

Christ is essentially Intelligence:

> His prophetical function consists of two parts; one external, namely, the promulgation of divine truth; the other internal, to wit, the illumination of the understanding.[3]
>
> Regeneration is that change operated by the Word and the Spirit, whereby the old man being destroyed, the inward man is regenerated by God after his own image, in all the faculties of his mind, in so much that he becomes as it were a new creature. . . .[4]
>
> The intent of SUPERNATURAL RENOVATION is not only to restore man more completely than before to the use of his natural faculties as regards his power to form right judgement, and to exercise free will; but to create afresh, as it were, the inward man, and infuse from above new and supernatural faculties into the minds of the

---

[1] *Treatise,* in *Prose Works,* IV, 285.   [3] *Ibid.,* IV, 290.
[2] *Ibid.,* IV, 288.                        [4] *Ibid.,* IV, 328.

renovated. This is called REGENERATION, and the regenerate are said to be PLANTED IN CHRIST.[5]

The new creation, in other words, takes place through Christ's descent into the elect.

### III. CHRIST, THE GREATER MAN

Christ incarnates into a number of men, who become his mystical body; he is in each, he is in all, they are one in him. He restores reason to its throne in them. Even as " all of us are of God," so " all the elect are of Christ."

Believers are said TO BE INGRAFTED IN CHRIST, when they are planted in Christ by God the Father, that is, are made partakers of Christ, and meet for becoming one with him.[6]
. . . from this union and fellowship of the regenerate with the Father and Christ, and of the members of Christ's body among themselves [The Communion of Saints], results the mystical body called THE INVISIBLE CHURCH, whereof Christ is the head. . . .
Seeing then that the body of Christ is mystically one, it follows that the fellowship of his members must also be mystical, and not confined to place and time, inasmuch as it is composed of individuals of widely separated countries, and of all ages from the foundation of the world.[7]

In order to understand fully this conception, we must remember that Milton does not believe in the soul, in the spirit. Christ is therefore in us materially; probably, in Milton's mind, as a sort of very subtle material substance, as effectually as Adam is in us by the continuity of physical generation. Christ is in the elect, or, rather, as he is greater, they are in him " transplanted," " engrafted." He is the whole, they are parts.

It is therefore the expression " second creation " that

---

[5] *Ibid.*, IV, 327–28.        [6] *Ibid.*, IV, 342.        [7] *Ibid.*, IV, 363.

best renders Milton's thought. Christ drew the elect
from his substance, as the Son drew the Creation from
his. This is closely connected with Milton's materialism.
We are, physically, parts of Adam. In the material substance he has transmitted to us lies concupiscences, his
"innate propensity to sin." [8]   Therefore, it can only be
through the pouring into us of a new, and better substance that we are regenerated; and in that substance,
which is Christ, we are members of Christ. He is the
"Greater Man" of *Paradise Lost:*

> Till one Greater Man
> Restore us, and regain the blissful seat.[9]

Not only morally Greater, but really, as a being of whom
the elect are parts. For Christ has not really reconquered
the old Paradise in Eden, he has established

> A Paradise within thee, happier far.[10]

Even like Paradise, Hell is in us, and Satan declares

> Myself am Hell.[11]

The archangel tells Adam how to imagine the struggle
between Satan and Christ:

> . . . Dream not of their fight
> As of a duel, or the local wounds
> Of head or heel. . . .
> Not by destroying Satan, but his works
> In thee and in thy seed,[12]

will Christ triumph.

Christ is thus materially the creator of the new human
race, and this explains an expression strange in Milton,
who calls Mary

> blest Mary, second Eve.[13]

[8] *Ibid.*, IV, 259.      [10] *Ibid.*, XII, 587.      [12] *Ibid.*, XII, 386-95.
[9] *P. L.*, I, 4-5.      [11] *Ibid.*, IV, 75.      [13] *Ibid.*, V, 387.

The poet's violent hatred of Catholicism tallies little with
the glorification of Mary.  But Milton expresses a physical fact.  Mary is the mother of the new mankind that
comes out of Christ, just as materially as Eve is the
mother of the whole of mankind.  Hence Milton's insistence in *Paradise Regained* on the idea of Christ being
a man.  And Milton is in no way a Socinian.  Christ is
the Son of God, because regenerated Man is the Son of
God, created of Him.  But Christ is the creator of Regenerated Man, is Regenerated Man: that part of God
incarnated in the Elect.  God speaks of Christ:

> He now shall know I can produce a Man
> Of female seed, far abler to resist
> All his solicitations, and at length
> All his vast force, and drive him back to hell,
> Winning by conquest what the first man lost
> By fallacy surprised.  But first I mean
> To exercise Him in the wilderness;
> There He shall first lay down the rudiments
> Of His great warfare, ere I send Him forth
> To conquer Sin and Death, the two grand foes,
> By humiliation and strong sufferance.
> His weakness shall o'ercome Satanic strength,
> And all the world, and mass of sinful flesh;
> That all the angels and ethereal powers
> (They now, and men hereafter) may discern
> From what consummate virtue I have chose
> This perfect Man, by merit called my Son,
> To earn salvation for the sons of men.[14]

" By merit called my Son " — because all beings are
Sons of God, as Satan boldly tells Christ:

> By voice from heav'n
> Heard thee pronounced the Son of God beloved.
> Thenceforth I thought thee worth my nearer view

[14] *P. R.*, I, 150–67.

And narrower scrutiny, that I might learn
In what degree or meaning thou art called
The Son of God, which bears no single sense.
The son of God I also am, or was,
And if I was I am; relation stands;
All men are sons of God; yet thee I thought
In some respect far higher so declared.[15]

All men are Sons of God, but Christ is doubly so, through birth and through merit; therefore he has a special title. Not because he is a man of superior merit, or because of the Virgin birth — Milton insists in no wise on these facts; the two corner stones of Christianity, the Crucifixion and the Birth from the Holy Spirit, play no noticeable part in his conception of things — but because Christ is the Greater Man, the body of the blest; because Mankind is regenerated in him, because in Him Satan is tempting the whole of the new man. The historical fact of the life of Jesus is not very important for Milton. Regenerated Man existed before Jesus came on Earth. Adam himself was saved, having expiated his fault,

And one bad act with many deeds well done.[16]

The Patriarchs were part of Regenerated Man, and probably all the great men of antiquity, whom Milton considered as inspired by God, although Jesus had not yet come. They were all members of Christ, whose mystical body is " not confined to place and time, inasmuch as it is composed of individuals of widely separated countries, and of all ages from the foundation of the world." [17]  For in them all divine Reason spoke, and Christ is divine Reason. Man cannot be saved by any external power; the regeneration must take place in himself through his

[15] *Ibid.*, IV, 512–21.        [16] *P. L.*, XI, 256.        [17] *Treatise*, IV. 363.

own will, that will which is a fragment of God's; in every man Christ descends.  Vicarious atonement is no Miltonic conception, and that is why the crucifixion plays so small a part in his conception of human destiny.  He speaks little of it in *Paradise Lost,* and not at all in *Paradise Regained,* which was the poem for it.

In order to be saved in Christ, we must participate in his merits, save ourselves; even as we participate in Adam's fall by allowing " evil concupiscence," " the old man," to dominate in us.  The ancients who mastered " the old man " in them were saved, were in Christ even before Jesus lived.  God says to the Son when he agrees to become Christ:

> . . . Be Thou in Adam's room
> The head of all mankind, though Adam's son.
> As in him perish all men, so in Thee,
> As from a second root, shall be restor'd
> As many as are restor'd, without Thee none.
> His crime makes guilty all his sons; Thy merit
> Imputed shall absolve them who renounce
> Their own both righteous and unrighteous deeds,
> And live in Thee transplanted, and from Thee
> Receive new life.  So man, as is most just,
> Shall satisfy for man, be judg'd and die,
> And dying rise, and rising with Him raise
> His brethren, ransom'd with His own dear life.
> So heav'nly love shall outdo hellish hate,
> Giving to death, and dying to redeem,
> So dearly to redeem what hellish hate
> So easily destroy'd, and still destroys
> In those who, when they may, accept not grace.[18]

This passage is one of the keys of the poem and gathers together several essential ideas.  We must remember here what Blake calls " the double vision."  It is true that the

[18] *P. L.,* III, 285-302.

Son of God became a man among men and sacrificed himself; the life of Christ as told in the Gospels is literally
true. But that would have no value if, at the same time,
or rather from all time, Christ had not made himself into
the regenerate part of each of the elect, recreating them
in him. This second creation takes place through the
will of the creatures,

> them who renounce
> Their own both righteous and unrighteous deeds,
> And live in Thee transplanted.

The last five lines give a key to the " double vision " of
the whole poem of *Paradise Lost:* the drama takes place
not only in the outside world — in Paradise for the Fall,
in Jesus's life for the Regeneration — but also in each of
us; at every moment of our lives Satan is " hellish hate,"
Christ is " heav'nly love." In the last two lines, God
transcends the time of the action, which is the beginning
of the world, and speaks from the higher sphere of his
divinity, above time, for all times:

> and *still* destroys
> In those who, when they may, accept not grace.

The poet is in the seventeenth century. Even like the
twin expressions, " A Paradise within thee " and " myself
am hell," these two lines transfer the whole drama into
man's consciousness, and make it eternally present.
Thus Milton believes (when he thinks fit) in the letter,
and yet considers the facts as symbols of spiritual realities.

God causes man's will to be accomplished. Therein
lies destiny. This is true in psychology as in politics.
After the Fall, man may have the will, but he has no

longer the power to carry out his will.  But to God, will
is sufficient; he will give the power: that is grace.  Thus
will predestines to salvation; Christ gives the possibility.
God says,

> All hast thou spoken as My thoughts are, all
> As My eternal purpose hath decreed:
> Man shall not quite be lost, but sav'd who will;
> Yet not of will in him, but grace in Me
> Freely vouchsaf'd; once more I will renew
> His lapsed pow'rs, though forfeit, and enthrall'd
> By sin to foul exorbitant desires.[19]

The power of man is small, for evil even as for good.
Therefore God, even as he helps the good in their virtue,
will help the wicked in their evil:

> But hard be hard'nd, blind be blinded more
> That they may stumble on, and deeper fall.[20]

And thus for Satan:

> . . . the will
> And high permission of all-ruling Heaven
> Left him at large to his own dark designs;
> That with reiterated crimes he might
> Heap on himself damnation.[21]

But none is predestined to perdition; predestination
" must always be understood with reference to election," [22]
by the will of the elect, who are parts of God fulfilling
themselves.  For each may carry out the will that is in
him; in him take place his fall and his regeneration.

[19] *P. L.*, III, 171–77.
[20] *Ibid.*, III, 200–01; and *Treatise*, IV, 50–51, where Pharaoh's heart is
hardened by God.
[21] *P. L.*, I, 211–15.
[22] *Treatise*, IV, 45, and the whole of chapter IV.

## POLITICS

IT is finally, in applying his ideas to the affairs of men, that Milton tries to justify the ways of God. On that ground the question originally arose; here the whole philosophy of Milton reaches its ends.

Milton, in his system of politics, sets down the principles of what man ought to be, claiming complete liberty for regenerated man, and delivering into the avenging forces of destiny unregenerate men and nations.

## I. LIBERTY

Christian liberty is that whereby we loosed as it were by enfranchisement, through Christ our deliverer, from the bondage of sin, and consequently from the rule of the law and of man; to the intent that being made sons instead of servants, and perfect men instead of children, we may serve God in love through the guidance of the Spirit of Truth.[1]

. . . Paul expressly asserts that "the law is not made for a righteous man," I Tim. i. 9. Gal. v. 22, 23.[2]

Such is the basis of liberty; since Christ is in the elect, the laws of men do not apply to them.

## A. *Moral liberty: no law*

The old moral law, the Mosaic decalogue, is abolished:

. . . the entire Mosaic law was abolished. . . . we are therefore absolved from subjection to the decalogue as fully as to the rest of the law.[3]

The spirit of the law abides in each of us:

[1] *Treatise*, IV, 398–99; *cf.* the whole of chapter XXVII.
[2] *Ibid.*, IV, 391.          [3] *Ibid.*, IV, 387.

. . . the end for which the law was instituted, namely, the love of God and our neighbour, is by no means to be abolished; it is the tablet of the law, so to speak, that is alone changed, its injunctions being now written by the Spirit in the hearts of believers. . . .[4]

Consequently the judgment will take place according to an individual rule for each: " the rule of judgment will be the conscience of each individual." [5]

A curious application of this theory, which is a claim for the legitimacy of the instincts of each regenerated man, is the admission of polygamy. Milton had probably come to consider, from his own experience, that having three wives successively came to much the same thing as having them simultaneously. He demonstrates at length that polygamy was allowed to the Hebrews [6] and ends with the aphorism, " The practice of the saints is the best interpretation of the commandments." [7]

### B. *Religious liberty; no priests*

Every believer has a right to interpret the Scriptures for himself, inasmuch as he has the Spirit for his guide, and the mind of Christ is in him.[8]

Scripture is the sole judge of controversies; or rather, every man is to decide for himself through its aid, under the guidance of the Spirit of God.[9]

. . . the same Spirit which originally dictated them, enlightening us inwardly, through faith and love.[10]

And Scripture itself is

not but by the Spirit understood.[11]

Christ is in each of us; Christ is in the communion of the Saints, and governs his Church directly, without need of any other government:

[4] *Ibid.*, IV, 394.   [7] *Ibid.*, IV, 237.   [10] *Ibid.*, IV, 446.
[5] *Ibid.*, IV, 483.   [8] *Ibid.*, IV, 444.   [11] *P. L.*, XII, 514.
[6] *Ibid.*, IV, 225–37.   [9] *Ibid.*, IV, 445.

Christ hath a government of his own, sufficient of itself to all his ends and purposes in governing his church, but much different from that of the civil magistrate . . . it deals only with the inward man and his actions, which are all spiritual, and to outward force not liable.[12]

The consequence is the suppression of the ecclesiastical ministry. Professional priests are not only useless, but harmful:

A man may be a heretic in the truth; and if he believes things only because his pastor says so, or the assembly so determines, without knowing other reason, though his belief be true, yet the very truth he holds becomes his heresy.[13]

All the members of the Church are priests, and the so-called " priests " are usurpers:

And this all Christians ought to know, that the title of clergy St. Peter gave to all God's people, till pope Higinus and the suc-ceeding prelates took it from them, appropriating that name to themselves and their priests only; and condemning the rest of God's inheritance to an injurious and alienate condition of laity, they separated from them by local partitions in churches. . . . Although these usurpers could not so presently overmaster the liberties and lawful titles of God's freeborn church; but that Origen, being yet a layman, expounded the Scriptures publicly. . . .[14]

## C. Intellectual liberty: no censors

Liberty is equally essential to the operations of the mind. Each man is to search for truth in his own way, for all we can know is made up of fragments of truth, and therefore the search must proceed in all directions. We need but set down a few arguments from the *Areopagitica*.

[12] *Treatise of Civil Power*, in *Prose Works*, II, 533.
[13] *Areopagitica*, in *Prose Works*, II, 85.
[14] *Reason of Church Government*, in *Prose Works*, II, 493. See above, pp. 77-78, for the development of these ideas.

Truth is not known in its entirety:

Truth indeed came once into the world with her divine master, and was a perfect shape glorious to look on: . . . then straight arose a wicked race of deceivers, who, as that story goes of the Egyptian Typhon with his conspirators, how they dealt with the good Osiris, took the virgin Truth, hewed her lovely form into a thousand pieces, and scattered them to the four winds. From that time ever since, the sad friends of Truth, such as durst appear, imitating the careful search that Isis made for the mangled body of Osiris, went up and down gathering up limb by limb still as they could find them. We have not yet found them all, lords and commons, nor ever shall do. . . . Suffer not these licensing prohibitions to stand at every place of opportunity forbidding and disturbing them that continue seeking, that continue to do our obsequies to the torn body of our martyred saint.[15]

Besides, on many points truth is not settled yet and therefore no law is possible:

Yet is it not impossible that she may have more shapes than one? What else is all that rank of things indifferent, wherein truth may be on this side, or on the other, without being unlike herself?[16]

Lastly — Milton hits here upon one of the ideas made most use of by Cardinal Newman (let us mark one more point where he is in agreement with his most hated adversaries, the Catholics) — truth changes with the ages of mankind:

For who knows not that truth is strong, next to the Almighty; she needs no policies, nor stratagems, nor licensings to make her victorious, those are the shifts and the defences that error uses against her power: give her but room, and do not bind her when she sleeps, for then she speaks not true, as the old Proteus did, who spake oracles only when he was caught and bound, but then rather she turns herself into all shapes except her own, and perhaps tunes her voice according to the time, as Micaiah did before Ahab, until she be adjured into her own likeness.[17]

15 *Prose Works*, II, 89.    16 *Ibid.*, II, 96-97.    17 *Ibid.*, II, 96.

Truth is compared in scripture to a streaming fountain; if her waters flow not in a perpetual progression, they sicken into a muddy pool of conformity, and tradition.[18]

The necessity for liberty of thinking is thus solidly established.  Milton points out that, besides, political liberty is necessary to the full development of intellectual life.  Thus, in Italy, the fall of liberty brought intellectual decadence.[19]  But political liberty is the main object of the prose works.

### D. *Political liberty: no tyrants*

Milton applies to politics his fundamental principles. Man is a part of God; therefore he is free.  But he is free only when reason dominates over the passions in him; otherwise, he is not " of Christ," and he has no right to external liberty.

Milton develops those ideas in the fine pages at the end of the *Defensio secunda*.  Institutions in themselves have no value; the vote has a meaning only if the citizens are enlightened and freed from passions.  Man must first govern himself, and then choose as leaders men who can govern themselves:

For it is of no little consequence, O citizens, by what principles you are governed, either in acquiring liberty, or in retaining it when acquired.  And unless that liberty which is of such a kind as arms can neither procure nor take away, which alone is the fruit of piety, of justice, of temperance, and unadulterated virtue, shall have taken deep root in your minds and hearts, there will not long be wanting one who will snatch from you by treachery what you have acquired by arms.  War has made many great whom peace makes small.  If after being released from the toils of war, you neglect the arts of peace, if your peace and your liberty be a state of warfare, if war be your only virtue, the summit of your praise, you

---

[18] *Ibid.*, II, 85.                    [19] See above, p. 75.

will, believe me, soon find peace the most adverse to your interests.

Your peace will be only a more distressing war; and that which you imagined liberty will prove the worst of slavery. Unless by the means of piety, not frothy and loquacious, but operative, unadulterated, and sincere, you clear the horizon of the mind from those mists of superstition which arise from the ignorance of true religion, you will always have those who will bend your necks to the yoke as if you were brutes, who, notwithstanding all your triumphs, will put you up to the highest bidder, as if you were mere booty made in war; and will find an exuberant source of wealth in your ignorance and superstition. Unless you will subjugate the propensity to avarice, to ambition, and sensuality, and expel all luxury from yourselves and from your families, you will find that you have cherished a more stubborn and intractable despot at home, than you ever encountered in the field; and even your very bowels will be continually teeming with an intolerable progeny of tyrants. Let these be the first enemies whom you subdue; this constitutes the campaign of peace; these are triumphs, difficult indeed, but bloodless; and far more honourable than those trophies which are purchased only by slaughter and by rapine. Unless you are victors in this service, it is in vain that you have been victorious over the despotic enemy in the field. . . . But from such an abyss of corruption into which you so readily fall, no one, not even Cromwell himself, nor a whole nation of Brutuses, if they were alive, could deliver you if they would, or would deliver you if they could. For who would vindicate your right of unrestrained suffrage, or of choosing what representatives you like best, merely that you might elect the creatures of your own faction, whoever they might be, or him, however small might be his worth, who would give you the most lavish feasts, and enable you to drink to the greatest excess?

Thus not wisdom and authority, but turbulence and gluttony, would soon exalt the vilest miscreants from our taverns and our brothels, from our towns and villages, to the rank and dignity of senators. For, should the management of the republic be entrusted to persons to whom no one would willingly entrust the management of his private concerns; and the treasury of the state be left to the care of those who had lavished their own fortunes in an infamous prodigality? Should they have the charge of the public purse, which they would soon convert into a private, by their unprincipled peculations? Are they fit to be the legislators of a whole people who themselves know not what law, what reason, what right and wrong, what crooked and straight, what licit and illicit means? who think that all power consists in outrage, all dignity in the parade of insolence? who neglect every other consideration for the corrupt gratification of their friendships, or the prosecution of their resentments? who disperse their own relations and creatures through the provinces, for the sake of levying taxes and confiscating goods; men, for the greater part, the most profligate and vile, who buy up for themselves what they pretend to expose to sale, who thence collect an exorbitant mass of wealth, which they fraudulently divert from the public service; who thus spread their pillage through the country, and in a moment emerge from penury and rags to a state of splendour and of wealth? . . . It is also sanctioned by the dictates of justice and by the constitution of nature, that he who from the imbecility or derangement of his intellect, is incapable of governing himself, should, like a minor, be committed to the government of another; and least of all should he be appointed to superintend the affairs of others or the interest of the state. You, therefore, who wish to remain free, either instantly be wise, or, as soon as possible, cease to be fools; if you think slavery an intolerable evil, learn obedience to reason and the government of yourselves, and finally bid adieu to your dissensions, your jealousies, your superstitions, your outrages, your rapine, and your lusts.[20]

*Learn obedience to reason and the government of yourselves.* Such is Milton's fundamental principle, from religion to politics. But the regenerate man in whom reason rules, is " of Christ," and therefore free. We read in the *First Defence:*

If one should consider attentively the countenance of a man, and inquire after whose image so noble a creature was framed, would not any one that heard him presently make answer, that he was made after the image of God himself? Being therefore peculiarly God's own, and consequently things that are to be given to him, we are entirely free by nature and cannot without the greatest sacrilege imaginable be reduced into a condition of slavery to any man, especially to a wicked, unjust, cruel tyrant.[21]

[20] *Prose Works,* I, 295–99.   [21] *Ibid.,* I, 63.

Had men remained in their normal state, no government would have been necessary. The origin of all government is in the Fall.[22] Consequently, for true men, government is not needed. In a country, government is only a necessary evil; therefore there must be as little as possible. The best government is that which governs least.

There must be few laws. Milton tells Cromwell in the *Second Defence:* " you will do well,

Since there are often in a republic men who have the same itch for making a multiplicity of laws, as some poetasters have for making many verses, and since laws are usually worse in proportion as they are more numerous, if you shall not enact so many new laws as you abolish old, which do not operate so much as warnings against evil, as impediments in the way of good; and if you shall retain only those which are necessary, which do not confound the distinctions of good and evil, which while they prevent the frauds of the wicked, do not prohibit the innocent freedoms of the good, which punish crimes, without interdicting those things which are lawful only on account of the abuses to which they may occasionally be exposed. For the intention of laws is to check the commission of vice; but liberty is the best school of virtue, and affords the strongest encouragements to the practice.[23]

Especially must the State not legislate for the church. We have seen all the bitterness of Milton against his hero Cromwell who had not abstained on this point. That ruined in Milton's mind the whole of the Protector's work. Then the government must ensure free discussion:

If you permit the free discussion of truth without any hazard to the author, or any subjection to the caprice of an individual, which is the best way to make truth flourish and knowledge abound, the censure of the half-learned, the envy, the pusillanimity, or the prejudice which measure the discoveries of others, and in short

---

[22] *Tenure* in *Prose Works,* II, 9.  See above, p. 82.
[23] *Prose Works,* I, 293–94.

every degree of wisdom, by the measure of its own capacity, will
be prevented from doling out information to us according to their
own arbitrary choice.[24]

The only positive duty of a government is to spread education. We have seen that Milton was not pleased with
the state of education in England. Here again he advises
Cromwell:

> Then, if you make a better provision for the education of our
> youth than has hitherto been made, if you prevent the promiscuous
> instruction of the docile and the indocile, of the idle and the
> diligent, at the public cost, but reserve the rewards of learning for
> the learned, and of merit for the meritorious.[25]

For all power belongs to the people, returns to the people
when the king and magistrates use it unwisely [26] — but
then the people must be enlightened: that remains the
basis of the whole system.

The central idea is given in the lines of *Paradise Lost:*

> But man over men
> He made not lord; such title to himself
> Reserving, human left, from human free.[27]

In these lines, Milton establishes a distinction between
the true ruler and the tyrant. For Milton, absolute
power may be welcome; tyranny alone is abhorred. Tyrants are the rulers who follow their personal interests or
passions — we have seen Charles I attainted on these
grounds [28] — even though they may have been elected
by the suffrage of the people:

> Who could endure such thievish servants, such vicegerents of
> their lords? Who could believe that the masters and the patrons
> of a banditti could be the proper guardians of liberty? or who
> would suppose that he should ever be made one hair more free by

[24] *Ibid.*          [25] *Ibid.*          [26] See above, p. 89, for the texts.
[27] XII, 70.          [28] *Cf. First Defence* in *Prose Works*, I, 97.

such a set of public functionaries, though they might amount to five hundred elected in this manner from the counties and boroughs? [29]

It is not therefore the manner in which he acquired power that makes the tyrant, but the manner in which he wields his power and the uses he puts it to.  The type of the tyrant is Satan, who

with necessity,<br>The tyrant's plea, excus'd his devilish deeds.[30]

Since the tyrant, like Satan, tries to take God's place, he desires " most unreasonably, and indeed sacrilegiously, that we should be subject to him, though not further, yet as far as all of us may be subject to God; to whom this expression leaves no precedency." [31]   And Milton declares in the *Tenure of Kings* that the tyrant's power comes from the devil and is to be combated.[32]

But the true leader, who devotes himself to the public good, may be entrusted with the most extended power, so long as he respects the liberty of the people, which means, to Milton, intellectual and religious liberty. Cromwell is, as a rule, the model of such a leader, who must begin by a befitting mastery of himself and whose dignity is to be " the preserver of our liberties." [33]

. . . and lastly, revere yourself; and, after having endured so many sufferings and encountered so many perils for the sake of liberty, do not suffer it, now it is obtained, either to be violated by yourself, or in any one instance impaired by others.  You cannot be truly free unless we are free too; for such is the nature of things, that he who entrenches on the liberty of others, is the first to lose his own and become a slave.[34]

[29] *Second Defence*, in *Prose Works*, I, 297–98.
[30] *P. L.*, IV, 393–94.
[31] *Eikonoklastes*, in *Prose Works*, I, 449.
[32] See above, p. 83.
[33] *Second Defence*, in *Prose Works*, I, 289.
[34] *Ibid.*, I, 289–90.

In the ruler's moral worth Milton sees the ultimate guar-
antee of liberty.    Besides, the true ruler never rules
alone:

> . . . render our liberty at once more ample and more secure.    And
> this you can, in my opinion, in no other way so readily effect, as
> by associating in your councils the companions of your dangers and
> your toils.[35]

Here also Milton was disappointed.    Indeed, as he
grew older, inveterate idealist as he was, he could not
but see that his whole system was largely based on illusions, desirable no doubt, but not to be established in
practice.    More and more he was forced to see that his
clear-sighted picture of " turbulence and gluttony, that
would exalt the vilest miscreant from our taverns and
brothels, to the rank and dignity of senators," [36] covered
practically the whole of political life.    None had seen
better than himself the vices of the representative system.
He came to see that the elect, the men " of Christ," are
ever in the minority.    Hence his bitterness against " The
general defection of the misguided and abused multitude."
This disappointment was finally expressed in *Paradise
Regained*.    Let us remember what the man who wrote the
following passage had written in the flush of his great
hopes in 1642, of " the capacity of a plain artisan." [37]
This is what he wrote about 1670; he had suffered much
in the interval:

> And what the people but a herd confused,
> A miscellaneous rabble, who extol
> Things vulgar, and, well weighed, scarce worth the praise?
> They praise and they admire they know not what,
> And know not whom, but as one leads the other;
> And what delight to be by such extolled,

[35] *Ibid.*, I, 290.        [36] See above, p. 102.        [37] See above, p. 47.

To live upon their tongues and be their talk,
Of whom to be dispraised were no small praise,
His lot who dares be singularly good.
Th' intelligent among them and the wise
Are few.[38]

The poet takes refuge in God. After all, false leaders and inconstant nations have but little power. God alone reigns. Above all the efforts and infamies of men and peoples, for the consolation of the few sages, destiny rules, unswerving and unavoidable, and deals out justice on the Earth.

## II. DESTINY: GOD AND HISTORY

The rule of the destiny of nations is clear to Milton's mind. Men have their liberty in themselves. If they lose that, if they allow their passions to rule them, they become slaves. There are two reasons for this: first, a human reason — man, once a slave of passion, becomes a slave to those who can flatter him or make him fear them; and second, a divine reason — God's justice delivers corrupt nations into the hands of tyrants. And as God ever works from the inside, the two reasons are one: corrupt nations, through their vices, unavoidably deliver themselves into the hands of tyrants.

This is Milton's answer to his original question; and the whole of his thinking ends in this result. Thus he undertakes

To justify the ways of God to men.

The cause of all his trials is in man himself. Milton has built an ontology to show man that he is originally free, and comes from God; a cosmology, to prove that man is

[38] *P. R.*, III, 49–59.

fundamentally good, being made of divine matter; a psychology, to teach him when and how he sins, by allowing
passion to rule him; a religion, to bring him God's help
if only he will amend himself.   Now he draws the pitiless
conclusion.   God's plans are well constructed; men's wills
get carried out and destiny brings catastrophe to corrupt
men and nations, through the weight of their own deeds.
Man is responsible, not only for his deeds, but for his
destiny, for his destiny is but a translation into events of
the psychological drama enacted in man's free soul.

Milton can therefore look upon the vicissitudes of history with something of the exultant spirit of the old
prophets applauding the justice of God:

For if you think that it is a more grand, a more beneficial, or a
more wise policy, to invent subtle expedients for increasing the rev-
enue, to multiply our naval and military force, to rival in craft the
ambassadors of foreign states, to form skilful treaties and alliances;
than to administer unpolluted justice to the people, to redress the
injured, and to succour the distressed, and speedily to restore to
every one his own, you are involved in a cloud of error; and too
late will you perceive, when the illusion of those mighty benefits has
vanished, that in neglecting these, which you now think inferior
considerations, you have only been precipitating your own ruin and
despair.   The fidelity of enemies and allies is frail and perishing,
unless it be cemented by the principles of justice; that wealth and
those honours, which most covet, readily change masters; they forsake the idle, and repair where virtue, where industry, where
patience flourish most.   Thus nation precipitates the downfall of
nation; thus the more sound part of one people subverts the more
corrupt; thus you obtained the ascendant over the royalists.

If you plunge into the same depravity, if you imitate their ex-
cesses, and hanker after the same vanities, you will become royalists as well as they, and liable to be subdued by the same enemies,
or by others in your turn; who, placing their reliance on the same
religious principles, the same patience, the same integrity and dis-
cretion which made you strong, will deservedly triumph over you

who are immersed in debauchery, in the luxury and the sloth of kings. Then, as if God was weary of protecting you, you will be seen to have passed through the fire, that you might perish in the smoke; the contempt which you will then experience will be great as the admiration which you now enjoy; and, what may in future profit others, but cannot benefit yourselves, you will leave a salutary proof what great things the solid reality of virtue and of piety might have effected, when the mere counterfeit and varnished resemblance could attempt such mighty achievements, and make such considerable advances towards the execution. For, if either through your want of knowledge, your want of constancy, or your want of virtue, attempts so noble, and actions so glorious, have had an issue so unfortunate, it does not therefore follow, that better men should be either less daring in their projects or less sanguine in their hopes. . . .

. . . among them who are the very guardians of liberty, and to whose custody it is committed, there must be so many, who know not either how to use or to enjoy liberty, who neither understand the principles nor merit the possession? But, what is worthy of remark, those who are the most unworthy of liberty are wont to behave most ungratefully towards their deliverers. Among such persons, who would be willing either to fight for liberty, or to encounter the least peril in its defence?

It is not agreeable to the nature of things that such persons ever should be free. However much they may brawl about liberty, they are slaves, both at home and abroad, but without perceiving it; and when they do perceive it, like unruly horses that are impatient of the bit, they will endeavour to throw off the yoke, not from the love of genuine liberty, (which a good man only loves and knows how to obtain,) but from the impulses of pride and little passions. But though they often attempt it by arms, they will make no advances to the execution; they may change their masters, but will never be able to get rid of their servitude. This often happened to the ancient Romans, wasted by excess, and enervated by luxury: and it has still more so been the fate of the moderns; when, after a long interval of years, they aspired, under the auspices of Crescentius, Nomentanus, and afterwards of Nicolas Rentius, who had assumed the title of Tribune of the People, to restore the splendour and re-establish the government of ancient Rome. For, instead of fretting with vexation, or thinking that you can lay the blame on any one but yourselves, know that to be free is the same thing as to be pious, to be wise, to be temperate and just, to be frugal and abstinent, and lastly, to be magnanimous and brave; so to be the opposite of all these is the same as to be a slave; and it usually happens, by the appointment, and as it were retributive justice, of the Deity, that that people which cannot govern themselves, and moderate their passions, but crouch under the slavery of their lusts, should be delivered up to the sway of those whom they abhor, and made to submit to an involuntary servitude.[39]

*It is not agreeable to the nature of things that such persons ever should be free.* Such was Milton's contemptuous judgment of his contemporaries when they fell back into slavery. And in 1669, he concludes his *History of Great Britain* on this note:

If these were the causes of such misery and thraldom to those our ancestors, with what better close can be concluded, than here in fit season to remember this age in the midst of her security, to fear from like vices, without amendment, the revolution of like calamities? [40]

*Paradise Lost* ends on the same ideas:

> Therefore, since he permits
> Within himself unworthy powers to reign
> Over free reason, God in judgment just
> Subjects him from without to violent lords,
> Who oft as undeservedly enthral
> His outward freedom.  Tyranny must be,
> Though to the tyrant thereby no excuse.
> Yet sometimes nations will decline so low
> From virtue, which is reason, that no wrong
> But justice, and some fatal curse annexed,
> Deprives them of their outward liberty,
> Their inward lost.[41]

And this shows *Paradise Lost* to be largely a political poem, culminating in this judgment, which explains the

[39] *Second Defense,* in *Prose Works,* I, 295-98.
[40] *Prose Works,* V, 392-93.          [41] *P. L.,* XII, 90-101.

conception of history set forth in the XIIth book: no
after-thought to round off an epic poem, but the plain
and large statement of Milton's answer to the problems
of human destiny:

> So shall the world go on,
> To good malignant, to bad men benign,
> Under her own weight groaning till the day
> Appear of respiration to the just,
> And vengeance to the wicked, at return
> Of Him. . . .[42]

A remarkable thing is that in this summary of history,
at the end of *Paradise Lost,* Milton does not even mention
the Reformation.  He never suggests that it brought back
liberty.  From the death of the Apostles to the day of
judgment, the world follows its course in unrelieved evil.
This shows how little Protestantism satisfied Milton: all
priests are a horror to him, and the succession of Protestant to Catholic priest does not seem to him worth a
mention.

But Milton, the old incorrigible dreamer, kept for the
end his most fantastic — his most logical — dream.
Christ will come at last, in his glory, to reign for a thousand years over the Earth.  This will be " on earth "[43]
and will last until " the expiration of a thousand years." [44]
Without this " day of respiration to the just and vengeance to the wicked," the history of mankind would be
too lamentable, and God too unjust; for as the wicked
triumphed on the Earth, so retribution must take place
on the Earth also.  Milton does not believe in spirits.
He wants a solid material triumph, to begin with.  Thereafter will come Armageddon, the end of Satan, the Com-

[42] *Ibid.,* XII, 537–42.
[43] *Treatise,* in *Prose Works,* IV, 484–85.
[44] *Ibid.,* IV, 486.

munion with God in Heaven, the final carrying out of God's plans:

> . . . there shall be no end of his kingdom, *for ages of ages,* . . . until *time itself shall be no longer,* . . . until everything which his kingdom was intended to effect shall have been accomplished; . . . it will not *pass away* as insufficient for its purpose; it will not be *destroyed,* nor will its period be a period of dissolution, but rather of perfection and consummation, like the end of the law.[45]

The aims of God are attained, politics have come back to ontology, the cycle is over, the philosophy is complete.

[45] *Ibid.,* IV, 488.

## CHAPTER VI

## CONCLUSION: A GENERAL VIEW OF MILTON'S PHILOSOPHY

### I. PRINCIPLES

MILTON'S chief ideas may be grouped under five heads:

I. The idea of God as the un-manifested Infinite, in whom is the Son (Creator and Creation), in whom is Christ (the elect);

II. The idea of free wills, liberated by the retraction of God, and the union of the idea of reason to the idea of liberty, which is an original proof of free will (intelligence is impossible without free will);

III. The idea of Matter as good, imperishable and divine, a part of God himself from which all things issue spontaneously; so that there is no soul, and all beings are parts of God, arranged on an evolutionary scheme;

IV. The idea of the duality of man: reason and passion; the necessity of the triumph of reason; the fall as the triumph of passion;

V. The idea of liberty, based on the goodness of the normal being made of divine matter and on the presence in the elect of the Divine Intelligence.

Of these five groups of ideas, the first and fifth seem to me to be interesting chiefly in view of an explanation of Milton's works; the second to contain an original and interesting conception of the necessity of liberty which has lost none of its interest; the third, to contain in germ a conception of the universe in full harmony with the views of science; the fourth, a view of human nature, deep, dramatic and valid, as founded on psychological experience.

## II. A Systematic Scheme, Chronologically Arranged

I. God: the latent Infinite, and also Perfect Being. Wisdom forms in him the plan of the World: destiny.

II. Creation: the Son; primitive matter.

The retraction of God; liberation of individual wills.

Evolution of matter: things, animals, men.

The Fall: triumph of passion over reason.

III. The Second Creation: Christ-Intelligence; the Greater Man subdues passion

incarnates in the elect, giving them

(1) intelligence

(2) triumph over passion

$\left.\right\}$ liberty $\left\{\begin{array}{l}\text{moral} \\ \text{philosophical} \\ \text{political}\end{array}\right.$

IV. Death: a cosmological incident; a total, but temporary extinction, to wash away sin.

V. Resurrection and final Perfection: Union of the Elect in God.

## III. A Translation into Abstract Vocabulary

It has been said too often that Milton's subject was unfavorable to him, since the loss of religious beliefs has ruined the chief philosophical interest of his poem. This can in no way be accepted, since Milton's use of religious terms is a wide and philosophical one; and it is easy to translate his system into the more abstract vocabulary of

nineteenth-century absolutism, which is the philosophy
his is most akin to.  This can be done from two equiva-
lences: for Milton, all beings are parts of God; and Christ
is Intelligence in the elect.  Thus we have:

| *In abstract language* | *In Milton's language* |
|---|---|
| Infinite Being | God |
| to express its latent possibili-ties forms Finite Being. | the eternal plan of Wisdom the Son |
| But its freed possibilities pre-vent its self mastery, | the Fall |
| until, in the course of its evo-lution in its highest crea-tures, | the Elect |
| appears Intelligence, | Christ |
| which dominates passions | regeneration |
| and makes them good. | Christian liberty |
| Beings thus made perfect unite into a Communion, | the Communion of Saints |
| which incorporates into the Infinite Being. | Resurrection |
| Thus the General Being has chosen, among its possibili-ties, those it wanted to ex-press and made them con-scious, | Final Perfection |
| casting the others out of Itself. | Hell |

PART III

THE GREAT POEMS

CHAPTER I

## FAITH, PHILOSOPHY, AND POETRY
## IN MILTON'S WORK

I T is necessary to examine the purely poetical part of
Milton's work to see what it adds to the results of
our previous survey of his thought and character, and
also to apply to his art the knowledge so far obtained of
his philosophy and of his general characteristics. The
two parts of his production, the abstract and the artistic,
throw much light on each other.

The *De doctrina* is at once more abstract and clearer
than the poems. There is in it, at bottom, very little
dogma. For instance, in the treatise, Milton does not
venture to risk a firm opinion on the date of the creation
of the angels (relatively to that of the world) nor on the
reasons of the rebellion of the angels or of the creation
of the world.[1] This silence amounts to a confession of
ignorance. Yet the poetry is built on most precise data
on all these points, which shows that Milton looked upon
dogma as a sort of myth, chiefly useful for poetical purposes. Anyhow, he always supplemented it with an inner,
psychological meaning, which gives to the poetry its
human, permanent value, whatever may happen to the
dogma. But even so, there remain obscure points.
Milton's pride and reserve kept him from giving away the
whole of his thought. Although his personality is so
strongly marked, the personal element in his work often
escapes us. Even as he wrote on divorce in the fury of

[1] Cf. *Prose Works*, IV, 184, 213.

thwarted passion and yet never mentioned his own case, so he seems to have kept back some of his most intimate beliefs from us, even in the *De doctrina,* where, as he says in the dedication, he gives mankind his " best and richest possession." One often feels, in reading him, a resistance and a reticence; and our hypotheses are not completely satisfactory. There remain in his expression gaps which so systematic a mind can hardly have left in his thought. Thus on the question of Christ's personality: perhaps Jesus was only a man for Milton; one feels obliged to give up that idea, confronted as one is by precise assertions; but doubt comes again and again as one re-reads *Paradise Regained* or *Samson Agonistes.*[2] Thus again on the question of the crucifixion, which Milton hardly mentions. Then again on the nature of God: Milton takes all attributes away from God with a zeal which must seem excessive to the right-minded. Justice seems the only attribute he leaves him, and even then he is careful to show us that justice always takes its course naturally, that it flows from the very constitution of man, without God's interference. The advanced sects in Milton's time went very far indeed. We shall see that he occasionally helped them.[3]

We know, at any rate, that he believed in a double revelation:

. . . we possess, as it were, a twofold Scripture; one external, which is the written word, and the other internal, which is the Holy Spirit; . . . that which is internal, and the peculiar possession of each believer, is far superior to all namely, the Spirit itself.[4]

---

[2] Cf. Raleigh, *Milton,* p. 168: "the central mystery of the Christian religion occupied very little space in Milton's scheme of religion and thought."
[3] See below, pp. 320–22.
[4] *Treatise of Christian Doctrine,* in *Prose Works,* IV, 447.

But there is frequently a conflict between the two, and then

even on the authority of Scripture itself, every thing is to be finally referred to the Spirit and the unwritten word.[5]

Milton boasted his belief in the Word. With what restrictions, we have seen in the case of God;[6] but he knew how to explain, on occasion, that the Old Testament is full of poetical images not to be taken literally, and that in a passage of Proverbs where some have seen an allusion to the Son of God, there is only " a poetical personification of wisdom." [7] He knew, too — and this is worse — that the text of Scripture had been corrupted, in many places designedly; and he found an all too ingenious justification of God for allowing the frauds or errors to take place:

. . . the written word, I say, of the New Testament, has been liable to frequent corruption, and in some instances has been corrupted, through the number, and occasionally the bad faith of those by whom it has been handed down, the variety and discrepancy of the original manuscripts, and the additional diversity produced by subsequent transcripts and printed editions. . . .

It is difficult to conjecture the purpose of Providence in committing the writings of the New Testament to such uncertain and variable guardianship, unless it were to teach us by this very circumstance that the Spirit which is given to us is a more certain guide than Scripture, whom therefore it is our duty to follow.[8]

And especially he had discovered the terrible doctrine that the sacred writer adapted himself to the times and men for whom he wrote, and that consequently we have to translate him into our own terms of thought.[9] Lastly, and worst of all perhaps, he accounted himself directly

---

[5] *Ibid.*, IV, 450.    [7] *Treatise*, IV, 174.
[6] See above, pp. 113-15.    [8] *Ibid.*, IV, 447-49.
[9] Cf. *Areopagitica*, in *Prose Works*, II, 98-99; *Tetrachordon*, III, 391, 420, etc.; and above, pp. 184-85.

inspired.   His widow is reported to have said (and, of
course, this was an echo of his own words) that " he stole
from nobody but the muse that inspired him, and that was
God's Holy Spirit." [10]   And he certainly had very broad
ideas about inspiration.   " These abilities," he declared in
the *Reason of Church Government*,[11] " wheresoever they
be found, are the inspired gift of God, rarely bestowed, but
yet to some . . . in every nation."   Thus Euripides was
useful to explain a point of Scripture,[12] and Spenser was
a better master than Aquinas and Scot.[13]

The rationalist critic's arguments against Milton are
therefore as much out of court as the orthodox theologian's.   Milton has his answer ready on both sides.
Neither must it be said that his faults were imposed upon
him by his subject.   He did exactly what he liked with
his subject; he added much to it; he retrenched what he
disliked.   Not only did he not keep to the letter, but frequently he did not even keep to the spirit of Christianity.
It is therefore exclusively the human truth of the poetry
that may justify the poet.   His " faults " — often they
are beauties; for instance, the false situations he gets
into when his sympathies are on the side he is obliged to
condemn intellectually — come from his character and
not from his faith.   What really preoccupied Milton was
the political-moral problem — this much more than the
metaphysical or cosmological problem.   The history of
Creation has been made difficult for us by modern science.
In former days, the creation of the world was not so big
or so interesting an affair as in our eyes.   God had created
it, and there was an end of it; it was considered to be
specifically God's business.

10 Masson, VI, 746.                12 *Ibid.*, IV, 270.
11 *Prose Works*, II, 479.          13 *Ibid.*, II, 68.

It is important also to point out that Milton needed dogma. The need of mythical thought, so strong in many poets, corresponds to a deeper tendency than the intellectual one. Certainly it helped to keep Milton in his faith — such as it was — at a time when minds less profound than his — Hobbes, Herbert of Cherbury, for example — were apparently more advanced than he. Frequently depth of mind, in men like Milton or Pascal, is an obstacle to their liberation from dogma — or, if you like, a force that keeps them in the faith. Such depth makes them find in the dogma meanings which are not there, and which satisfy them. But such adhesion is of doubtful value. Poets in particular need myths. Shelley re-built a mythology out of Greek fragments. Blake made up one out of the queerest materials, and possibly believed in it. For poets are always sorry when they cannot believe in their fictions. Therefore Milton believed through his poetical needs and his high need of sincerity, whereas intellectually he was very near to not believing. He insists with pride — and a certain amount of bad faith, so mixed are human motives — on the fact that his myths are truth whereas the ancients' were false. But we shall see that he used myth — or dogma — less and less in his later work. *Paradise Regained* and *Samson* are practically devoid of it.

On the whole, the only two things we can be sure he believed in are: a divine spirit, essentially unknowable, of whom we are all parts; and a moral fall, which takes place in every man, and from which every man can rise by his own strength, which is the divine spirit in him. Everything else is imagination, consciously or unconsciously. This is proved by the way he allowed himself to tamper with dogma, and by the little trouble he took to avoid contradiction.    Thus the descriptions of Hell and its inhabitants in the first books of *Paradise Lost* are pure literature, even as is the allegory of Sin and Death.    The dialogues between God and the Son in Book III are merely dramatic, and meant to enlighten the reader, since the course of the world is fixed from all eternity, and God can really be neither seen nor heard.    The wars in Books V and VI are entirely foreign to dogma, or all but the vaguest idea of them, and the invention of gunpowder by the rebel angels has always been a scandal to true believers.    Books V, VII, and VIII contain no particularly Christian dogma, and are consistent with mere deism, or even pantheism, like nearly the whole of Books XI and XII.    Books IX and X contain dogma, certainly, but much addition to it, on the subject of sensuality, for instance, and always interpretation of it.    Milton thus nowhere gives pure dogma, and how are we to know whether he believes more in the dogma proper than in his own poetical fancies?    Lastly, on one of the most important points of his story, he obviously contradicts himself.    In Book III he lays down the true doctrine:

> Thee next they sang of all Creation first,
> Begotten Son. . . .
> He Heaven of Heavens and all the powers therein
> By thee created. . . .[14]

Yet God declares in Book V:

> This day I have begot whom I declare
> My only Son, and on his holy hill
> Him have annointed. . . .
> . . . Your Head I him appoint.[15]

[14] III, 383–91.          [15] *Ibid.,* V, 603–06.

Milton certainly believed in the possibility of no such appointment. But he was looking for a valid poetical reason for Satan's rebellion. The appearance of the Son at a certain date was necessary to his drama. Had the Son been created first, and, as in the *Treatise of Christian Doctrine*, been really the only God the angels could possibly have known, Satan would have had no cause for rebellion on that particular day of Heaven's great year. Nor would his angels have seen any cause to follow him and call him

Deliverer from new lords.[16]

The whole economy of Books V and VI would have been different, and dramatically inferior.

Thus it can be said that Milton did not believe in the possibility of the events of several of his cantos; and this is a warning to us not to take the rest of his mythology too seriously. Milton has warned us not to take too literally what God says of himself. What, then, of the things Milton sings of Him? Milton uses dogma as myth; his constant intrusion of Greek myth into it is a most characteristic trait. Another order of considerations must also be brought forward. Blake, in a celebrated passage of the *Marriage of Heaven and Hell*, says:

Those who restrain Desire do so because theirs is weak enough to be restrained; and the restrainer or Reason usurps its place and governs the unwilling.

And, being restrained, it by degrees becomes passive till it is only the shadow of Desire.

The history of this is written in *Paradise Lost* and the Governor, or Reason, is called Messiah.

And the original Archangel, or possessor of the command of the Heavenly Host, is call'd the Devil or Satan, and his children are called Sin and Death.

[16] *Ibid.*, VI, 451.

But in the Book of Job, Milton's Messiah is called Satan.

For this history has been adopted by both parties.

It indeed appeared to Reason as if Desire was cast out; but the Devil's account is that the Messiah fell, and formed a Heaven of what he stole from the Abyss.

This is shown in the Gospel, where he prays to the Father to send the Comforter, or Desire, that Reason may have Ideas to build on; the Jehovah of the Bible being no other than he who dwells in flaming fire.

Know that after Christ's death, he became Jehovah.

But in Milton, the Father is Destiny, the Son a Ratio of the five senses and the Holy ghost Vacuum.

Note. — The reason Milton wrote in fetters when he wrote of angels and God, and at liberty when of Devils and Hell, is because he was a true poet and of the Devil's party without knowing it.[17]

This passage, on the part of Blake, who did not know the *De doctrina,* is sheer genius, and the proof of a fundamental harmony of mind between him and Milton.[18]

We have seen that Christ is, in truth, Reason triumphing over Desire. Is Satan, then, a symbol of passion, as Blake asserts? This raises the question of symbolism in Milton.

I do not think that Milton should be interpreted in totality, as has been attempted with Blake, by finding for each character and each event an allegorical, hidden meaning. Milton, unlike Blake, is a clear and precise poet, perfectly in command of his ideas and art, who says what he wants to say, all he wants to say, and no more. But we are not to stop at the letter of his writing either, because, in Milton, behind the letter, there is intensity of conviction and depth of idea. Moreover, behind the ideas, there are powerful feelings, which feed them like a nutritious sap. If we do not know his ideas, we shall unduly restrict the meaning of his words. If we do not

---

[17] *Poetical Works,* ed. Sampson (Oxford, 1914), pp. 248–49.
[18] See my *Blake and Milton* (Paris, Alcan, 1920).

know his feelings, we shall unduly restrict the importance of his ideas.

Thus Christ is " Reason," but not through allegory: he is truly the reasonable part of each believer, each man being part of God. As for Satan, it is doubtful whether Milton did him the honor of spreading him thus into every human soul. Satan is therefore not " passion " as Christ is " reason " — that is to say, not Satan in the poems; in Milton's mind, it is quite possible that the devil is the evil element in every man, and even in God, that is to be combated severally; the conception seems to me in perfect harmony with the whole of Milton's doctrine, and gives a new depth to his art and thought. We have seen repeatedly that Satan is the prototype of all that Milton execrates — tyrants, kings, popes, priests even. They come dangerously near to being " of the devil " [19] even as the elect are " of Christ," that is to say, made of him, parts of him. This is one of the points on which Milton kept his inmost thought to himself. But it is helpful to keep the idea in mind while reading him. And anyhow, Satan is the great champion of passion in revolt against divine reason. Milton had too much poetical instinct to spoil his wonderful Satan by making an allegory of him. Yet he had diversified him and had given him all the necessary passions, that he might be, on the intellectual plane, a worthy adversary of deified reason. For it is quite true, as Blake says, that *Paradise Lost* is the struggle of passion against reason. But that is not the whole of *Paradise Lost*. It is only the general meaning, and Milton rambles at his pleasure, for he is a poet and a man of letters and he believes in bringing everything that is fit subject for literature into his poem.

[19] See above, p. 83.

His embroidery on the main theme is rich, and rarely inspired by philosophical ideas. The philosopher in him had ideas, but the poet it was that expressed them, and the poet had many things to express besides, on his own account.

Yet, as we have seen, in speaking of Christ Milton uses symbol in a particular way, which is warranted, as we shall see, by Augustine's authority. He believes in a physical fact, and yet that fact, real in itself, is a symbol of moral facts. The events of Scripture, the life of Jesus himself, are a sort of poetical allegory used by God, who, instead of writing in a book words that have two meanings, a literal and a figurative, causes to happen on earth events that have two senses: the plain solid fact, that Jesus lived, and the moral fact, that, concurrently, divine reason came into men. Even so, Satan is an image of passion in all men — even if he is not passion in all men — and also a reprobate angel cast down from Heaven by thunder. Thus, even when Milton did not interpret dogma so as to destroy it, as he occasionally did, he built, parallel to it, a course of psychological events that were as a sort of lining to that cloth, and were an integral part of the finished garment.

We must not, therefore, make a mere allegory of *Paradise Lost*. There is allegory in it, and myth and symbol. But at bottom Milton is a clear rationalist mind who despises " superstitions " when they correspond to no clear ideas of his own. He submitted to no symbolism, and to no dogma, further than he liked. The element of clearness, reason, culture is predominant in his mind, and his whole work is a sane and vigorous effort towards light and freedom.

## CHAPTER II

*PARADISE LOST*

### I. MILTON IN *PARADISE LOST*

PARADISE LOST is built round two great themes which are harmoniously balanced: the fall of the angels and the fall of man. The first books describe the state of the fallen angels; in contrast to this, after an interval in Heaven, the following books picture man before his fall, in Paradise; then comes the fall of the angels, and the creation of the world which compensates it; and finally, the fall of man and the history of the world which will make up for it. The dramatic interest in the first half is in Satan's efforts; in the second, in the human drama between Adam and Eve. The two parts are linked, Satan's efforts being the cause of the human drama. The scheme is simple, clear, and grand, and bears the imprint of Milton's mind.

From the psychological and philosophical point of view we have taken in this work, *Paradise Lost* is first of all, as we have seen in Part II, the working out of Milton's ideas; but it is also — and this remains to be studied — a sort of transposition of his private and political experience. Milton has drawn upon his own life to depict situations similar to those he had known. Hence the false position he frequently puts himself into; for analogy in the events has driven him to take from himself or from his friends the traits wanted for the picture of the fallen angels.

Thus Satan's character, as Milton presents it, cannot but inspire feelings of sympathy and admiration. The traditional motive of Satan's fall was pride. Milton had then to describe the pride of Satan. But, as we have seen, pride was the ruling passion in his own soul. Consequently, the character of Satan is drawn with a power unique in literature. In reality, Milton pours out his own feelings. Satan's first speeches are pure Miltonic lyricism. For, in addition, Milton's pride had known defeat, even as Satan's had. What matters failure and the triumph of the enemy if one is resolved not to submit? Here we have the rage and defiance which Milton himself felt when he saw the Restoration coming, and which we have seen him expressing in prose in his *Ready and Easy Way*.[1] Now, it must be pointed out that it was probably at the same time, since he began work on the epic about 1658, that he expressed the same feelings in verse:

> . . . Yet not for those
> Nor what the potent victor in his rage
> Can else inflict, do I repent or change,
> Though changed in outward lustre, that fix'd mind
> And high disdain from sense of injured merit.
> . . . What though the field be lost?
> All is not lost: th' unconquerable will,
> And study of revenge, immortal hate,
> And courage never to submit or yield,
> And what is else not to be overcome.
> That glory never shall his wrath or might
> Extort from me: to bow and sue for grace
> With suppliant knee, and deify his pow'r,
> Who from the terror of this arm so late
> Doubted his empire; that were low indeed!
> That were an ignominy and shame beneath
> This downfall; since by fate the strength of Gods

---

[1] See above, p. 99.

And this empyreal substance cannot fail,
Since through experience of this great event,
In arms not worse, in foresight much advanced,
We may with more successful hope resolve
To wage by force or guile eternal war,
Irreconcilable to our grand foe,
Who now triumphs, and in th' excess of joy
Sole reigning holds the tyranny of heav'n.[2]

No one is vanquished who remains strong in his own spirit.

Fallen cherub, to be weak is miserable
Doing or suffering. . . .[3]

Milton, in hiding at the Restoration, sought for, and, in theory at least, in danger of death, remembering all his dreams of what the Kingdom of the Saints was to be, and seeing the reign of Belial in London itself —

In courts and palaces he also reigns,
And in luxurious cities, where the noise
Of riot ascends above their loftiest tow'rs,
And injury and outrage; and when night
Darkens the streets, then wander forth the sons
Of Belial, flown with insolence and wine — [4]

Milton must have thought of the condition of the Elect somewhat in this strain:

Is this the region, this the soil, the clime,
Said then the lost Arch-Angel, this the seat
That we must change for heav'n, this mournful gloom
For that celestial light?   Be it so, since he
Who now is Sovran can dispose and bid
What shall be right: farthest from him is best,
Whom reason hath equall'd, force hath made supreme
Above his equals.   Farewell happy fields,
Where joy for ever dwells: Hail horrors, hail
Infernal world, and thou profoundest Hell

[2] *P. L.*, I, 94–124.       [3] I, 157–58.       [4] I, 497–502.

> Receive thy new possessor; one who brings
> A mind not to be changed by place or time.
> The mind is its own place, and in itself
> Can make a Heav'n of Hell, a Hell of Heav'n.[5]

And when Beelzebub cries

> The mind and spirit remains
> Invincible,[6]

he expresses the invincible spirit of the great Pur'.ans as it appears, for instance, in Harrison's speeches before his execution or at his trial. He told his judges, " My lords, this matter . . . was not a thing done in a corner," and argued to the end the case for the legality of the King's judgment. Like Vane, Hugh Peters, and all the friends of old, he was sentenced to be hanged, then drawn and quartered while still alive, and only after that, beheaded. And he told the people from the scaffold:

If I had ten thousand lives, I could freely and cheerfully lay down them all to witness in this matter. By God I have leaped over a wall; by God I have run through a troup, and by God I will get through this death, and he will make it easy to me. However men presume to call it by hard names, there was more of God in it than men are now aware of.[7]

Miltonic speech this; and the rage of the fallen Puritans has gone into Satan's first speeches.

But Satan is not only pride. He is passion in general. He is, in particular, sensuality — and Milton gratuitously put this upon him.[8] A sensual passion unites him to his daughter Sin, and their common ideal is to reach, as she says,

> To that new world of light and bliss, among
> The gods who live at ease, where I shall reign
> At thy right hand voluptuous, as beseems
> Thy daughter and thy darling, without end.[9]

[5] I, 242-55.      [7] See Masson, VI, 82, 95, 96.
[6] I, 139-40.      [8] See below, pp. 154-55.     [9] II, 867-70.

Envy and anger and all the passions are in him: he thus
addresses the Sun:

> O thou that with surpassing glory crowned
> Look'st from thy sole dominion like the god
> Of this new world, at whose sight all the stars
> Hide their diminished heads, to thee I call,
> But with no friendly voice, and add thy name,
> O Sun, to tell thee how I hate thy beams,
> That bring to my remembrance from what state
> I fell, how glorious once above thy sphere.[10]

And

> Thus while he spoke, each passion dimmed his face,
> Thrice changed with pale ire, envy and despair.[11]

Dr. Johnson, in his wicked essay on Milton, charges the
poet with these very vices; and for all his wickedness,
Johnson was not deficient in penetration, and Sir Walter
Raleigh's witticisms, true though they be in spirit —
Milton was not so bad as all that — do not yet quite
cover the case:

> It may, at least, be credited to Johnson for moderation, that
> he requires only four of the Seven Deadly Sins, to wit, Pride,
> Envy, Anger, and Sloth, to explain Milton's political tenets. Had
> he permitted himself another sentence, an easy place might surely
> have been made for Gluttony, Luxury, and Covetousness, the three
> whose absence cannot fail to be remarked on by any lover of
> thorough and detailed treatment in these intricate problems of
> human character.[12]

Last of all, there is no lack of sympathy on intellectual
subjects between Satan and Milton. Satan is naturally a
great heretic; his peculiar position gives him a liberty of
mind which is rarely attained. Bishop Sumner accuses
him of being a Manichean.[13] At any rate, he sees faults

---

10 IV, 32–39.      12 *Milton*, p. 52.
11 IV, 114–15.     13 *Prose Works*, IV, 184, n. 2.

in " the ways of God." And in those passages where he
affirms that everything has been produced by the Earth,
his materialism looks dangerously like Milton's: Milton
also thought that all beings were produced by matter:

> Who saw
> When this creation was?  Remember'st thou
> Thy making, while the Maker gave thee being?
> We know no time when we were not as now;
> Know none before us, self-begot, self-rais'd
> By our own quick'ning pow'r, when fatal course
> Had circled his full orb, the birth mature
> Of this our native heav'n, ethereal sons.[14]

And:

> The gods are first, and that advantage use
> On our belief, that all from them proceeds;
> I question it, for this fair Earth I see
> Warmed by the Sun, producing every kind,
> Them nothing.[15]

Satan, again, is particularly contemptuous of God's proceedings in the matter of the apple.  Why should Science
be forbidden?  A slip of the adversary this, and Satan is
not slow to take advantage of it:

> One fatal tree there stands, of Knowledge call'd,
> Forbidden them to taste.  Knowledge forbidden?
> Suspicious, reasonless.  Why should their Lord
> Envy them that?  Can it be sin to know?

[14] V, 853–60.

[15] IX, 718–22. The doctrine of the Earth and Sun is in Spenser, " a
better teacher than Aquinas." See *Faerie Queene*, III, vi, 9:

> " Great father he of generation
> Is rightly cald, th' authour of life and light;
> And his faire sister for creation
> Ministreth matter fit, which, tempred right
> With heate and humour, breedes the living wight."

Professor Greenlaw (*Studies in Philology*, XVII [1920], 331–332) interprets
this passage as referring to the Sun (" father ") and the River Nile (" sister ").
For my reasons for dissenting from this interpretation, see *Revue germanique*, XIV (1923), 119n.

Can it be death?  And do they only stand
By ignorance? . . .
O fair foundation laid whereon to build
Their ruin!  Hence I will excite their minds
With more desire to know, and to reject
Envious commands, invented with design
To keep them low whom knowledge might exalt
Equal with gods: aspiring to be such,
They taste and die.  What likelier can ensue? [16]

And Satan is as quick as a modern rationalist to see the
disproportion between the eating of an apple and all the
ensuing disturbance.  Milton was therefore not blind
to it:

Him by fraud I have seduced
From his Creator, and the more to increase
Your wonder, with an apple!  He thereat
Offended (worth your laughter) hath given up
Both his beloved Man and all his world,
To Sin and Death a prey, and so to us,
Without our hazard, labour, or alarm,
To range in, and to dwell, and over Man
To rule, as over all he should have ruled. [17]

Satan in these passages is merely harping on the insuffi-
ciency of dogma when taken literally.  And the whole of
the *De doctrina* is based on a similar attitude.  Satan is
not only a part of Milton's character, he is also a part of
Milton's mind.

And yet Satan is not the hero of the poem: he is intellectually condemned, in spite of all the poet's — and
the reader's — sympathy.

Since neither Christ nor God nor Adam is a fitting
counterpart for Satan, Milton has been charged with having no hero, or with having an evil one.  The charge,

[16] IV, 514-27.                    [17] X, 485-93.

apparently well founded — and artistically, too, perhaps
— is groundless psychologically.  Milton has not felt a
lack of equilibrium between the powers of good and the
powers of evil because, in fact, there is in *Paradise Lost*
a greater character than Satan, an adversary of the
Adversary.  The hero of *Paradise Lost* is Milton himself.

Milton throws himself personally into the struggle
against Satan, and from the reading of *Paradise Lost* one
derives two inevitable impressions: the greatness of Satan
and the greatness of Milton.  Hence the lyricism which
occasionally explodes through the stiff conventionalism
of the epic.  Milton brings his own self into the poem
just as he did into the pamphlets: in both cases he is one
of the duellists; he has a personal share in the fighting.
He it is, and not God or the Son, that overcomes Satan.
He follows him in all his enterprises, stigmatizes them
with one adjective, one line.  He exposes Satan so pas-
sionately that he forgets Satan's natural enemies: he
takes their place before the Enemy.  What need has
Milton of a hero in his poem?  He is his own hero.

Nor was it entirely his egotism, however largely unconscious, that lured him into this attitude.  There was a
deeper cause: Milton had Satan in him and wanted to
drive him out.  He had felt passion, pride, and sensuality.
The deep pleasure he takes in his creation of Satan is the
joy of liberating, purging himself of the evil in himself,
by concentrating it, outside himself, into a work of art.
A joy peculiar to the artist — a joy that, perhaps, was
God's ultimate aim in creating the world, as we have
seen.  Hence that strange monster Satan.  Whereas inferior artists build their monsters artificially, Milton takes
his, living and warm with his own life, out of himself.

In this his ideas were in harmony with his feelings. The struggle between Reason and Passion takes place in Man:

> Dream not of their fight
> As of a duel, or the local wounds
> Of head or heel.

Under the epic, Milton had therefore to picture the human drama. Now God is no actor in that drama: God holds the scales. He cannot be the hero. Man is the hero. But Man, in the poem, is the poet. It was not possible for Adam to follow Satan foot by foot, look him unflinchingly in the eye, and confound him at every moment. The poet-chorus-hero alone could do that. Adam, admirable as he is, is only secondary, as are God and Messiah and the angels — artistically, I mean. The lyrical drama which is the subject-matter of *Paradise Lost* has Milton and Satan as actors. The scene is the soul of the poet: the soul of Man.

Hence our high idea of Milton: he is the man that could look evil in the face, see its force, its grandeur, its fascination even, and then judge, condemn, and reject it. That is why Milton had to give up the dramatic form, in which he could not have thus introduced himself — later on he found the trick of the chorus in *Samson Agonistes* to fulfil the same function. In this sense, as has often been pointed out, his genius is essentially lyrical. His whole life went to the building of *Paradise Lost*. He was of the Devil's party without knowing it; but he was also of God's party, and, what is more important, he knew it. He knew he had passion in him, and he wanted, not to suppress, but to master it. That is why he depicted it so well and combated it so fiercely.

Here is Milton entering upon his enterprise, and praying for help:

> . . . or if Sion hill
> Delight thee more, and Siloa's brook that flow'd
> Fast by the oracle of God; I thence
> Invoke thy aid to my advent'rous song,
> That with no middle flight intends to soar
> Above th' Aonian mount, while it pursues
> Things unattempted yet in prose or rhyme.
> And chiefly Thou, O Spirit, that dost prefer
> Before all temples th' upright heart and pure,
> Instruct me, for Thou know'st: Thou from the first
> Wast present, and with mighty wings outspread
> Dove-like sat'st brooding on the vast abyss,
> And mad'st it pregnant.  What in me is dark
> Illumine, what is low raise and support,
> That to the height of this great argument
> I may assert eternal Providence,
> And justify the ways of God to men.[18]

Here is Milton escaped from hell and invoking holy
Light:

> Thee I revisit now with bolder wing,
> Escaped the Stygian pool, though long detain'd
> In that obscure sojourn, while in my flight
> Through utter and through middle darkness borne
> With other notes than to th' Orphean lyre,
> I sung of Chaos and eternal Night,
> Taught by the heav'nly Muse to venture down
> The dark descent, and up to reascend,
> Though hard and rare: thee I revisit safe,
> And feel thy sov'reign vital lamp: but thou
> Revisit'st not these eyes, that roll in vain
> To find thy piercing ray, and find no dawn;
> So thick a drop serene hath quench'd their orbs,
> Or dim suffusion veil'd.  Yet not the more
> Cease I to wander where the Muses haunt
> Clear spring, or shady grove, or sunny hill,

[18] I, 10–26.

Smit with the love of sacred song; but chief
Thee, Sion, and the flow'ry brooks beneath,
That wash thy hallow'd feet, and warbling flow,
Nightly I visit: nor sometimes forget
Those other two equall'd with me in fate,
So were I equall'd with them in renown,
Blind Thamyris and blind Mæonides,
And Tiresias and Phineus, prophets old;
Then feed on thoughts, that voluntary move
Harmonious numbers; as the wakeful bird
Sings darkling, and in shadiest covert hid
Tunes her nocturnal note.  Thus with the year
Seasons return, but not to me returns
Day, or the sweet approach of ev'n or morn,
Or sight of vernal bloom, or summer's rose,
Or flocks, or herds, or human face divine;
But cloud instead, and ever-during dark
Surrounds me, from the cheerful ways of men
Cut off, and for the book of knowledge fair
Presented with an universal blank
Of Nature's works, to me expunged and rased,
And Wisdom at one entrance quite shut out.
So much the rather thou, celestial Light,
Shine inward, and the mind through all her pow'rs
Irradiate, there plant eyes, all mist from thence
Purge and disperse, that I may see and tell
Of things invisible to mortal sight.[19]

Here he is, in danger, praying to the holy muse for pro-
tection, spiritual and earthly:

Up led by thee
Into the Heav'n of Heav'ns I have presumed,
An earthly guest, and drawn empyreal air,
Thy temp'ring.  With like safety guided down,
Return me to my native element;
Lest from this flying steed, unrein'd (as once
Bellerophon, though from a lower clime),
Dismounted, on th' Aleian field I fall
Erroneous there to wander, and forlorn.

[19] III, 13-55.

Half yet remains unsung, but narrower bound
Within the visible diurnal sphere;
Standing on earth, not rapt above the pole,
More safe I sing with mortal voice, unchanged
To hoarse or mute, though fall'n on evil days,
On evil days though fall'n, and evil tongues;
In darkness, and with dangers compass'd round,
And solitude; yet not alone, while thou
Visit'st my slumbers nightly, or when morn
Purples the east: still govern thou my song,
Urania, and fit audience find, though few;
But drive far off the barb'rous dissonance
Of Bacchus and his revellers, the race
Of that wild rout that tore the Thracian bard
In Rhodope, where woods and rocks had ears
To rapture, till the savage clamour drown'd
Both harp and voice; nor could the Muse defend
Her son. So fail not thou, who thee implores;
For thou art heav'nly, she an empty dream.[20]

And, in sight of the port, here is Milton vindicating the greatness of his enterprise and claiming divine inspiration:

If answerable style I can obtain
Of my celestial patroness, who deigns
Her nightly visitation unimplored,
And dictates to me slumb'ring, or inspires
Easy my unpremeditated verse,
Since first this subject for heroic song
Pleased me, long choosing, and beginning late;
Not sedulous by nature to indite
Wars, hitherto the only argument
Heroic deem'd. . . .
. . . Me of these
Nor skill'd nor studious, higher argument
Remains, sufficient of itself to raise
That name, unless an age too late, or cold
Climate, or years, damp my intended wing
Depress'd, and much they may, if all be mine,
Not hers who brings it nightly to my ear.[21]

[20] VII, 12–39.          [21] IX, 20–47.

Thus Milton, at each great turning point of his epic, comes openly to the front of the stage and claims his part among the actors.  As for Milton the adversary, critic, and companion of Satan, he is to be found wherever Satan and his angels are.  No impartial and cold historian he: he adds his personal curse to all the disadvantages Satan is laboring under:

Who first seduc'd them to that foul revolt?
Th' infernal serpent, he it was, whose guile,
Stirr'd up with envy and revenge, deceiv'd
The mother of mankind, what time his pride
Had cast him out from heav'n, with all his host
Of rebel Angels, by whose aid aspiring
To set himself in glory above his peers,
He trusted to have equall'd the Most High,
If he oppos'd; and with ambitious aim,
Against the throne and monarchy of God,
Rais'd impious war in heav'n, and battle proud,
With vain attempt.  Him the Almighty Pow'r
Hurl'd headlong flaming from th' ethereal sky,
With hideous ruin and combustion, down
To bottomless perdition. . . .
        . . . he with his horrid crew
Lay vanquish'd, rolling in the fiery gulf,
Confounded, though immortal.  But his doom
Reserv'd him to more wrath; for now the thought
Both of lost happiness and lasting pain
Torments him.  Round he throws his baleful eyes,
That witness'd huge affliction and dismay,
Mix'd with obdurate pride, and stedfast hate.[22]

Note the adjectives: " foul," " infernal," " impious," " vain," " horrid," " baleful," " obdurate " : all could be suppressed; each is a personal insult of Milton to his foe. Similarly, Satan's first speech is followed by this comment:

[22] I, 33–58.

So spake the apostate angel, though in pain
Vaunting abroad, but racked with deep despair.[23]

And the first gesture of the great rebel calls for this
malediction:

So stretch'd out huge in length the Arch-fiend lay,
Chain'd on the burning lake; nor ever thence
Had ris'n, or heav'd his head, but that the will
And high permission of all-ruling heaven,
Left him at large to his own dark designs,
That with reiterated crimes he might
Heap on himself damnation, while he sought
Evil to others; and enrag'd might see,
How all his malice serv'd but to bring forth
Infinite goodness, grace, and mercy shewn
On man by him seduc'd; but on himself
Treble confusion, wrath, and vengeance pour'd.[24]

There is a note of terrible rejoicing in Satan's disaster,
as in the lines,

With hideous ruin and combustion, down
To bottomless perdition.[25]

To his description of the cursed ground of hell, Milton
adds:

Such resting found the sole
Of unblessed feet.[26]

Here are, in the midst of the all-too-successful delibera-
tions of the infernal council, two short half-lines which
interrupt the explanation of Satan's diplomacy:

But their spite still serves
His [God's] glory to augment.[27]

Here is Satan's magnificent journey through chaos.
Milton admires him; but he does not forget himself:
note the " ill chance " :

[23] I, 125–26.    [25] I, 46–47.    [27] II, 385–86.
[24] I, 209–20.    [26] I, 237–38.

All unawares,
Flutt'ring his pennons vain, plumb down he drops
Ten thousand fathom deep, and to this hour
Down had been falling, had not by ill chance,
The strong rebuff of some tumultuous cloud,
Instinct with fire and nitre, hurried him
As many miles aloft.[28]

And Milton cannot end the second book without an extra malediction:

Thither, full fraught with mischievous revenge,
Accursed, and in a cursed hour he hies.[29]

In the third book, when Satan goes by the bottom of Jacob's ladder, Milton does not overlook his chance:

The stars were then let down, whether to dare
The Fiend by easy ascent, or aggravate
His sad exclusion from the doors of bliss.[30]

And Book IV opens on another outburst:

O for that warning voice, which he who saw
The Apocalypse heard cry in Heav'n aloud,
Then when the Dragon, put to second rout,
Came furious down to be revenged on men,
Woe to th' inhabitants on earth! that now,
While time was, our first parents had been warn'd
The coming of their secret foe, and 'scaped,
Haply so 'scaped his mortal snare; for now
Satan, now first inflamed with rage, came down,
To wreck on innocent frail man his loss
Of that first battle and his flight to hell.[31]

And so on through the poem. We have seen Milton at this sort of work, relentlessly pursuing and insulting the author of *Eikon Basilike*, or Salmasius or More in the *Defences*. The insult which ends Book II is particularly

[28] II, 932–38.
[29] II, 1054–55.
[30] III, 523–25.
[31] IV, 1–12.

reminiscent of the ending of many chapters in the *Defensio prima,* where Salmasius receives each time a surplus hit.    Milton treats Satan as he had treated the anonymous Gauden or the celebrated Salmasius: as a personal enemy.

But not only in the fierceness of his personal relationship to Satan is Milton discoverable in *Paradise Lost.* The whole experience of his life has been poured into the poem.    The wonderful eloquence of the council in hell is an echo from a period of passionate Parliamentary life. Each orator gives such powerful arguments that one feels he must carry the assembly; but each succeeding orator is more powerful than his predecessor, and the whole culminates in Satan's finest piece of diplomacy.    And the war in heaven is a civil war, characterized by the bitterness of feeling and language peculiar to internal broils.

The summary of Milton's experience of private life, too, is here, in the charming and deeply human relationship between Adam and Eve.    And we cannot refrain from pointing out one more proof of the humanity of the poet in that scene, admittedly imitated from Milton's reconciliation with his wife, in which Eve's humble affection opens the way back to life.    Here Milton happily forgets his theories of the predominance of reason, and the influence of " female charm " on Adam is this time his salvation:

> Forsake me not thus, Adam.    Witness, Heav'n,
> What love sincere, and rev'rence in my heart
> I bear thee, and unweeting have offended,
> Unhappily deceived.    Thy suppliant
> I beg, and clasp thy knees.    Bereave me not,
> Whereon I live, thy gentle looks, thy aid,
> Thy counsel in this uttermost distress,

My only strength and stay.   Forlorn of thee,
Whither shall I betake me, where subsist?
While yet we live, scarce one short hour perhaps,
Between us two let there be peace. . . .
   She ended weeping, and her lowly plight,
Immoveable till peace obtain'd from fault
Acknowledged and deplored, in Adam wrought
Commiseration.   Soon his heart relented
Tow'rds her, his life so late and sole delight,
Now at his feet submissive in distress,
Creature so fair his reconcilement seeking,
His counsel, whom she had displeased, his aid;
As one disarm'd, his anger all he lost,
And thus with peaceful words upraised her soon.[32]

And here again Milton is the hero of his own epic.


## II. God in *Paradise Lost:* the Divine Irony

Compared with the intense and active life of the party of Satan, and with the pathetic and richly human life of the first human couple, the life of the heavenly party can hardly be said to count.   Yet there is one feeling Milton has touched upon — one feeling that might have been susceptible of rich development, both poetical and philosophical, in his treatment of the Divinity.

Since the divine plans are laid from all eternity, since God has foreseen all the manifestations of the free creatures and has provided for them — or against them, — the only feeling that may yet move God with regard to the efforts directed against him, or even those that aim at knowledge of him, is a feeling of irony: the irony of intelligent Fate looking on at the vain struggles of beings submitted to inevitable law.   In order, however, to deal adequately with this subject, perhaps a poet should be a

[32] X, 914-46.

heathen — Goethe himself got some of this irony only into Mephistopheles — and he should not believe so thoroughly as did Milton in the essential freedom of beings. Besides, Milton had not the intellectual agility, nor the perfect tact, nor the deep bitterness of feeling, necessary to paint such a picture. Therefore his traits are heavy and lacking in poetry and depth. He saw the possibilities of the theme, but he could not fully exploit them. Nevertheless, he had the merit of seeing the situation. Thus, he makes God say to his Son when the angels rebel:

> Nearly it now concerns us to be sure
> Of our omnipotence, and with what arms
> We mean to hold what anciently we claim
> Of Deity or empire; such a foe
> Is rising, who intends to erect his throne .
> Equal to ours, throughout the spacious north;
> Nor so content, hath in his thought to try
> In battle what our pow'r is, or our right.
> Let us advise, and to this hazard draw
> With speed what force is left, and all employ
> In our defence, lest unawares we lose
> This our high place, our sanctuary, our hill.
>     To whom the Son, with calm aspect and clear,
> Lightning divine, ineffable, serene,
> Made answer. Mighty Father, thou thy foes
> Justly hast in derision, and, secure,
> Laugh'st at their vain designs and tumults vain.[33]

The same irony accompanies man's fruitless efforts towards knowledge:

> Or if they list to try
> Conjecture, he his fabric of the Heav'ns
> Hath left to their disputes, perhaps to move
> His laughter at their quaint opinions wide

[33] V, 718-34.

Hereafter, when they come to model Heav'n
And calculate the stars, how they will wield
The mighty frame, how build, unbuild, contrive
To save appearances, how gird the sphere
With centric and eccentric scribbled o'er,
Cycle and epicycle, orb in orb.[34]

And the laughter of Heaven is on men's confusion over
the Tower of Babel:

But God, who oft descends to visit men
Unseen, and through their habitations walks
To mark their doings, them beholding soon,
Comes down to see their city, ere the tow'r
Obstruct Heav'n-tow'rs, and in derision sets
Upon their tongues a various spirit to rase
Quite out their native language, and instead
To sow a jangling noise of words unknown.
. . . Great laughter was in Heav'n,
And looking down, to see the hubbub strange,
And hear the din; thus was the building left
Ridiculous, and the work Confusion named.[35]

On two occasions, however, this divine irony is tempered
with compassion — a feeling befitting the Divinity. The
first is when Adam asks for a suitable mate,

Whereto th' Almighty answer'd, not displeased:
A nice and subtle happiness I see
Thou to thyself proposest, in the choice
Of thy associates, Adam, and wilt taste
No pleasure, though in pleasure, solitary.
What think'st thou then of me, and this my state?
Seem I to thee sufficiently possess'd
Of happiness, or not, who am alone
From all eternity? [36]

And the second is when God allows himself a last remark,
quite justified after all, before accepting, as is befitting,

[34] VIII, 75–84.          [35] XII, 48–62.          [36] VIII, 398–406.

Adam and Eve's repentance.  He speaks to the faithful
angels:

> O Sons, like one of us Man is become
> To know both good and evil, since his taste
> Of that defended fruit! [37]

So that, even in Milton's God, there are traces of the
poet's humaneness.  Divine reason, with some admixture
of irony and pity, is reconciled with human feeling.

[37] XI, 84–86.

## CHAPTER III

*PARADISE REGAINED* AND *SAMSON AGONISTES*

P*ARADISE REGAINED* sings Man's Regeneration. The most remarkable thing about it, from our point of view here, is that such a title should be given to such a work.

The drama remains entirely intellectual. There is no action and no passions come into play. The purely emotional side of Jesus's story, his suffering and crucifixion, has not attracted Milton. Divine love, God's love for the world, which makes him sacrifice his only Son for the salvation of his creatures, Christ's love for men which makes him give his blood as an offering to Eternal Justice, has no appeal for Milton either. Milton was not sentimental; he was not a mystic. He had his strong share of human feelings and passions, but he was simple and natural, and satisfied his desires in the plain normal human way, without refining overmuch. Besides, he wanted to understand things. The incomprehensibility of God is to him an intellectual fact, a perception by the mind of its own limitations. It is not a mystery of love and blind self-forgetfulness.

Therefore, even as the Fall had been an argument in which man had been deceived, so the Restoration is an argument in which man, in the person of Jesus, triumphs. *Paradise Regained* is a tale of Reason and Passion discussing who shall win in man. It comes as near as it can to being an allegory, and barely escapes being one through Milton's poetical scheme, which includes the persons of Satan and Christ.  Christ is hardly a success artistically.  It is agreed that the poet had his own child-hood in mind in the lines

> When I was yet a child, no childish play
> To me was pleasing, all my mind was set
> Serious to learn and know, and thence to do
> What might be public good.[1]

Milton has for once made a bad mistake in bringing in his own autobiography.  He may have been a child with a passion for learning — there are such children — and an abnormal pride.  The fact, transmitted into Jesus's experience, sounds like the worst sort of cant; and the whole of the presentation of Christ in the first book is vitiated by intolerable self-consciousness.

Satan is not the grand Rebel of the first books of *Paradise Lost*, but the subtle tempter of Eve; and in that part, he is worthy of his glory.  He shows true psycho-logical acumen when he decides that the evident tempta-tions of sensuality will be of no avail on Jesus and that only legitimate desires, like hunger, must be made use of. It is curious to point out that this should have driven the theme of sensuality out of the poem, but not at all: the loveliest part of *Paradise Regained* (and it contains many beautiful passages) is on women.  Listen to Belial:

> Set women in his eye, and in his walk,
> Among daughters of men, the fairest found;
> Many are in each region passing fair
> As the noon sky: more like to goddesses
> Than mortal creatures, graceful and discreet,
> Expert in amorous arts, enchanting tongues
> Persuasive, virgin majesty with mild

[1] I, 201–04.

And sweet allay'd, yet terrible to approach,
Skill'd to retire, and in retiring draw
Hearts after them tangled in amorous nets.

. . . . . . . .

To whom quick answer Satan thus return'd:
Belial, in much uneven scale thou weigh'st
All others by thyself; because of old
Thou thyself doat'st on womankind, admiring
Their shape, their colour, and attractive grace,
None are, thou think'st, but taken with such toys.[2]

And never has Milton evoked any visions more fascinating than that

Of fairy damsels met in forest wide
By knights of Logres or of Lyones,
Lancelot, or Pelleas or Pellenore.[3]

However, on the whole, outside these and other well-known passages, the poem yields small reward. Landor's judgment on it is both picturesque and sound:

Milton is caught sleeping after his exertions in *Paradise Lost*, and the lock of his strength is shorn off; but here and there a prominent muscle swells out from the vast mass of the collapsed.[4]

To this mood of fatigue, no doubt, is to be attributed Milton's surly *boutade* against books:

However, many books
Wise men have said, are wearisome; who reads
Incessantly, and to his reading brings not
A spirit and judgment equal or superior
(And what he brings, what needs he elsewhere seek?)
Uncertain and unsettled still remains,
Deep versed in books and shallow in himself,
Crude or intoxicate, collecting toys
And trifles for choice matters, worth a sponge;
As children gathering pebbles on the shore.[5]

[2] II, 153–77.          [4] *Southey and Landor.*
[3] II, 259–61.          [5] IV, 321–30.

There is much truth in it, and it is forcibly put; but let us rather remember the *Areopagitica*: " For books are not absolutely dead things, but do contain a progeny of life. . . ." Where is the Milton of 1644, and all the youthful enthusiasm?

*Samson Agonistes* is Milton's literary and philosophical testament. It is a pure jewel, nearly as splendid and much more human than *Paradise Lost*. Did not the majestic proportions of the epic forbid all comparison, one might be tempted, sacrilegiously, to give *Samson* the first rank among Milton's works.

In *Samson*, Milton takes up once more all the main themes of his thinking, and works them out in a simpler and broader manner than in *Paradise Lost*.

First, we find here the particular subject of the fall through woman, that is, through sensuality. Then, the more general triumph of passion over reason. Like Adam, Samson yields to Dalila:

> Against his better knowledge, not deceived,
> But fondly overcome by female charm.

Regeneration is here also: the rejection of woman, and the triumph of reason; with a great heroic deed added. Then there is the interrogation of Destiny which is the bottom of Miltonic thought:

> God of our fathers, what is man?

And the answer: the fall of man in himself is translated into disaster outside him; his inner regeneration, into external victory.

*Samson Agonistes* is a return to simplicity. Milton gives up the complications of dogma, fall and restoration, and frankly sets his drama in Samson's soul — a drama which is led towards precise aims by Destiny, by God. God is more mysterious and more dreadful; he is no longer the all-too-clear logician of *Paradise Lost;* he is the incomprehensible and yet just Power that presides over the course of the World. In *Paradise Regained* Milton took a first step away from dogma: his action is purely intellectual and psychological. In *Samson,* he takes the next step and frees himself from dogma; all he keeps of it is God-Destiny. Now, it must be remembered that these three modes of thought are not properly successive, but practically simultaneous. *Paradise Regained* and *Samson Agonistes* were written immediately after *Paradise Lost,* so that Milton's ideas had undergone no change. We must therefore read *Paradise Lost* also in the simpler light of the other poems.

In *Samson,* Milton gives a threefold picture of life: first, of man's life in general: then of the history of England, Samson representing the fallen Puritan party, when the Royalist Philistines triumph in debauch and revelry, the end being a prophecy of justice to come; and lastly, of Milton's own life, wrecked in hope, blind and poor, and meditating and perpetrating the glorious revenge of *Paradise Lost.* The three themes are held together in a masterly manner under the simple Biblical tale. We have here a magnificent example of what Blake calls " fourfold vision." *Samson Agonistes* is thus the last word on the Miltonic conception of life. The most striking fact is the extent of what Milton has been able to omit from the scheme.

First of all, he has omitted the theory of original sin. This is all the more remarkable since, in a Hebrew subject, in harmony with the idea of the fall through woman,

there was a logical place for the old myth.  But the omission i₃ in harmony with Milton's character.  He disliked
the idea that human nature is evil from its origin, and
had never insisted much on original sin.  His natural
pride went against it.  The essential point to him was the
individual fall and regeneration.  Hence a greater depth
to the question, " God of our fathers, what is man? " since
man is not corrupt by nature.  The anxiety behind the
question is more pathetic, more human than in the description of Eve and the apple.  This over-simple solution
to the riddle of destiny no longer satisfies Milton.  He
insists, for the first time, on another point of view.
Divine justice is no longer the sole cause of man's trials;
the education of man is in view.  God's hand is heavy,
out of all proportion to the fault he punishes, because
God, through suffering, accomplishes our inmost education and brings about our regeneration.  God deals with
individuals as with nations.  Milton had learned much
through suffering; he hoped England would learn.

In the second place, Milton also gives up the idea of
salvation through Christ.  No allusion, no prophecy on
the subject of Christ in *Samson,* and yet, what a rich and
tempting poetical theme was there!  But Milton cared
little for vicarious atonement.  Death settles all accounts;
even the just have to die, and that expiates sufficiently.
Samson is buried in his victory.  Such death is not to be
dreaded; it is the final liberation from passion, the ultimate triumph of intelligence,

> And calm of mind, all passion spent.

Lastly, Milton gives up all precision in the idea of God.
The last remnants of the doctrine of the Trinity disappear.  The Son is not mentioned in *Samson.*  God alone

remains, a secret, incomprehensible God, whose ways call forth anxious questionings, and not precise explanations, as in *Paradise Lost*. The Holy Ghost had long been without an official existence in Milton's doctrine. The Christ-Son of God also tends to dissolve; as Son of God, he becomes identical with God, the Creator, whose name he assumes; as Christ, the Savior, he tends to be merely Divine Reason in each of the elect; as Jesus, he fades more and more into mere man. This dispersion of the second person of the Trinity, the most embarrassing for heretics and rationalists, brings Milton near mere deism — or pantheism. But as it becomes less precise, the idea of God becomes greater. For the first time in Milton's work, there appears an element which is lacking in *Paradise Lost*, the feeling of awe in the presence of God, respectful dread and trust.

Thus Milton, in his last work, deliberately gives up, in his attempt to find a solution to the problems of his life and thought, the whole fabric of dogma which had helped him so far. His explanation is now merely psychological, whereas previously the psychology had only run parallel to the dogma. Was not then Milton freer from dogma at the end of his life than is generally supposed? Milton's last poem is a last enigma. The fact obliges us to be very liberal in our interpretation of Milton's religion, and to look for the central fixed point of his thought not in dogma, but in philosophy. Milton is more intimately present in *Samson Agonistes* than in any of his other poems. Here he put the history of his own life. Did he not put here also the last and best expression of his thought? Being here more human, is he not also more sincere?

Here is Milton blind — and, for the first time, complaining:

> O loss of sight, of thee I most complain!
> Blind among enemies, O worse than chains,
> Dungeon, or beggery, or decrepit age!
> Light, the prime work of God, to me is extinct,
> And all her various objects of delight
> Annulled, which might in part my grief have eased.
>
> .    .    .    .    .    .    .    .    .
>
> The sun to me is dark
> And silent as the moon,
> When she deserts the night,
> Hid in her vacant interlunar cave.
> Since light so necessary is to life,
> And almost life itself, if it be true
> That light is in the soul,
> She all in every part; why was the sight
> To such a tender ball as th' eye confined,
> So obvious and so easy to be quenched? [6]

Here is doubt, at the very core of man.  Having so long called to account the great of the earth and the people, and Milton himself, in the name of God, the old prophet turns upon his master, like an old minister remonstrating with his king; and this time, in the name of the great, of the people, of Milton himself, the poet calls God to account:

> God of our fathers, what is man!
> That thou towards him with hand so various,
> Or may I say contrarious,
> Temper'st thy providence through his short course,
> Not evenly, as thou rul'st
> The angelic orders and inferior creatures mute,
> Irrational and brute. [7]

Why did God allow the Saints to come to complete disaster?

[6] Ll. 67–95.                    [7] Ll. 667–73.

Nor do I name of men the common rout,
That wandering loose about
Grow up and perish, as the summer fly,
Heads without name no more remembered,
But such as thou hast solemnly elected,
With gifts and graces eminently adorned
To some great work, thy glory,
And people's safety, which in part they effect:
Yet toward these thus dignified, thou oft
Amidst their height of noon,
Changest thy countenance, and thy hand with no regard
Of highest favors past
From thee on them, or them to thee of service.
  Nor only dost degrade them, or remit
To life obscured, which were a fair dismission,
But throw'st them lower than thou didst exalt them high,
Unseemly falls in human eye,
Too grievous for the trespass or omission;
Oft leav'st them to the hostile sword
Of heathen and profane, their carcasses
To dogs and fowls a prey, or else captived;
Or to the unjust tribunals, under change of times,
And condemnation of the ingrateful multitude.[8]

And Milton's own old age is bitterly described, his illnesses, which his life, made of temperance and dignity, ought not to have brought about; the loss of his fortune even he does not forget:

If these they scape, perhaps in poverty,
With sickness and disease, thou bow'st them down,
Painful diseases and deformed,
In crude old age:
Though not disordinate, yet causeless suff'ring
The punishment of dissolute days.

And is this to be the conclusion?
        . . . in fine,
Just or unjust, alike seem miserable,
For oft alike both come to evil end.[9]

[8] Ll. 674–96.      [9] Ll. 697–704.

Milton has faced the problem of destiny in all its difficulty.   Then comes the magnificent episode with Dalila,
which marks Samson's triumph over himself.   But Milton
does not believe as entirely as of old in the solidity of
such triumphs; the chorus closes the episode on a doubting and half angry mood.[10]   Here again Milton is more
human, and has looked more closely into human weakness.

But at last, to Samson, purified through suffering and
meditation, as the ultimate answer to God, his opportunity of heroic action is offered.   A new trait here also:
it is not enough for man to attain wisdom for himself;
he must help the course of the world, become the instrument of God's will, and act greatly.   Again the experience
of life had taught Milton something more.

Samson's victory is the defeat of the Philistines; they
fell through their passions, which blinded them, while
his suffering was regenerating Samson.   On this conclusion of the whole of his life's patient thought, Milton
closes his last, his most poignant poem; " blindness internal " is the cause of all disaster.

> While their hearts were jocund and sublime,
> Drunk with idolatry, drunk with wine,
> And fat regorged of bulls and goats,
> Chanting their idol, and preferring
> Before our living Dread who dwells
> In Silo His bright sanctuary;
> Among them He a spirit of frenzy sent,
> Who hurt their minds,
> And urged them on with mad desire
> To call in haste for their destroyer;
> They, only set on sport and play,
> Unweetingly importuned

[10] See above, p. 165.

Their own destruction to come speedy upon them.
So fond are mortal men,
Fallen into wrath divine,
As their own ruin on themselves to invite,
Insensate left, or to sense reprobate,
And with blindness internal struck.[11]

Thus the ways of God are again justified; calamity has taught man his lesson, and rid him of his passions; intelligence is increased, passion spent, harmony complete in the poet's soul:

Nothing is here for tears, nothing to wail
Or knock the breast; no weakness, no contempt,
Dispraise, or blame; nothing but well and fair,
And what may quiet us in a death so noble.

.        .        .        .        .        .        .        .

   *Chor.*   All is best, though we oft doubt,
What th' unsearchable dispose
Of Highest Wisdom brings about,
And ever best found in the close.
Oft He seems to hide His face,
But unexpectedly returns,
And to His faithful champion hath in place
Bore witness gloriously; whence Gaza mourns,
And all that band them to resist
His uncontrollable intent;
His servants He, with new acquist
Of true experience from this great event,
With peace and consolation hath dismissed,
And calm of mind, all passion spent.[12]

[11] Ll. 1669–86.                    [12] Ll. 1721–58.

PART IV

THE SOURCES

MILTON'S thought is essentially original. I mean that, although he has expressed only ideas which were current before him, and around him in certain circles, yet he has never accepted an idea from the outside. He has examined all the old notions of mankind, re-weighed them in his own scales, and accepted or rejected them for reasons peculiar to his own mind. I have tried to show in Part I how he acquired the ideas he held at the end of his life; that is to say, how he caught up with those ideas, so to speak, as his own personal experience progressed. In this Part IV, I wish to study what he adopted them from. Having seen the workings of his internal inspiration, let us now see his external sources. What he says of Scripture in the *De doctrina* applies to all his sources; we must remember that he saw no fundamental difference between the Bible and other great " inspired " books, whatever nation or creed they came from:

. . . we possess, as it were a twofold Scripture; one external, which is the written word, and the other internal, which is the Holy Spirit . . . that which is internal, and the peculiar possession of each believer, is far superior to all, namely the Spirit itself.[1]

Through this Spirit, his own peculiar possession, he judged of the necessity of accepting external suggestions. As I see the evolution of his mind, his outlook on life changed with his own personal experience, which decided what he would adopt and what he would reject among the ideas so far brought forward by mankind.

[1] *Prose Works*, IV, 447. See above, p. 204.

In fact, the expression " sources," which is retained here
for reasons of convenience, is totally inadequate; I hold
it impossible to investigate properly the sources of Milton's ideas, because that would mean writing a history of
philosophy, and setting on parallel pages what Milton
may — or may not — have borrowed from each successive
phase of human thought. Milton is a unit of a whole
that goes together; to take up a thread at the beginning
of human culture and follow it up till it reaches Milton
is a pure illusion, a mere abstract fabrication of the critical mind. Yet we must do something to situate Milton
in the evolution of man's thought. In studying a man's
ancestry, in order to be complete, one would have to study
the whole of mankind, since the number of his ancestors
increases into the infinite as one works backwards. But
it is possible to study his own parents and even his grandparents with tolerable precision. Thus I shall try to see
what Milton's immediate ancestry was, to study, so to
speak, his parents and his grandparents, and to find the
" sources " of his thought — or at least thought akin to
his (it will be difficult often to fix on the precise degree
of relationship, to say, if I may follow up my simile,
whether we have discovered a real parent or a mere uncle)
in movements of the sixteenth and seventeenth centuries.

This applies to the ideas proper. It applies in a lesser
degree to his " myths," because here Milton followed a
precise tradition of dogma, at least in so far as he used
Christian myth. Here, in Milton's own mind — which is
the all-important fact — a thread did exist which led from
the beginning of the world to himself.

I shall therefore divide this part into two sections. In
the first, I shall study the traditions on the Fall handed

down to Milton, and try to see how he used the myth; I
shall stop when I reach a period at which the myth he
used was fully formed, namely, at the time of Augustine.
In the second section I shall study those contemporary
movements which allow us most precision in our search
for influences received or deliberately accepted by Milton.

I make no claim to any sort of completeness. The field
is new, and many scholars are engaged upon it. Many
important questions, such as the theme of Reason versus
Passion in the sixteenth and seventeenth centuries, or the
influence of Spenser on Milton's thought, for instance, I
shall hardly glance at. I merely bring here my personal
contribution to the search. In a bibliographical appendix,
I shall give a cursory view of what others are doing at
the present moment in the same field.

## SECTION I

## THE MYTH OF THE FALL: SOURCES
## AND INTERPRETATION

English critics seem to me to have exaggerated Milton's
originality in this field. Huxley complained with some
bitterness that most people's idea of the origins comes
from Milton and not from the Bible. Mark Pattison
writes: " In Genesis it is the serpent who tempts Eve.
. . . In Milton it is Satan who has entered into the body
of a serpent, and supplied the intelligence. Here, indeed,
Milton was only adopting a gloss, as ancient at least as
the Wisdom of Solomon (2:24). But it is the gloss, and
not the text of Moses, which is in possession of our minds,
and who has done most to lodge it there, Milton or the

commentators? "[1]   Sir Walter Raleigh also says: " The Miltonic account of the Fall of the Angels . . . is not borrowed from the Fathers, but corresponds rather with the later version popularised in England by the cycles of Miracle Plays."[2]   And finally, one of Milton's last biographers, Mr. John Bailey, remarks: " To this day if an ordinary man is asked to give his recollections of the story of Adam and Eve, he is sure to put Milton as well as Genesis into them.   For instance, the Miltonic Satan is almost sure to take the place of the Scriptural serpent."[3]

Now, the idea that Satan was in the serpent is a very orthodox idea, introduced into dogma, so to speak, by St. Augustine, and developed by Calvin in his commentary on the first chapters of Genesis.   It is found in catechisms of the Reformation previous to Milton's time; its popularity is due to ministers and Sunday-school teachers far more than to Milton in Protestant countries; and it is part of the usual Catholic teaching in countries where Milton is practically unknown.

Milton is heir to an extremely complex tradition; his originality lies in selection and not in invention.   But in his selection we find the principles that directed his whole thinking.

[1] *Milton*, p. 185.         [2] *Milton*, p. 99.
[3] *Milton* (Home University Library; New York, 1915), p. 143.

## CHAPTER I

### HEBRAIC SOURCES

#### I. THE FALL OF MAN [1]

THE probable aim of the tales on the fall of man among the ancient Hebrews seems to have been the investigation of the origin of suffering and not of moral evil. Why is man obliged to work hard to feed himself and his family? Why has woman to bear children in pain and why is she submitted to the slavery of marriage?

The answer seems to have been that man's misery is connected with his intelligence, with his knowledge of good and evil. This knowledge is considered as good and desirable: " for as an angel of God, so is my lord the king to discern good and bad." [2] Children acquire the knowledge as they grow up: " your children, which in that day had no knowledge between good and evil." [3] Childhood is a period of happiness and play, and also a period of ignorance. But as the child grows up, knowledge comes to him; he knows good and evil. Then play and happiness are over. The girl is given a husband, who is her master, and she is doomed to child-bearing. The young man is set to work and begins a life of trouble,

---

[1] I am indebted for guidance in this field to Professor Ad. Lods, Professor of Hebrew at the Sorbonne; and for later times to Dr. de Faye, of the École des Hautes Études and to Professor Charles Guignebert, of the Sorbonne. The *Zohar* texts I quote in Section II, Chapter I, have been verified in the original by Dr. Liber, of the Hautes Études.

[2] II Samuel 14:17, 20; 19:35.

[3] Deuteronomy 1:39, and *cf.* Isaiah 7:15, 16.

fatigue, and suffering.  Even thus mankind went through
a period of happiness, in Paradise, and then grew up and
was condemned to know good and evil, work and child-
bearing.[4]

The divine will, in Adam's own interest, had forbidden
him to acquire the knowledge of good and evil.  By remaining in the blessed ignorance of childhood, mankind
might have remained in a state of perpetual happiness.
But man disobeyed.  He wished to become as the gods,
knowing good and evil.  Pride possessed him; and God
was obliged to put down his pride by sending him tribula-
tion.  This idea is one of the most frequent themes of
the prophets: "And the loftiness of man shall be bowed
down, and the haughtiness of men shall be made low,
and the Lord alone shall be exalted in that day."[5]

On the whole, then, the sufferings of life are the price
paid for knowledge; and the price is worth paying.  Anyhow, man chose his lot, against God's will and warning.

What did Milton know of the old texts that might have
allowed him to get into contact with the primitive ideas
of the Hebrews?  He had at his disposal the Polyglot
Bible published by Walton in 1657.  He seems even to
have known Walton personally; Walton had been curate
in Milton's native street, Bread Street, in 1624, and it
seems probable that it was on Milton's initiative that the
Council of State voted money to help him with his
publication.  A particular friend of Milton's, one of his
former pupils, was one of Walton's collaborators.[6]  In

---

[4] Cf. Bousset, Die Religion des Jundentums in neutestamentlichen Zeit-
alter, Ch. XX, especially p. 466; R. M. Charles, The Book of Enoch
(Oxford, Clarendon Press, 1912), pp. civ ff.  Even in this comparatively
recent text, "moral evil is not brought into causal connection with the
transgression of Adam, save in one passage."

[5] Isaiah 2: 17.                    [6] Masson, VI, 417.

Walton's recension appeared the great commentaries of
Onkelos and Jonathan the Targoum. Milton knew them
before this, however, for he speaks of them in 1649, in
the *Apology for Smectymnuus*.[7] He had therefore access
to sufficient sources. The constant communion with the
Bible in which he lived seems to have allowed him to
catch more of the old meanings than subsists of them in
orthodox interpretation. Thus he came to the conclusion that the ancient Hebrews did not believe in the
survival of the soul after death, in spite of the general
opinion before and around him.[8] He was also in sympathy with the old beliefs in thinking that, after all, the
price paid for knowledge had not been too much,[9] and
he saw advantages in the Fall.[10] He was equally ready
to profit by the naïve primitiveness of Bible folk, who
saw nothing wrong in it, to justify legitimate sensuality:

As saints and patriarchs used.

## II. The Fall of the Angels

The first record of Hebrew speculations on the fall of
the angels is in Genesis 6:1–5:

And it came to pass, when men began to multiply on the face
of the earth, and daughters were born unto them, that the sons of
God saw the daughters of men that they were fair; and they took
them wives of all which they chose. . . . There were giants in the
earth in those days; and also after that, when the sons of God
came in unto the daughters of men, and they bare children to
them. . . . God saw that the wickedness of man was great in the
earth. . . .

[7] *Prose Works*, III, 131.
[8] See above, p. 146, and *Prose Works*, IV, 271–72; *cf.* Bousset, p. 460.
[9] See *Areopagitica*, in *Prose Works*, II, 67–68.
[10] *P. L.*, XII, 474 ff.

In this primitive form of the myth, it is important to note
that (1) the fall of the angels comes later than that of
man; (2) the cause of the angels' fall is sensuality; (3)
the origin of evil is in the fall of the angels and not in
that of man.

The legends of the Fall, based on these three fundamental ideas, were developed in the course of history,
and gathered, about the second or first century B.C., in
the Book of Enoch.    In the time of Milton all that was
known of this book was a rather long fragment preserved
by the Byzantine historian, Georgius Syncellus, in his
*Chronographia*.    This book was published by Goar in
Paris in 1657.    Professor Hanford, in his article on the
" Chronology of Milton's Private Studies," [11] gives a list
of the Byzantine historians that were in Milton's library
in 1658, and Syncellus is in the list under his other name
of Georgius Monachus.[12]    Besides, in his letter XXI,
Milton asks his correspondent to send him Theophanes's
book, which is a sequel to Syncellus's — a fair proof that
he had read the latter.

We find in *Paradise Lost* a passage which proves that
Milton knew that part of the Book of Enoch contained
in Syncellus:

> Then straight commands that at the warlike sound
> Of trumpets loud, and clarions, be uprear'd
> His mighty standard; that proud honour claim'd
> Azazel as his right, a Cherub tall;
> Who forthwith from the glittering staff unfurl'd
> Th' imperial ensign; which, full high advanc'd,
> Shone like a meteor streaming to the wind,
> With gems and golden lustre rich emblaz'd.[13]

---

[11] *Publications of the Modern Language Association*, XXXVI (1921),
284, note.
[12] There is another Georgius Monachus; that Syncellus is meant is proved
by letter XXI.  See *Prose Works*, III, 513.        [13] *P. L.*, I, 531–38.

Azazel has always been a hard angel to explain with
Milton's commentators.  Newton, who is perhaps the
most qualified to speak on such questions, writes, " The
name is used for some demon or devil by several ancient
authors," and translates the Hebrew as a sneer — " brave
in retreating."  But Milton certainly never thought of his
devils as cowards.  Now, it is only in the Book of Enoch
that Azazel is mentioned as one of the leaders of the fallen
angels.[14]  The word is in Leviticus 16:8, but is rendered
by " scapegoat."  Jonathan and Raschi in Walton's Bible
make of Azazel the name of a place in the desert where
the goat is sent.  Milton, had he thought about the subject at all, would probably have adopted either sense —
but for the Book of Enoch.[15]  I suggest, therefore, that
Milton got his Azazel from the Book of Enoch.  One
special phrase in the Miltonic text that has particularly
exercised the commentators is " as his right."  Milton
must have meant it, to risk the inelegant jingle, " Azazel
as his right."  Now we have, an Enoch (in Goar's text): [16]

Primus Azael [the name is variously given as " Azael," " Azal-
zel," or " Azazel "] qui gladios, thoracas, et omne bellicum instru-
mentum, et terræ metalla conflare, aurum quoque et argentum qua
tractarent arte mulienem mundum compositiori adimverint; qua
polirent etiam, et electis lapidibus nitorem adjicerent, et colores
fucarent, instruxit.

Azazel evidently was the chemist, jeweller, and goldsmith
of the infernal band; he dealt in women's ornaments, but
also in men's weapons.  So I suggest further that he was

14 See *Encyclopedia Biblica* and Hastings' *Dictionary of the Bible,* art.
" Azazel."
15 Irenæus (*Haer.* I, 12) and Origen (*Cels.* VI, 305) render Azazel as
Satan — which does not fit in with Milton either.
16 I am indebted to Mr. F. A. Pompen, of Heerlen, Holland, for a cor-
rection in the text as I gave it in 1920 in *La Pensée de Milton,* p. 239.

the maker of the " imperial ensign," and that this was the reason why he carried it " as his right."  Note that

> With gems and golden lustre rich emblaz'd

follows Goar's "*et electis lapidibus nitorem . . . et colores. . . .*"

The point is of interest because the fragment known to Milton [17] and more generally, the Book of Enoch, insist on a part of the myth which Milton used, against orthodox tradition: sensuality as a motive in the angel's fall. Not that Milton derived the idea from there; I have shown the importance of it in his scheme, and shall come back to it; but he would naturally be in sympathy with texts that bore him out.

It may be thought also that the five verses from Genesis quoted above are a slender basis for more than one hundred lines in Book XI of *Paradise Lost*, in which Enoch, who is but scantily referred to in the Old Testament,[18] and given no prophetic part in the trouble period, plays a noble rôle

>          . . . till at last,
> Of middle age one rising, eminent
> In wise deport, spake much of right and wrong,
> Of justice, of religion, truth, and peace,
> And judgment from above: him old and young
> Exploded, and had seiz'd with violent hands,
> Had not a cloud descending snatch'd him thence,
> Unseen amid the throng: so violence
> Proceeded, and oppression, and sword-law,
> Through all the plain, and refuge none was found.[19]

[17] In Syncellus (Dindorf edition, Bonn, 1829, pp. 20–24 and 42–47). For modern versions see Ad. Lods, *Le livre d'Hénoch* (Paris, Leroux, 1892), pp. 72–76; and R. M. Charles, *The Book of Enoch*, pp. 13–25. It comprises 6:1 to 10:14 of *Enoch*, the two fragments of Syncellus being consecutive in the text.

[18] Jude 14 may also have helped Milton to his conception.

[19] XI, 660–69.

Milton, however, would find ample material for the picture in the Book of Enoch.

The question of the "sons of God," and especially of who they were, is also interesting for Miltonic criticism. Milton was of course bound by his subject to reject the notion that they were angels, since his angels had to fall before man did. But he rejected it with a bad conscience. I have pointed out already that in the *De doctrina* he does not become too precise on the point. In Book XI of *Paradise Lost* he follows Augustine and orthodox tradition, and speaks of

> that sober race of men, whose lives,
> Religious titl'd them the sons of God,[20]

but who fell to the lures of women. (This was surely the appropriate time to make Satan say

> The Son of God I also am,

and claim his share of feminine booty.) But then Enoch had evidently made a deep impression on Milton's mind, and when off his guard he contradicts himself very beautifully. In *Paradise Regained*, in a burst of rhetorical ardor against Belial, he adopts the version that the "sons of God" were the fallen angels — pure Enoch doctrine. Satan says to Belial:

> Before the Flood, thou, with thy lusty crew,
> False titl'd sons of God, roaming the Earth
> Cast wanton eyes on the daughters of men
> And coupl'd with them and begot a race.[21]

This is all the more amusing for that comment of Satan's on the inspired writer's words: "False titl'd sons of God." Satan (or Milton?) corrects Moses. Finally, in the fifth

[20] XI, 617–18.      [21] *P. R.*, II, 178–81.

book of *Paradise Lost*, Milton again forgets his orthodoxy, and reverts to the Book of Enoch:

> Meanwhile at table Eve
> Ministered naked, and their flowing cups
> With pleasant liquors crowned.  O innocence
> Deserving Paradise! if ever, then,
> Then had the sons of God excuse to have been
> Enamour'd at that sight; but in those hearts
> Love unlibidinous reigned.[22]

The sons of God here are certainly the angels, Adam
being already " enamour'd."

[22] *P. L.*, V, 443-49.

## CHAPTER II

## THE CHRISTIAN ERA

IN Jewish speculation immediately before and about the beginning of the Christian era, there developed a tendency to refer the origin of evil to the fall of man, seen especially in the fourth Esdras. Paul is, to a certain extent, heir to this general tradition. But his importance is such that it is preferable to consider him separately.

### I. PAUL

For Paul, Satan as yet seems to play no part in the fall of man: "by one man sin entered the world, and death by sin; and so death passed upon all men, for that all have sinned." [1] For Paul, as for the ancient Hebrews, the serpent who tempted Eve was merely a serpent, and Paul nowhere identifies him with Satan: "the serpent beguiled Eve through his subtilty." [2] Paul's chief interest is not in the myth, but in the human psychology of the Fall. He seeks the source of evil in man himself; and he finds it in "the flesh," that is to say, passion in general, and more particularly, sensuality. Milton, naturally, follows Paul as closely as he can, and grounds his own opinions as frequently as possible on this solid basis of Christianity; the *De doctrina*, in many of its most important parts is mainly a commentary on Paul; [3] naturally also Milton uses Paul,

[1] Romans 5:12.
[2] II Corinthians 11:3.
[3] The necessary work on this has been done by Sumner in his edition of the *De doctrina*, as has most of the theological work. It is the historian of religions that must investigate Milton now.

as he uses the whole Bible, to prove what he likes, and follows Paul no further than he cares to go.

Here are the chief Paulinian texts from our point of view:

> Now the works of the flesh are manifest, which are these; Adultery, fornication, uncleanness, lasciviousness, idolatry, witchcraft, hatred, variance. . . .[4]
>
> The body is not for fornication, but for the Lord.
>
> Flee fornication. Every sin that a man doeth is without the body; but he that committeth fornication sinneth against his own body.[5]

And I Corinthians 7, entirely:

> It is good for a man not to touch a woman. Nevertheless, to avoid fornication, let every man have his own wife and let every woman have her own husband. . . . I speak this by permission, and not of commandment. For I would that all men were even as I myself. . . . I say therefore to the unmarried and widows, It is good for them if they abide even as I. But if they cannot contain, let them marry; for it is better to marry than to burn.

Ephesians 5:22–23 is likewise important:

> Wives, submit yourselves unto your own husbands, as unto the Lord. For the husband is the head of the wife, even as Christ is the head of the Church. . . .

This enables us to see how far Milton follows Paul. " To avoid fornication " becomes:

> By thee adulterous lust was driven from men
> Among the bestial herds to range.

And " the husband is the head of the wife " becomes:

> He for God only, she for God in him.

But Milton refuses to follow Paul in accepting marriage as a necessary concession; and in a passage com-

---

[4] Galatians 5:19-20.        [5] I Corinthians 6:18.

menting on " the body is for the Lord, and the Lord for the body," he concludes: " for marriage must not be called a defilement." [6] The flesh is not naturally evil for Milton. Fornication is the Fall, but " wedded love, as saints and patriarchs used," is holy and good. Milton has on this essential point entirely broken away from Paul; he knows of a sensuality that is legitimate, and even " commanded." [7]

Yet another of Milton's most important ideas is sanctioned by Paul: " Adam was not deceived, but the woman being deceived was in the transgression." [8] For Paul, as for Milton, Adam fell

> Against his better knowledge, not deceived,
> But fondly overcome by female charm.

## II. LATER JUDAISM

Before and around Paul, the elements of what was to become the Christian tradition on the Fall were being shaped. About the first half of the first century after Christ, the Jews came to the idea that Satan and the Serpent were one. [9] The ways had been prepared for this notion. The Wisdom of Solomon [10] had said: " Through the envy of the devil death entered the world." But that was not very precise yet. The Book of Enoch [11] had said that one of the fallen angels had seduced Eve, but this was contradicted by the rest of the book, in which the angels fell later than man, and it remained a passing trait.

---

[6] *Apology for Smectymnuus,* in *Prose Works,* III, 122. See above, p. 46.
[7] See above, pp. 155 ff.
[8] I Timothy 2:14.
[9] Bousset, p. 469. A Jewish *Life of Adam* of the 1st century is the principal proof.
[10] 2:24.
[11] 73:4. *Cf.* Charles, p. 137.

But at last the Jews in the first century connected the two origins of evil. The fall of man, from being a confused and obscure legend, took on a definite meaning, and became the source of all evil and suffering for mankind. A curious legend of the same time [12] tells that after the creation of man, God ordered the angels to worship Adam. Satan refused, and was consequently driven out of Heaven. But he avenged himself by inducing Adam to eat the apple. This legend is extremely logical, and ought to have prevailed. Adam is here the direct cause of Satan's misfortune, and not an innocent victim. Satan's behavior is much more human (if the expression is permissible in this case) than in the orthodox tradition.

But there was more. Jewish Gnosis [13] identified Adam with the Son of God, the promised Messiah. So here is perhaps the first origin of the idea that Satan rebelled through envy of the Son; Milton adopts this for poetical purposes without believing it. But there were theologians at the Reformation who held the theory. Calvin condemns them severely in his *Commentary on Genesis*.

The Jewish beliefs about Satan's rebellion and the war in Heaven probably passed into The Revelation. In any case The Revelation is an important source for Milton's tale:

> . . . a great red dragon. . . . And his tail drew the third part of the stars of heaven, and did cast them to the earth. . . . And there was war in heaven: Michael and his angels fought against the dragon; and the dragon fought and his angels. . . . And the great dragon was cast out, that old serpent, called the Devil, and Satan . . . and his angels were cast out with him.[14]

[12] Bousset, p. 469. This is found also in the Koran, 20:115.
[13] *Cf.* Bousset, p. 558.
[14] Revelation 12:3–9.

This applies to the end of the world. But it is a sort of law in prophetic imagination that the end should be like the beginning, and these texts became, in the tradition, a precious source of knowledge about the origins. Milton in the *De doctrina* quotes them as proofs for the war in Heaven.[15] Here also the Serpent is called Satan; later this will be thought a further proof that Satan was the serpent who tempted Eve.

Lastly, the beginnings of the Christian era saw the birth of an erroneous interpretation of a few verses in Isaiah, and this mistake became also an important document:

> How art thou fallen from heaven, O Lucifer, son of the morning! . . . For thou hast said in thine heart, I will ascend into heaven, I will exalt my throne above the stars of God: I will sit also upon the mount of the congregation, in the sides of the north . . . I will be like the most High. Yet thou shalt be brought down to hell, to the sides of the pit.[16]

The imprecation is aimed at the King of Babylon, and Lucifer is only the morning star. So far as we know, Tertullian and Gregory were the first to apply the passage to Satan, who kept the name Lucifer. From this came the mountain in the North and the chief motive of Satan's revolt: the ambition to be like the most High.

The different elements of the tale are now all evolved: Satan's revolt through ambition; sensuality in the fall of the angels; the temptation of Eve by the Serpent, who is Satan; of Adam through Eve; sensuality in the fall of man.

[15] *Prose Works*, IV, 216–17.

[16] 14:12–15. Gunkel suggests (*Schöpfung und Chaos*, 1895, pp. 132–34) that this may be an allusion to a myth, perhaps Babylonian, recording the ambition and failure of the Morning Star, which disappears in the light of the sun — "hides its diminished head," as Milton puts it (*P. L.*, IV, 35).

## CHAPTER III

## THE FATHERS

THE elements of the tale of the Fall were put together and more or less worked out by the Fathers. Yet most of the Fathers, before Augustine, seem to the modern reader hopelessly backward and chaotic. It is only Augustine who gives a coherent tale. The astonishment of the modern reader at the eccentric ideas of the early Fathers was fully shared by Milton, who, consequently, frequently looks upon them with open contempt.

### I. MILTON'S OPINIONS OF THE FATHERS

In 1641, in the pamphlet *Of Prelatical Episcopacy*, Milton expressed picturesquely his feelings about the Fathers, thus:

. . . when men began to have itching ears, then not contented with the plentiful and wholesome fountains of the gospel, they began after their own lusts to heap to themselves teachers, and as if the divine scripture wanted a supplement, and were to be eked out, they cannot think any doubt resolved, and any doctrine confirmed, unless they run to that indigested heap and fry of authors which they call antiquity. Whatsoever time, or the heedless hand of blind chance, hath drawn down from of old to this present, in her huge drag-net, whether fish or seaweed, shells or shrubs, unpicked, unchosen, those are the fathers.[1]

Further on,[2] Irenæus is sharply rebuked, and called " the patron of idolatry " to the papist for having said that

[1] *Prose Works*, II, 422.          [2] *Ibid.*, II, 430.

" the obedience of Mary was the cause of salvation to herself and all mankind . . . that the virgin Mary might
be made the advocate of the virgin Eve." Did Milton
change his opinion of Irenæus when he came to call Mary
" Blest Mary, second Eve " ? Tertullian also was to
return to favor, but here he is vigorously blamed:
" Should he move us, that goes about to prove an imparity
between God the Father and God the Son? " [3] Still, he
feels a certain amount of respect for Clement of Alexandria, and tries to prove that Clement was not in favor of
bishops.[4]

In *The Reason of Church Government* (1641) Milton
calls Jerome " the learnedest of the fathers." [5] Yet in the
same year, in *Reformation in England,* he violently attacks the early Fathers, and Clement is not spared:

Who is ignorant of the foul errors, the ridiculous wrestling of
Scripture, the heresies, the vanities thick sown through the volumes
of Justin Martyr, Clemens, Origen, Tertullian, and others of
eldest time? Who would think him fit to write an apology for
Christian faith to the Roman senate, that would tell them " how of
the angels," which he must needs mean those in Genesis, called the
sons of God, " mixing with women were begotten the devils " as
good Justin Martyr . . . told them.[6]

But Cyprian, Lactantius, and especially Augustine are
praised for having refused to submit to the authority of
the ancients:

St. Austin writes to Fortunatian that " he counts it lawful, in
the books of whomsoever, to reject that which he finds otherwise
than true; and so he would have others deal by him." He neither
accounted, as it seems, those fathers that went before, nor himself,
nor others of his rank, for men of more than ordinary spirit, that
might equally deceive, and be deceived.[7]

[3] *Ibid.,* II, 432.   [5] *Ibid.,* II, 458.   [7] *Ibid.,* II, 385.
[4] *Ibid.,* II, 433–34.   [6] *Ibid.,* II, 379–80.

On that understanding, " so he would have others deal by him," Milton seems, as we shall see, to enter into a sort of pact with Augustine.  In 1641 again, in his *Animadversions,* he declares:

I shall not intend this hot season to bid you the base through the wide and dusty champaign of the councils, but shall take counsel of that which counselled them — reason: . . . the gift of God in one man as well as in a thousand.[8]

But it is in 1642, in the *Apology for Smectymnuus,* that the councils are finally disposed of thus:

I have not therefore, I confess, read more of the councils, save here and there; I should be sorry to have been such a prodigal of my time; but, that which is better, I can assure this confuter, I have read into them all.  And if I want any thing yet I shall reply something toward that which in the defence of Murena was answered by Cicero to Sulpitius the lawyer: If ye provoke me (for at no hand else will I undertake such a frivolous labour) I will in three months be an expert councilist.[9]

In 1644, in the *Doctrine and Discipline of Divorce,* Milton quotes the fathers, Tertullian and Jerome in particular, chiefly to give instances of ancient prejudice on the subject of marriage.

In *Tetrachordon* (1645), as we have seen, he attacks Augustine for his " crabbed opinion " on a similar subject. But the attack shows the weight he attaches to Augustine's opinion:

Car il l'attaque à part, comme un noble adversaire.

Then he quotes, in regular battle order, the Fathers that are on his side.  He is rather shamefaced about it, for they are the very same Fathers so derided in 1641: Justin, Clement, Origen, and Tertullian.  He is brazen enough

---

[8] *Ibid.,* III, 56–57.       [9] *Ibid.,* III, 162–63.

even to appeal to the councils of Eliberis in Spain, Neocæsaria, and Agatha, " although testimony be in logic and
argument rightly called inartificial," [10] etc., etc., the end
being that the Fathers are called " wisest heads heretofore." Long discussions follow, of opinions of Justin,
Tertullian, Origen, Lactantius, Epiphanius, Jerome, Ambrose, and we come at last to Augustine, the most important of them all, because he interprets fornication (as a
cause for divorce) " in a general sense," to mean " that
which draws the mind from God's law." [11] Milton is very
grateful to Augustine for this timely help, since this is
his principal argument all through the divorce tracts.

*Areopagitica* (1644) yields a precious indication:
" Who finds not that Irenæus, Epiphanius, Jerome, and
others discover more heresies than they can well confute,
and that oft for heresy which is the truer opinion? " [12]
Irenæus and Epiphanius having written mostly against
the Gnostics, Milton thus seems not disinclined to approve the latter.

In the *Defensio* (1651), the Fathers are frequently
quoted to confound Salmasius.[13] Tertullian is still
thought little of: " who is no orthodox writer, notorious
for many errors." [14] Athanasius and Ambrose are " miser-
ably raw in divinity, and unacquainted with the doctrine
of the gospel." [15] Augustine, here again, is oftenest
quoted and thought most of. His opinion of Sulpitius
Severus proves the latter " a man of great wisdom and
learning." [16] Milton tries to interpret Augustine in his
favor,[17] or combats him in such a manner as to show his

---

[10] *Ibid.*, III, 414–19.      [11] *Ibid.*, III, 419.      [12] *Ibid.*, II, 69.
[13] E.g., *Prose Works*, I, 39, 80, 81: on Jerome, Origen, Tertullian,
Irenæus.      [14] *Ibid.*, I, 101.      [15] *Ibid.*, I, 81.
[16] *Ibid.*, I, 38. *Cf.* I, 62 and 172.      [17] *Ibid.*, I, 82.

importance.[18]  His general idea is again stated: "Whatever they [the Fathers] say, which is not warranted by
the authority of the Scriptures, or by good reason, shall
be of no more regard with me, than if any other ordinary
man had said it."[19]  Still there is no denying that he
likes having them on his side.

In 1659, in his *Means to remove Hirelings*, Milton is
in a very bad temper.  The Fathers, after all, are priests,
and therefore more or less likely to be of the King's
party; so he speaks bitterly of them all:

> Of fathers, by custom so called, they quote Ambrose, Augustin,
> and some other ceremonial doctors of the same leaven: whose as-
> sertion, without pertinent scripture, no reformed church can admit;
> and what they vouch is founded on the law of Moses, with which,
> everywhere pitifully mistaken, they again incorporate the gospel;
> as did the rest also of those titular fathers. . . .[20]

And later he speaks of " the obscure and entangled wood
of antiquity, fathers and councils fighting one against
another,"[21] and declares that it is useless to know them,
and still more to go to the Universities to study them.
His opinion at the time is rather Hamlet's " Reform them
altogether," and all together, Fathers and theologians,
clergy and Universities.

But in the *De doctrina* Milton is in a quieter mood.
He quotes the Fathers little, but calls them to the rescue
in perilous moments, when he feels he is alone against the
crowd; he mentions them with dignity and respect.  Thus,
when he wants to prove that the angels were created and
fell before the beginning of the world (the point is
ticklish; there are no Biblical texts, and the whole structure of *Paradise Lost* is concerned), he says: " Many at

18 *Ibid.*, I, 107.                    20 *Ibid.*, III, 17.
19 *Ibid.*, I, 101.                    21 *Ibid.*, III, 38.

least of the Greek, and some of the Latin Fathers, are of opinion that angels, as being spirits, must have existed long before the material world,"[22] etc. Augustine is a particularly valuable ally. When Milton wants to prove one of his most important points, to wit, that souls are not created by God at each birth, he proudly quotes Augustine, who " was led to confess that he could neither discover by study, nor prayer, nor any process of reasoning, how the doctrine of original sin could be defended on the supposition of the creation of souls."[23] Tertullian himself has become worthy of consideration by this time: " . . . the human soul . . . is propagated from father to son . . . which was considered as the more probable opinion by Tertullian and Apollinaris, as well as by Augustine," etc.[24]

For Milton, therefore, and this is the most important conclusion of our survey, from 1641 till the end of his life, Augustine is the most highly considered, oftenest quoted of all the Fathers; the weightiest when he is on Milton's side, the most elaborately refuted when he is against Milton. A special study of Augustine is therefore necessary, but we must first cast a glance over those early Fathers, whom Milton generally thought so little of.

## II. THE FATHERS BEFORE AUGUSTINE

Tertullian is one of the first who connected sensuality with the Fall. Woman was for him the cause of all evil and " *janua diaboli.*"[25] He described the fall of the angels after Genesis 6.

[22] *Ibid.*, IV, 185.  [23] *Ibid.*, IV, 193
[24] *Ibid.*, IV, 189–90.
[25] *De cultu feminarum*, cap. I; see also *De exhortatione castitatis;* and *De monogamia.*

Origen starts from the same text, but is much more philosophical: the fall of the spirits occurred before the Creation and they chose evil knowingly; free will is the cause of the Fall, and, possibly, pride. The lower a spirit falls, the more material he becomes.[26]  Matter is thus a degradation — and this is against Milton; yet matter is essentially the same as spirit, only in a grosser form — and this Milton concurs in.  M. de Faye writes: [27]

> Naturellement, seules les âmes obtiennent le salut. La chair doit périr. Quiconque possédait alors une sérieuse culture philosophique et qui réfléchissait, considérait le salut de la chair, donc sa résurrection comme inadmissible. Les efforts que font d'une part Tertullien pour sauver la chair, Origène de l'autre pour sauver le corps sans chair, sont singulièrement significatifs à cet égard.

So here is a direction in which Milton went further than either.

The Gnostics were then known — as now still largely — by quotations of their adversaries, particularly Irenæaus and Epiphanius. Milton had more sympathy for heretics than for Fathers of the Church, but it is difficult to see what he could derive from the Gnostics. Some of them, exaggerating the old notion that found some good in the Fall, came to worship the Serpent, the cause of the Fall, as the great benefactor. It was probably as a polemical device, and to confute these Ophites, that Epiphanius declared that the Serpent who had tempted Eve was no other than Satan.[28]  It is only then, about 380 A.D., that the tradition of the Fathers at last caught up with Jewish myth. The Jews had reached that conclusion during the first century.

[26] De principiis II.
[27] Gnostiques et gnosticisme (Bibliothèque de l'École des Hautes Études), p. 164.      [28] Cf. de Faye, p. 348.

The works of Lactantius prove that in the fourth century the tradition was far from settled. In his *Divine Institutes* (II, 9), he explains the origin of the Son of God and of the Devil. God first created a spirit like unto himself; then a second in whom the divine perfection was not maintained. This second son envied the first, became evil and is now called the Devil. God, however, gave him power over the Earth, after he had corrupted Adam and Eve; and then sent angels to protect mankind against him. But the Devil drew angels into vice and made them commit fornication with the daughters of men.[29] The *Epitome of the Divine Institutes*, of the same father, however, gives another version. Chapter XXVII of that work relates that the Serpent, one of God's servants, envied man because man had been made immortal, and induced man to break God's commandment. This Serpent was the cause of all evil, beginning with the murder of Abel. Then God again sent his angels to protect mankind, and the rest follows Enoch: the angels fell, etc. This shows the incoherence of the tradition, even in the writings of one Father.

In the *Clementine Homilies*, an earlier and spurious production, we find more information on this principle of evil. In the XXth homily it is explained that God, in the beginning, created two powers, one for evil, one for good (the Son). The Devil is to reign over the Earth first, and then make way for the Kingdom of the Son, which will be endless. No revolt here. The XIXth[30] goes further, and says that the Devil has had no beginning; God is not to be blamed for not destroying him; that is impossible, even for God. This is sufficient justifi-

---

[29] II, 15.     [30] Chapter V.

cation for Milton's opinion of the early Fathers; and one cannot but feel sympathetic as one rereads his ringing summing up:

> Whatsoever time, or the heedless hand of blind chance, hath drawn down from of old to this present, in her huge drag-net, whether fish or seaweed, shells or shrubs, unpicked, unchosen, those are the fathers.

Let us, however, note two more ideas of the Fathers that were found useful by Milton.

Hilarius suggests [31] that the elect were meant to occupy the room left vacant in Heaven by the fallen angels. Milton's God says, speaking of Satan:

> But lest his heart exalt him in the harm
> Already done, to have dispeopled heav'n,
> My damage fondly deemed, I can repair
> That detriment, if such it be to lose
> Self-lost, and in a moment will create
> Another world, out of one man a race
> Of men innumerable, there to dwell,
> Not here, till by degrees of merit raised,
> They open to themselves at length the way
> Up hither.[32]

Jerome [33] and Lactantius [34] and some more of the Fathers held that the gods of the heathen were none other than the fallen angels.[35] Hooker promulgated the doctrine during the English Reformation.[36] Milton used it as a precious instrument, which allows him to pour at will into his epic the whole of Greek mythology:

[31] *Matth.* XVIII, 6.
[32] *P. L.*, VII, 150–59.
[33] *Contra Vigilantium*, 10.
[34] *Inst. div.*, II, 15, 17.
[35] The idea is of course much older. It is found, for example, in Leviticus 17:7, and II Chronicles 11:15.
[36] *Ecclesiastical Polity*, I, 4.

Nor had they yet among the sons of Eve
Got them new names, till wand'ring o'er the earth,
Through God's high sufferance for the trial of man,
By falsities and lies the greatest part
Of mankind they corrupted to forsake
God their creator, and the invisible
Glory of Him that made them to transform
Oft to the image of a brute, adorned
With gay religions full of pomp and gold,
And Devils to adore for Deities:
Then were they known to men by various names,
And various idols through the heathen world.[37]

## III. AUGUSTINE

With Augustine at last we find a coherent account of
the Fall. Augustine's ideas underwent great changes during his long life.[38] But of all his works, Milton, like the
whole of his century, knew chiefly the *City of God*.[39]
He took no trouble to reconcile Augustine's ideas in that
work with his ideas at other periods of his life, and was
only too happy, according to his wont, to find Augustine
contradicting himself — that is, if he cared about Augustine's other books at all.

Augustine sets the fall of the angels at the beginning of
creation, before the birth of the world; he finds, as its
motive, pride; he definitely identifies the Serpent as
Satan; he connects sensuality with man's fall, and no
longer with that of the angels. Except on this last point,
Milton has therefore followed Augustine's version entirely. Even the sensual trait in the angels' fall is only

[37] *P. L.*, I, 364–75.
[38] See P. Alfaric, *L'Évolution intellectuelle de Saint Augustine* (Paris,
Nourry, 1918).
[39] This is confirmed by Hanford, *Publications of the Modern Language
Association*, XXXVI, 304.

marked in the case of Satan, and, however heavily insisted upon, is used allegorically and philosophically,
rather than dogmatically; in the *De doctrina* we hear
nothing of it. So we can say that on the Fall Milton's
dogma is Augustine's.

The angels were created before any other things or
beings, with " heaven " or " light." [40] Some of the angels
fell before the creation of the world. This is the meaning
of the phrase " God divided the light from the darkness,"
and they were thrown into the lowest part of the world.[41]
Milton entirely adopts all this in the *De doctrina*: " the
angels . . . are considered as comprehended under the
general name of *heavens* " ; [42] his angels rebel " before
the foundations of this world were laid," [43] and his hell
is in the lowest part of creation " beyond the limits of
this universe." [44] The " sons of God " of Scripture are
merely a race of good men.[45] We have seen that Milton
officially adopts this opinion, whatever slips his reminis-
cences of Enoch (severely condemned by Augustine)
may produce. The motive of the Fall is pride: " This
superb and envious angel, this prince of devils who turns
away from his creator towards himself, and makes himself into a tyrant." [46] For Milton also, the devil is the
archetype of the tyrant. Satan is the Serpent. " He
chose the Serpent, a wily and cunning animal, and used
it to speak to the woman." [47]

In the account of the Fall, the same parallelism is to
be found. Adam was not deceived by his wife, but he
could not resist his love for her,[48]

[40] *De civitate Dei* XI, 32.
[41] *Ibid.*, XI, 33.
[42] *Prose Works*, IV, 184.
[43] *Ibid.*, IV, 185.
[44] *Ibid.*, IV, 490

[45] *De civitate* XV, 13, 23, and XVIII, 38.
[46] *Ibid.*, XIV, 11; *cf.* XI, 15 and XII, 1.
[47] *Ibid.*, XIV, 11.
[48] *Ibid.*, XIV, 11.

> Against his better knowledge, not deceived,
> But fondly overcome by female charm.

But it is in the description of the degraded state that the resemblances are most striking. Augustine is very crude. As soon as man has disobeyed God, man's body ceases to obey him. " The motion of concupiscence is the sequel of sin." [49] Man's sexual organs no longer followed his will, but rebelled against him, at their pleasure.[50] Even so Milton makes of sensuality the first consequence of the Fall.

Augustine also opposes concupiscence to wisdom, reason: " They [passions] need to be led and moderated by reason; reason must allow them to effect only good actions, as anger to punish justly; concupiscence to beget children." [51] Adam's reason ought to have made him safe against Eve's charm. " As though there were some one to be believed and obeyed in preference to God." [52] Milton says:

> Was she thy God? that her thou didst obey
> Before his voice. . . .[53]

Man's fall generally is in this triumph of passion over reason and will: " a revolt of himself against himself, so that he cannot effect what he wills." [54] Then man is no longer free in himself. " Man, because of his evil will, becomes a slave to his own passions." [55]

> For understanding ruled not, and the will
> Heard not her lore.

But again here, as with Paul, Milton goes thus far and no further. He will hear nothing against the flesh as such,

[49] *Ibid.*, XIII, 24.
[50] *Ibid.*, XIII, 13, 15, 16, and XIV, 17.
[51] *Ibid,* XIV, 19.
[52] *Ibid.*, XIV, 14.
[53] *P. L.*, X, 145–46.
[54] *De civitate* XIV, 15; *cf.* XIX, 15.
[55] *Ibid.*, XIX, 15, title.

which is good in itself. He refers to Augustine's thoroughgoing ideas as " crabbed opinions." He puts sensuality in Paradise, before the Fall, whereas Augustine devotes long pages to proving that in Paradise sensual pleasure did not exist.[56] He acknowledges the sacredness of the text which caused Milton to ask

Who bids abstain?

But he has found a way out: in Paradise, children " were to be begotten without any motion of concupiscence." And yet Augustine admits that " the flesh in itself is not to be blamed, since it is good in its way." [57]  So that Milton may be said to be carrying Augustine's principles further than Augustine himself. But for Augustine the flesh has become evil, whereas for Milton matter and the flesh are still " the source of every subsequent good." What is only a concession for Augustine as for Paul, to which " shame attaches even in marriage," [58] is for Milton the sane, normal law, " for marriage must not be called a defilement."

With this central difference, we may say, therefore, that Milton follows Augustine's ideas on the Fall. Since the tale of the myth is here completed, and as a transition between this and the next section, let us point out the resemblances between Augustine's and Milton's general ideas. They will confirm the hypothesis of a special influence of the Father on the poet, in so far as Milton can submit to influence; he preserves, that is, always his independence, and accepts only what his reason approves of, and violently rejects what he dislikes, even when it is intimately mixed with what he accepts, as we have seen on the subject of the Fall.

[56] *Ibid.*, XIV, 21 ff.    [57] *Ibid.*, XIV, 5.    [58] *Ibid.*, XIV, 18, title.

It is curious that even in Augustine, whose name and influence have been weighty on the opposite side, Milton may have found authority for his belief in free will. Whatever others may have seen in Augustine — whatever Augustine himself may have really thought — Milton was sure to be impressed only by what he agreed with. And one of the chapters of the *De civitate* has for its subject: That man, created innocent, was lost only through evil use of his free will.[59]  For both, sin is foreseen by God, and provided for.  Augustine has a chapter " On prevaricating men and angels whose sin does not disturb the order of divine providence." [60]  God could have prevented the fall of both angels and men, but he preferred to let them follow their will, in order to show what his divine grace was capable of.[61]  These very considerations comfort Adam in his fall.[62]

In the account of the creation of man, the resemblances are also striking: Augustine devotes as much attention as Milton to the text " and man became a living soul."  And the Father proves at length [63] that the passage does not refer to man's immortal soul, and that the word " soul " in Scripture applies to animals.  This is only a secondary point in Augustine, who believes in the dualism of soul and body, but becomes all important for Milton.  The coincidence of interpretation is all the more notable.

The conception of Christ is also very similar in both systems.  For Augustine, Christ is the Second Man, the Father of the Elect; his spiritual body comprehends all men who have received grace " to be together one and the same Christ." [64]  This is Milton's Greater Man.  For

---

[59] XIII, 14.
[60] XIV, 27.
[61] XIV, 27, *in fine*, and XIV, 11.

[62] *P. L.*, XII, 470 ff.
[63] *De civitate* XIII, 24.
[64] *Ibid.*, XIII, 23.

both, Christ is Man regenerated by triumph over passion.[65]  Let us note also in the *De civitate* that the terrestrial life of Christ occupies but little room, but two
chapters in Book XVIII (49 and 50).  We have seen that
this is also the case with Milton.  And the *De civitate*
speaks but little of the Crucifixion, as little as Milton:
Man's regeneration is brought about by the advent of
Christ in Man.  And Augustine thinks also [66] that there
were men, outside the Hebrew people, and before the
coming of Christ, that belonged already to the divine
body.  Yet both believe literally in the Gospel; but they
have the same methods of interpretation, and Augustine
speaks for Milton when he says: " Such allegorical explanations are very good, as long as one believes at the
same time in the very exact truth of the historical
account." [67]

Lastly, they agree in politics.  Augustine admirably
expresses Milton's views when he writes:  " It is through
sin that man is subject to man . . . that only happens
through the judgment of God." [68]  Men not free in themselves by their triumph over passion are submitted to
external servitude; but " It was not God's will that man
should reign over men." [69]  We have studied Milton's
texts:

> . . . But man over men
> He made not lord: such title to Himself
> Reserving, human left from human free.
>
> .  .  .  .  .  .  .  .  .  .
>
> But justice, and some fatal curse annexed,
> Deprives them of their outward liberty,
> Their inward lost. . . .[70]

[65] *Ibid.*, XIV, 2: "live according to the Spirit "; XIV, 4: "according
to truth and not to lies."          [66] XVIII, 47.
[67] XIII, 21. For Milton, see above, pp. 204-05.    [69] *Ibid.*, XIX, 15.
[68] *De civitate* XIX, 15 ff.          [70] *P. L.*, XII, 69-71, 99-101.

To sum up, all the differences between Augustine and Milton can be reduced to one essential one: for Augustine, God created matter out of nothing,[71] and consequently matter tends towards evil, being radically void, and nothing, from its origin. For Milton, matter has been drawn from God himself and is good and divine. This is Milton's central idea, the idea that makes of him a modern man. Let us study in our next section, the intellectual milieu from which he imbibed that conception.

[71] *De civitate* XIV, 11.

## SECTION II

## CONTEMPORARY SOURCES AND INFLUENCES

M ILTON'S relationship to movements of his own time may be summed up thus: roughly speaking, the whole of Milton's philosophy is found in the Kabbalah,[1] except his materialism; his materialism is found in Fludd, except his mortalism; and his mortalism is connected with the ideas of the contemporary English Mortalist group. The three stages are connected and form developments, one from the other: Fludd starts from the Kabbalah, and the Mortalists have their general principles in common with Fludd, and probably derived them from him.

[1] Renaissance Neo-Platonism may be counted as a parallel influence; in popular exposition of theories, the two practically coincide; only many things in Milton are in the Kabbalah and not in Neo-Platonism proper. Besides, I agree with those who maintain that the chief differences between Renaissance Neo-Platonism and ancient Neo-Platonism are mostly due to the influence of the Kabbalah. For instance, the new theory that matter, the flesh, and nature are good, not a degradation but an expression of the Divinity, is first brought forward properly by Pico della Mirandola, in his *Heptaplus,* as derived from the Kabbalah.

## CHAPTER I

### THE *ZOHAR* AND THE KABBALAH

THE *Zohar* was put together in Spain in the thirteenth century as a compendium of all the non-orthodox Jewish traditions. Some of the material used probably goes back centuries earlier. From the beginning of the Renaissance, its influence on European thought was considerable. It was printed at Mantua and Cremona in 1559–60, another edition coming out at Lublin in 1623. The most celebrated commentators of the *Zohar*, Cordovero and Loria, belong to the middle of the sixteenth century. Pico della Mirandola, Reuchlin, and Agrippa had, during the fifteenth and sixteenth centuries, prepared the scholars of Europe to receive kabbalistic ideas and had made known many of the principles of the Kabbalah. In 1635 Joseph Voysin published in Paris a Latin translation of some passages of the *Zohar*. Father Kircher published his study of the Kabbalah in Rome from 1652 to 1654. In England, Robert Fludd (1574–1637) gave to the public the most interesting among the kabbalistic conceptions, and, as we shall see, there are many striking resemblances between Fludd's and Milton's ideas. Last of all Henry More, who belonged to the same Cambridge college as Milton, published in 1654, in London, his work on the Kabbalah.

Such facts must here suffice to show that Milton could not be ignorant of the existence of the Kabbalah. Unani-

mous tradition and even the statement of the poet himself
leave us no doubt that he was able to read the Aramean
text of the *Zohar;* [1] and we know Milton sufficiently well
to be sure that, if once he became interested in the Kabbalah, he would go straight to the main text with his usual
contempt for commentators, since the text was accessible.
In such circumstances the proof that Milton knew the
*Zohar* and derived ideas from it must come from a comparison of the two systems of thought and a precise
investigation of texts.

I do not mean to maintain that Milton was a kabbalist
in the sense that he accepted the *Zohar* as a revealed
book in any other way than any other great book. His
mind was much too clear and exacting for that. Besides,
the *Zohar* is full of contradictions, owing to the way it
was put together or transmitted. Milton evidently took
only what suited him from that chaos of ideas. But
Milton used the *Zohar,* found there abundant confirmation of his general ideas, and drew thence many of the
ideas whch seem at first sight most particularly his own.

Many of his general conceptions belong to a traditional
stock, common to the *Zohar* and to other Jewish or Christian lines of development. But some of Milton's most
original notions are found only in the *Zohar;* and the
most striking fact of all is that in the *Zohar* can be found
all Milton's ideas, whether apparently peculiar to himself or not. With one reservation only, [2] it can be stated

---

[1] *Cf. Apology for Smectymnuus (Prose Works,* III, 131), where Milton
quotes the targoumists; *Of Education* (III, 473), where he recommends the
study of Aramean; and Phillip's statement (quoted in Johnson's *Lives of the
Poets,* ed. G. B. Hill, Oxford, 1905, I, 145).

[2] The idea of the non-existence of the soul; and even in this case all
the ideas on which Milton bases this notion are in the *Zohar:* pantheism,
matter as a divine substance, transformation of matter into spirit, unity between matter and spirit, vindication of sex-passion, etc. Milton only

that Milton's philosophy is in the *Zohar*, and Milton had only to disentangle it from extraneous matter.

Inversely, although Milton took from the *Zohar* only a very small part of its contents, there is really but one great idea of the *Zohar* which is not in Milton: the idea of reincarnation. Even in this case, however, there is a parallel conception in the poet. The basis of the theories of reincarnation is that the future life must take place on earth and debts contracted either by us or towards us must be paid in kind. This idea of justice as rendered in this world and not in another world is what drove Milton to adopt the notion of the Millenarians and Fifth Monarchy men: it is on this earth that Christ will come and reign and settle all accounts.[3]

Let us first see what Milton owes to the mythology of the *Zohar*. It is comparatively little. So reasonable a mind could not be much influenced by the extravagant development and complication of myths in which the kabbalists indulge.[4] Yet a few traits are very interesting.

In *Paradise Lost* Eve, after eating the apple, and before giving it to Adam (she had thought it better perhaps to keep superior science to herself), soliloquizes thus:

> But what if God have seen
> And death ensue? then I shall be no more,
> And Adam, wedded to another Eve,
> Shall live with her enjoying, I extinct;
> A death to think. Confirmed then I resolve
> Adam shall share with me in bliss or woe:
> So dear I love him, that with him all deaths
> I could endure, without him live no life.[5]

drew the conclusion, and was probably helped to it by an out-and-out kabbalist, Robert Fludd. See below, pp. 301 ff.

[3] See above, pp. 196–97.

[4] Milton follows the normal Christian tradition as to myth; see above, pp. 249 ff.  [5] IX, 826–33.

Splendid psychology, in splendid language.  The *Zohar* says:

> The woman touched the tree.  Then she saw the Angel of Death coming towards her, and thought: Perhaps I shall die, and the Holy One (Blessed be He) will make another woman and give her to Adam.  That must not happen.  Let us live together or let us die together.  And then she gave the fruit to her husband that he should eat it also.[6]

There is perfect correspondence in the sequence of ideas:

| | |
|---|---|
| But what if God have seen, And death ensue? then I shall be no more, | Perhaps I shall die, and the Holy One (Blessed be He) |
| And Adam wedded to another Eve, | will make another woman |
| Shall live with her enjoying, I extinct; | and give her to Adam |
| A death to think.  Confirmed then I resolve | That must not happen. |
| Adam shall share with me . . . | |
| . . . with him all deaths I could endure, without him live no life. | Let us live together or let us die together. |

A second trait seems more important still.  The allegory of the second book of *Paradise Lost,* in which Satan commits incest with his daughter Sin, issued from himself, and thus produces Death, has revolted many minds since Voltaire; the more so because the repulsive idea of incest

---

[6] *Zohar* I, 209b. (de Pauly, II, 637).  Eleazer of Worms has a similar passage derived from *Midrash, Genesis rabba* XIX.  But Eleazer of Worms or the *Zohar* is all one for my thesis, Eleazer being one of the most celebrated kabbalists.  I use the French translation of the *Zohar* by de Pauly (Paris, Leroux, 1906–1911), which is acknowledged to be sound.

seems quite gratuitous, a mere indulgence in the horrible
on Milton's part, since James 1:15 gives no hint of it:
" When Lust has conceived, it bringeth forth Sin, and Sin,
when it is full grown, bringeth forth Death." If, then,
we have been sorry to take from Milton's wreath that
flower of Eve's jealousy, it is a sort of compensation to
acquit him of this less graceful invention. Karppe [7] tells
us that in the kabbalistic myths, " it is a law, which applies also to the Sephiroth, that the female first issues
from the male, and then is fecundated by him." Hence
Sin came from Satan, and then incest was committed by
them. In the *Zohar*, the particular form of incest,
" father-daughter," becomes a law. God himself has
sexual intercourse with the Matrona, or Shekhina, his
daughter.[8] And there is a Matrona of the lower world
(Lilith perhaps) who has become Milton's Sin, daughter
and wife to Satan, as she boasts herself:

> At thy right hand voluptuous,
> Thy daughter and thy darling, without end.

A third trait, less important perhaps, is also interesting.
Whence comes chaos in Milton? Since in his philosophy
everything comes from God by his " retraction," which
produced first that divine matter from which the universe
is evolved naturally, it is difficult to explain the anterior
existence of chaos, and we may be tempted to see here a
purely poetical survival from a different cosmogony. But
the *Zohar* explains this chaos and, incidentally, suggests
a meaning for one of Milton's finest and most discussed

---

[7] S. Karppe, *Etude sur les origines et la nature du Zohar* (Paris, Alcan,
1901), p. 427.

[8] *Zohar* I, 173, 353; II, 432, etc. The *Zohar* insists somewhat too much
on this point for our modern European taste.

lines,[9] where chaos is " The womb of Nature and perhaps her grave." Why " perhaps her grave " ? The *Zohar* relates on several occasions[10] that God, before creating this world, had created several others and, not being pleased with them, had destroyed them; the remnants of such worlds being pointed to by the words: " and *the Earth* was *tohu* and *bohu*." It seems evident that, in Milton's mind, unless the Earth fulfil the aims for which God created it, it will be destroyed also and become part of this chaos of lost worlds. Hence a tragic significance to " perhaps her grave."

Such are the artistic traits in common between Milton and the *Zohar:* few indeed, but very curious. Let us now see the practically complete correspondence between the philosophical ideas.

The most striking feature here is the identity of views on the ontological relationship between God and the world.

In Milton's system, since God is all things, the creation of separate beings must be their separation from God. I have tried at length to show that this idea of free-will within a pantheistic system was the central point of Milton's thought both in *Paradise Lost* and the *De doctrina Christiana*. This creative liberation can only be accomplished by a " retraction " of God upon himself: the divinity, as Milton says, " retires " its will from certain parts of itself, giving them over, so to speak, to whatever latent impulses remain in them. God himself, at one of the decisive points of *Paradise Lost*[11] before the creation

---

[9] *Paradise Lost*, II, 911. See Greenlaw, in *Studies in Philology*, XVII (1920), 335.

[10] See especially I, 24b (de Pauly, I, 152) and I, 266b (II, 631).

[11] VII, 170 ff.

of this world, when Satan seems to have wrought havoc
in the divine scheme, gives out the theory:

> I uncircumscribed myself retire
> And put not forth my goodness, which is free
> To act or not.

The *Zohar* says: [12]

When we think that the Holy One (Blessed be He) is infinite
and that he fills everything, it is easily understood that any creation
would have been impossible without the *zimzum* [" retraction "].
How could it be possible to put more water into a cup which is
already filled to the brim?  The Holy One (Blessed be He) has
therefore contracted the Holy Light which is his essence; not
that he diminished himself — God preserve us from such an idea!
— being all things, he can neither increase nor decrease.  Only,
since the Light of God is of such purity and strength that it eclipses
all things, even the higher angels, even the Hayoth, even the Seraphim and the Cherubim,[13] the Holy One (Blessed be He), to make
possible the existence of celestial and material worlds, withdrew
his almighty Light from a part of himself.

If we go back to the complete passage in Milton, in
its very construction we shall find an exact reproduction
of these few lines of the *Zohar:*

| | |
|---|---|
| Boundless the deep, because I am who fill | When we think that the Holy One . . . is infinite and that he fills everything, |
| Infinitude, nor vacuous the space. | |
| Though I uncircumscribed my-self retire, | it is easily understood that any creation would have been im-possible without the *zimzum* [" retraction "]. . . . The |
| And put not forth my good-ness, which is free | |
| To act or not, | Holy One (Blessed be He) has therefore contracted the Holy |
| Necessity and Chance | Light which is his essence; |

---

12 *Tikunē Zohar*, XIX, quoted by de Pauly, VI, ii, 346.

13 Note Milton's insistence on this theme — " God is light " — and this
particular trait (*P. L.*, III, 383):

> "—— dazzle Heaven, that brightest Seraphim
> Approach not, but with both wings veil their eyes."

| Approach not me, and what I will is fate. | not that he diminished himself — God preserve us from such an idea! — being all things, he can neither increase nor decrease. |
|---|---|

In the two texts we find in the same order:

1. *The assertion that God is infinite,* repeated twice — " I am who fill infinitude " rendering " the Holy One is infinite," and " nor vacuous the space " rendering " he fills everything " ;

2. *The idea of " retraction,"* the English " retire " rendering *zimzum* ("*retrait*" in the French of de Pauly), and " put not forth my goodness " rendering " contracted the Holy Light," since " goodness " and " Light " are two names of the Shekhina, the essence that plays the principal part in the *Zohar;*

3. *The assertion* that, in spite of this " retraction," God remains all powerful, his greatness undiminished.

It appears, therefore, that the passage from *Paradise Lost* is simply an adaptation of, or properly a sort of free translation from, the passage in the *Tikunē Zohar.* Milton has omitted only the comparison to the cup of water, which was a hindrance to the logical impetuosity of his period.

It must be considered also that this is not a side issue, but that these six lines are the most important passage in *Paradise Lost* from the philosophical point of view, as well as the most characteristic. Here Milton expresses his most striking and, as it seems, his most original idea, from which is derived his conception of matter; since matter is that " space not vacuous " even after the contraction of God, that which remains of God's powers in

space when God has withdrawn his will.  It can therefore
be asserted that Milton has derived from the *Zohar* his
philosophical system.  Pantheism, materialism, doctrines
of free-will and of fate as God's will — by a truly remarkable *tour de force* Milton has logically tied these
four somewhat antagonistic conceptions into one solid
knot; he has done it in six lines, but only because the
*Tikunē Zohar* had done it in ten.

Should even some source, at present unknown, have
transmitted second-hand to Milton this idea of " retraction," the close correspondence of the two passages seems
to me to prove that anyhow in this particular case Milton
has gone back to the original text and that whatever other
inspiration may be found could have only indicated it to
him.

This central point once fixed, everything else derives
from it.  A volume would be necessary to study precisely
the relationship between Milton's ideas and the ideas of
the *Zohar*, and even such a study would be incomplete,
because other elements than either Milton or the *Zohar*
would have to be taken into account; these are only two
strands of a rope that is made up of many more besides.
I shall here point out only the chief resemblances, and
therefore, practically, only open the discussion.  I do not
assert in what follows that this or that particular passage
of the *Zohar* has inspired this or that passage in Milton,
but only that the same ideas exist in the two systems.

To Milton God is the infinite, immutable, unknowable,
non-manifested; that is, the " En-Sof," the Endless of
the *Zohar*, which is also " Ayin," Nothingness, so inconceivable is it: " Fountain of Light, Thyself invisible." [14]

[14] *P. L.*, III, 374.

"But God, as he cannot be seen, so neither can he be heard." [15] "The phrases *he did not think it,* etc. . . . appear inapplicable to the supreme God." [16] "Within the Supreme Thought," say the *Zohar,* [17] "no one can conceive anything whatsoever. It is impossible to know the Infinite, which does not come under the senses; every question and every meditation is vain to reach the essence of the Supreme Thought, centre of all, secret of secrets, without beginning or end, infinite."

In both systems, God is the absolute of the metaphysicians, equally incapable of manifesting itself and of being conceived. Consequently, in both systems there is a Demiurge, as it were an inferior God, who is at once the Creator and the Creation, since there is some sort of Pantheism in the two schemes. In Milton this Demiurge is the Son, who is the Finite, the Expressed, "the first of the whole creation . . . by whom afterwards all other things were made," [18] "not co-eval with the Father," [19] "not . . . from everlasting, but *in the beginning,*" [20] "the secondary and instrumental cause." [21] In the *Zohar,* the part of the Demiurge is played by the "World of Emanation," the first three Sephiroth taken as one whole — Crown, Wisdom, and Intelligence — because the *Zohar* carries the idea further and puts several steps between God and the world. [22] Milton follows suit on the few occasions when he feels inclined to admit of the Holy Ghost;

[15] *Prose Works,* IV, 109.
[16] *Ibid.,* IV, 145.
[17] See I, 21a (I, 129); *cf.* also Karppe, pp. 342, 352, etc.
[18] *Treatise,* in *Prose Works,* IV, 80–81.
[19] *Ibid.,* IV, 83.
[20] *Ibid.,* IV, 109.
[21] *Ibid.,* IV, 91.
[22] See Karppe, pp. 377, 378, etc. The quotations are too numerous to be given here; among others, see de Pauly, I, 98 and VI, 119.

he makes of that being a third step between the Son and the world, quite clearly inferior to the Son.

The three higher Sephiroth seem to have inspired Milton in his invocation to Urania, at the beginning of Book VII:

> Before the hills appeared, or fountain flowed,
> Thou with Eternal Wisdom didst converse,
> Wisdom thy sister, and with her didst play
> In presence of th' Almighty Father, pleased
> With thy celestial song.

We know " Eternal Wisdom " ; it is the Logos, the Creative Son. But who is Urania, who has a place with Wisdom in presence of the Father? Is she a purely poetical personification? It would seem very bold here on Milton's part. Besides, Milton insists on her reality: " Thou art heavenly, she [the Muse] an empty dream." The *Zohar* explains her. The Father is the Crown, the first Sephira, too near as yet to the En-Sof to be creative; Wisdom in Milton is, by name, the Wisdom of the Kabbalah: Urania then is the third Sephira, Intelligence, the sister of the second, as Milton well knows, and Milton addresses this Intelligence, which he disguises as Urania, so that he may be inspired by her — the proper power of inspiration.[23] And from these divine " recreations " the creation came. Milton ascribes to these acts within the bosom of divinity the sexual character which is so well marked in the *Zohar;* and that is the meaning of that terrible passage in *Tetrachordon,*[24] in which Milton invokes God's own example to justify man in his need of woman:

God himself conceals not his own recreations before the world

[23] See Karppe, p. 375.     [24] *Prose Works*, III, 331.

was built: " I was," saith the Eternal Wisdom, " daily his delight, playing always before him " . . . and [Solomon] sings of a thousand raptures between those two lovely ones far on the hither side of carnal enjoyment.

No doubt Milton is quoting sacred texts; but he adds another text: " before the world was built," and this is a relationship of cause to effect in the *Zohar* — the world is the outcome, the child, of sex-life within the divinity. Milton also makes use of another kabbalistic law: life here below is the image of the life within God; that is why man has need of woman.[25]

But let us pass on to less delicate subjects. Free-will is a natural consequence of the " retraction " of God both in the *Zohar* and in Milton.[26] A connected idea in both cases is that of the usefulness of evil. Milton's texts are rightly celebrated:

Good and evil we know in the field of this world grow up together almost inseparably. . . . What wisdom can there be to choose, what continence to forbear, without the knowledge of evil? . . . I cannot praise a fugitive and cloistered virtue unexercised and unbreathed. . . .[27]

Thus also the *Zohar:*

Had not the Holy One (Blessed be He) created the spirit of good and the spirit of evil, man could have had neither merit nor demerit; that is the reason why God created him a mixture of the two spirits.[28]

In both systems God has foreseen the use his creatures would make of their free-will and has provided for all the consequences by his " preliminary decree," so that, as

[25] *Zohar,* tr. de Pauly, I, 173, 353, 391, and II, 432, and *passim,* for the sex-life God-Matrona.
[26] Karppe, pp. 466, 478, etc.
[27] *Areopagitica,* in *Prose Works,* II, 67–68.
[28] I, 142.

the *Zohar* has it, " The Spirit of Evil works his Master's will." Thus Milton's Satan is himself an instrument of God, and it is " fondly " that he thinks he can do anything to " damage " his Master.[29]

The ontology is thus in complete concordance: God absolute and unmanifested, Demiurge, " retraction " of God and free-will, necessity and usefulness of evil, preliminary decrees of God — all are both in the *Zohar* and in Milton.

The same harmony exists in the cosmology, but for the difference insisted upon earlier. In the two systems the universe is made of one substance, and that unique substance is God himself. The theories of the *Zohar* on "emanation" are well known, and all through the *Zohar* flows a current of pantheism:[30] " All souls form one Unity with the essential soul."

And although the *Zohar* does not give up, as Milton does, the idea of a soul distinct from the body, yet it adopts this other idea, which bridges the difference, that there is no essential distinction between the body and the soul. This last is a Miltonic thesis also. M. Karppe sums up the doctrine of the *Zohar* as follows:

As the aim of the kabbalists is not to bring the En-Sof into direct contact with the Finite, it becomes necessary that the Crown [the first Sephira] be able to replace the En-Sof, and contain along with the spiritual principle the potentiality of the material — matter being for the *Zohar* a degradation of the spiritual substance — the Crown is the whole of this substance, with its full potentialities."[31]

This is all Miltonic thought; witness the following passages in the *De doctrina:*

[29] *Zohar*, IV, 105; " My damage fondly deemed," says God, of Satan's activities (*P. L.*, VII, 152).
[30] Karppe, pp. 375, 407, etc. " One first matter all," says Milton. *Cf.*
[31] Karppe, p. 375.          *Zohar*, V, 366.

For spirit being the more excellent substance, virtually and essentially contains within itself the inferior one; as the spiritual and rational faculty contains the corporal, that is, the sentient and vegetative faculty.[32]

For the original matter of which we speak, is not to be looked upon as an evil or trivial thing, but as intrinsically good, and the chief productive stock of every subsequent good. It was a substance, and derivable from no other source than the fountain of every substance [God].[33]

This divine origin of the substance of which all beings are made has the same consequence in psychology and ethics for Milton and for the *Zohar*. The physical instincts of the body are good and legitimate, and, especially, that of sex is good and legitimate; both the poet and the kabbalists find it in God himself, as we have seen. We need not, therefore, develop the point beyond marking the extreme limit, common to both.

The *Zohar* proclaims several times that it is a sin to abstain from lawful sexual intercourse;[34] Milton is just as positive with his

> who bids abstain,
> But our destroyer, foe to God and man?

And Milton, in a passage which causes Raphael himself to blush, has shown us the example of physical love among the angels also:

> Whatever pure thou in the body enjoy'st
> (And pure thou wert created) we enjoy.[35]

But there is an evil sensuality, which in both systems is associated with the Fall. "Sexual desires," says the *Zohar*, "are good or evil according to the spirit that prompts them." [36] The whole argument of Milton on the

---

[32] *Prose Works*, IV, 181.    [34] I, 290; II, 340, 642, etc.    [36] I, 142.
[33] *Ibid.*, IV, 179.    [35] *P. L.*, VIII, 622-23.

subject in the treatises on divorce is based upon that very principle. Therefore the history of the Fall is the same; the *Zohar* reads like a commentary on the ninth book of *Paradise Lost:*

The woman saw that the fruit was good to eat; she took and ate thereof. These words refer to the first union of Adam and Eve. At first Eve consented to the union solely because of her reflections on the usefulness of conjugal cohabitation [37] and also because of the pure affection that bound her to Adam. But as soon as the serpent came into it — Scripture says " and gave thereof to her husband " — their intercourse was no longer inspired by a pure affection, but she aroused in him carnal desires.[38]

All these elements are in the Miltonic tale of the Fall: the purity of sexual relationship before the Fall, the fruit considered as an aphrodisiac, sexual corruption following immediately upon the Fall, the first manifestation of it. And the *Zohar*, like Milton, can rise to a generalization from these facts: it has the great theory of the opposition between passion and reason, and derives it also from reflection upon sexual passion. " Man," says Rabbi Yehuda,[39] " has three guides: reason, inspired by the holy soul; passion, inspired by evil propensities; and the instinct of self-preservation common to all men. Note that the Evil Spirit can act only upon the last two guides. The guide called passion does not even wait for the Tempter — it runs to meet him; and it is this second guide which perverts the third, by nature inoffensive." This third guide Milton calls " desire " or " will," which is " inoffensive by nature." The poet describes the effects of sensuality on Adam and Eve:

[37] Let us note here another trait common to Milton and the *Zohar* — an occasional colossal lack of sense of humor.
[38] I, 287–88.
[39] On the daughters of Lot (II, 691).

For understanding [the 1st guide] ruled not, and the will [the 3rd]
Heard not her lore, both in subjection now
To sensual appetite [the 2nd].[40]

And again:

Reason in man obscured, or not obeyed [the 1st],
Immediately inordinate desires [the 3rd]
And upstart passions [the 2nd] catch the government
From reason.[41]

Consequently Milton's attitude to woman is much the same as that of the *Zohar.* For both, man without woman is an incomplete thing. The *Zohar* frequently asserts the fact: [42] " The male form alone and the female form alone are each only one half of a body." (The basis of these ideas is in the theories on primitive hermaphrodism, traces of which can thus be found in Milton's thought also.) Similarly, Adam explains to the Archangel that God

from my side subducting, took perhaps
More than enough.[43]

Man without woman is an incomplete being; hence his weakness before her. Then woman, being the instrument of passion, is not so directly as man in relationship with God. "He for God only, she for God in him," says Milton, and the *Zohar* reads: " Women do not possess the Light of the Law, which is reserved to men, but they have the candle of the Sabbath, which brings them rewards." [44]

But quite a special dignity is given woman in many passages. For the *Zohar,* woman remains on Earth the

[40] *P. L.,* IX, 1127–29.
[41] *Ibid.,* XII, 86–89.
[42] Karppe, pp. 426–27.
[43] *P. L.,* VIII, 536–37.
[44] IV, 119.

expression of the Matrona: "small in her exile, but powerful "; [45] " the house is hers, and man is to consult her for all matters relating to the household " ; " the union of man and woman must be voluntary on both sides." Woman must never be considered as the passive instrument of pleasure; her consent must be obtained " by words of friendship and tenderness." [46]  This attitude of superiority mixed with respect and tenderness is quite precisely Milton's attitude to woman.

If we pass on to Milton's more particularly religious ideas, the conception of the " Greater Man," of Christ, who is the whole body of the elect, of the intelligent, the problem becomes wider.  It is a larger tradition than that of the *Zohar* which comes down to Milton.  But the tradition is in the Kabbalah also.  The Heavenly Man, Adam Kadmon, who is One, the prototype and also the whole of mankind, may have helped Milton towards his idea of the Greater Man, Christ.  In any case there is harmony.

This parallelism could be carried on *ad infinitum*.  I shall only add here the simple statement that, among others, the following Miltonic conceptions are also found in the *Zohar:*

Original Sin takes place in each of us, and not once for all in Adam.
In God's intention our bodies were to become spirits without having to undergo death.
There is in the fall much that is good.
There exist mysteries which it is fatal to unveil.
God reveals himself to men according to their powers,
    and not such as he is.
Holy Scripture has many meanings.
External events, although real in themselves, are yet in a way only symbols of spiritual events, etc.

[45] VI, 117.                    [46] I, 286.

There is thus practically not one philosophical trait in Milton which is not to be found in the *Zohar*. Does this mean that Milton derived all his ideas from the Kabbalah? That cannot be reasonably asserted. It seems to me:

1. That he obviously derived from the *Zohar* such peculiar conceptions as are found nowhere else, *e. g.*, the idea of " retraction," his most fundamental idea;

2. That some ideas coming to him from other sources were strengthened by the *Zohar* into a maturity and importance they would not otherwise have reached;

3. That again he found in the *Zohar* confirmation of other ideas which belonged to a much wider tradition.

But it is perhaps practically impossible — and it is of no real utility — to try to work out this division in the detail of the ideas. What conclusions then are we to draw from the main facts?

The first is that Milton has used the *Zohar;* I see no other hypothesis covering the range of correspondences I have hardly done more than point out here.

The second is that Milton's originality as a thinker is practically reduced to the working of his intellect or feelings upon outside material which he appropriates and only arranges. Yet he remains a great thinker, because he is still the representative of the modern mind in presence of the tremendous chaos of impossible ideas, puzzling myths, and grotesque conceptions of the *Zohar*. Milton has chosen warily; he has drawn from this confusion practically all the original or deep ideas that were acceptable to the cultured European. He has never been swept away by the element of intellectual and sentimental perversity which plays so great a part in the *Zohar*. In the presence of this (for it) new world rising on the European horizon, an undeniable greatness of character and of intellect was needed to maintain such an attitude; few of those who dealt intimately with the Kabbalah were able to do so.

In the light of these data — Milton now appearing, not as the creator, but as the stage-manager only, of his philosophical ideas — the problem of the poet's thought is transformed and becomes: Why and how did Milton come to adopt such ideas? Why did he give up the orthodox tradition of his time and adopt this kabbalistic tradition?

The answer is to be found in the historical and psychological study of his life, of the evolution of his feelings and character, a study of which I have tried to lay the foundations in Part I.

Milton's original value may thus be diminished, but his historical significance becomes much greater. He is not an isolated thinker lost in seventeenth-century England, with predecessors or disciples. He becomes, at a given moment, the brilliant representative of an antique and complex tradition which continues and widens after him; for the problem becomes larger. "Milton among the kabbalists " — this is, as it were, a gap blown into the very fortress of English literature, and much may here come in: for example, the inexplicable relationship of Blake to Milton becomes clearer for this common light;[47] Blake himself in many points is less of a puzzle; and this current broadens into the nineteenth century from Shelley to Whitman. But here it is no longer simply Milton and only the *Zohar* that are in question;

[47] See on this my *Blake and Milton* (Paris, Alcan, 1920, and New York, Lincoln MacVeagh, The Dial Press, 1924).

other influences are at work, and on others besides Milton. It becomes necessary to trace a whole stream of semi-occult ideas, flowing through the whole of modern literature and taking in much of Goethe, Wagner, and Nietzsche, much of Lamartine and Hugo.[48]

[48] See on this point my article in the *Revue de littérature comparée*, III (1923), 337–68.

## CHAPTER II

ROBERT FLUDD (1574-1637)

A STUDY of Fludd is indispensable to a proper understanding of the evolution of ideas in the seventeenth century in England. His contemporaries held him in high esteem. Selden is known to have thought highly of him. Gassendi devoted two treatises to a courteous refutation of his ideas. His works are an encyclopedia of Kabbalism, Neo-Platonism, Hermetism, and of all sciences and arts of his time, from astrology and even astronomy, to the construction of musical instruments.

His system is extremely complicated, and it can be said at once that Milton has not adopted it, nor even probably been influenced by it except on some particular points which I shall examine in detail. That Milton knew Fludd I take for granted; every educated man of the time knew Fludd; to his great reputation as a philosopher he added celebrity as a medical practitioner and a somewhat scandalous notoriety for his independence towards the medical authorities, who, on several occasions, had to admonish him severely.

Of his general system of ideas, it is enough to say that practically all the kabbalistic conceptions which we went over in our last chapter are found in his works. It is therefore needless to prove the general similarly between Milton's philosophy and Fludd's.

There is, however, one particular doctrine which must be investigated more closely, because it can be said not

to exist explicitly in the Kabbalah (though many kabbalists derive it from their principles) and it is common to
Milton and Fludd: the doctrine of materialism.   Both
derive their materialism from a pantheism: God is everything; the original matter from which everything is made
is part of God.   Fludd also knows of the retraction.[1]
But Milton's use of pantheism to justify physical passion
is not paralleled in Fludd, who despises the body.   Also
of Milton's use of the retraction theory to prove man's
liberty and therefore to justify the ways of God, I find
no traces in Fludd, who seems to be disturbed by no
doubts or questionings relative to the justice of God.
Thus Milton's chief preoccupations are foreign to
Fludd.

But in the cosmology there are more precise analogies.
For Fludd, the original matter, part of God, from which
everything has been made, is light, of which fire is a
grosser form.   There might seem to be an influence of
Stoicism here, and probably the Neo-Stoicism of the
Renaissance has left traces in Fludd; but the only au-
thorities Fludd quotes in support of the theory, so far as
I have seen, are Zoroaster and the Kabbalists.   However
that may be, one passage of Fludd must be compared with
Milton's hymn to light at the beginning of Book III of
*Paradise Lost:*

Concludimus igitur, lucem esse vel increatam, scilicet Deum omnia
naturantem (nam in ipso Deo Patre est vera lux, deinde in Filio
ejus illustrans splendor et uberans, et in Spiritu Sancto ardens
fulgor superans omnen intelligentiam) vel ab ea increata creatam.[2]

---

[1] Though I have not been able to find in Fludd the passage of the
*Tikuné Zohar* I quote in the previous chapter, I will not go so far as to
say it is not there, as Fludd's complete works are a real cosmos, in which
it seems to me impossible to say that something is not to be found.
[2] Fludd, *De macrocosmi historia,* I, I, Caput VI, p. 28.

And Fludd examines at length the authorities for either hypothesis and will come to no precise conclusion.

Now, it is a peculiar fact that Milton also oscillates between the two opinions; and a poet who, in a lyrical effusion, stops to put in alternative saving clauses, must have been impressed by some considerable authority that the matter is not decided: [3]

> *Hail, holy light, offspring of Heav'n firstborn!*
> OR OF THE ETERNAL COETERNAL BEAM.
> AND NEVER BUT IN UNAPPROACHED LIGHT
> MAY I EXPRESS THEE UNBLAM'D.[4] SINCE GOD IS LIGHT
> DWELT FROM ETERNITY — DWELL THEN IN THEE
> BRIGHT EFFLUENCE OF BRIGHT ESSENCE INCREATE!
> *Or hear'st thou rather, pure ethereal stream*
> *Whose fountain who shall tell? Before the Sun,*
> *Before the Heavens thou wert.*

" Offspring of Heav'n first born " is certainly a designation of the Son, from whom all things are made, and therefore of the divine matter out of which they are made. So Milton seems to adopt the Fluddian theory of light as a *materia prima*, at least poetically, for the moment. And he emphasizes the point by adding

since God is light [5]

And we know that all things are of God. " Offspring of Heav'n first born " goes well with " *ab ea increata creatam*," but Milton adds at once: " Or of the Eternal Co-eternal beam," which recalls " *vel increatam lucem*" :

Bright effluence of bright essence increate!

And again, Milton hesitates and goes back to

---

[3] I italicize one hypothesis and set the other in capitals.

[4] " Unblam'd " because none should express the Eternal in the first hypothesis — hence the " hear'st thou rather "; in the second, it is permissible.   [5] *Cf.* Fludd: " *est vera lux.*"

pure ethereal stream
Whose fountain who shall tell? [6]

This extreme caution of the poet, in view of the contemporary philosopher's hesitation, is certainly worth noting.
And it is all the more remarkable that the poet should
stumble where the philosopher has been tripped, because
the poet ought not to have stumbled here.  He was quite
definitely committed to the doctrine that the Son was not
co-eternal; therefore the original matter, light, could not
be.  The fact points to strong external influence, which
made the poet forget at the time the inner coherence of
his own system.  He obviously did not care to contradict
Fludd on the subject of light, and as he does not make a
particular point of light being the *materia prima,* he let
Fludd have it his own way.

Even the end of the hymn,

So much the rather, thou Celestial Light
Shine inward, and the mind through all her powers
Irradiate,

is all the better for a little Fluddian commentary.  It
might seem to us that Milton is unduly passing from the
physical to the spiritual meaning of the word " light " ;
but Fludd explains in his Tome II [7] that the human mind
is also made of that same material light, only of subtler
variety, because it is received directly from God, whereas
external light is received from God through the inter-
mediary of the world.  The " shine inward " is then no
figure of speech, but expresses a true physical reality;

---

[6] *Cf.* Fludd: " *ab ea increata* [who shall tell] *creatam.*"
[7] Tome II, tractatus I, section I, p. 167, and *passim.*  The difference is
the same as that between the souls of the brute creation (external light) and
that of man (internal).

and here Milton uses Fludd aptly, since for Milton all is matter, and spirit only a more refined sort of matter.

Materialistic pantheism is naturally expressed by the image of the scale of beings. This scheme is replaced, or doubled, in Milton by the image of the tree, through which nutriment circulates from top to bottom and bottom to top:

> Till body up to spirit work, in bounds
> Proportion'd to each kind.  So, from the root
> Springs lighter the green stalk; from thence the leaves
> More aery; last, the bright consummate flow'r
> Spirits odorous breathes; flow'rs, and their fruit,
> (Man's nourishment) by gradual scale sublim'd,
> To vital spirits aspire, to animal,
> To intellectual; give both life, and sense,
> Fancy, and understanding.[8]

And the nutriment theme is again insisted upon:

> For know, whatever was created needs
> To be sustain'd and fed: of elements,
> The grosser feeds the purer; earth the sea;
> Earth and the sea feed air; the air those fires
> Ethereal; and as lowest, first the moon;
> Whence in her visage round those spots, unpurg'd
> Vapors, not yet into her substance turn'd.
> Nor doth the moon no nourishment exhale
> From her moist continent, to higher orbs.
> The sun, that light imparts to all, receives
> From all his alimental recompense
> In humid exhalations; and at ev'n
> Sups with the Ocean.[9]

Here again Fludd gives useful explanation.[10]  Matter goes from earth to heaven,

more arboris, a cujus radice sursum ascendendo molis ejus dimensio semper decrescit, cum inferior prima pars superiori sit grossior et

---

[8] *P. L.*, V, 478-86.    [9] *Ibid.*, V, 414-26.    [10] Tome I, I, V. 6, p. 137.

rami adhuc, quo eminentiores, eo mincitiores, foliadenique et flores omnium ejus partium enuissimi existunt.

And:

nonne etiam autoritate omnium fere prædictorum Philosophorum ignis in ærem, ær in aquam, aqua in terram inspissatione quadam convertuntur? per quod facilime quoque cernitur, quod terra vice versa in aquam, aqua in ærem, ær vero in ignem per subtiliationem transmutentur." [11]

So Milton:

> earth the sea;
> Earth and the sea feed air; the air those fires . . .

Thus the Sun is the centre of the distribution of fire in our system, the veritable God of this world, which is made of his substance. Fludd gets enthusiastic over the subject, and it is the only page where I have seen his Latin rise to within even a remote distance of literature. He explains at length that the Sun receives the " pyramidal exhalation " of all things, in the shape of subtler and subtler light; and, fed by them in this wise, gives them back the vital substance that makes them live. Curious engravings illustrate the thought; we see the pyramid rising to the Sun in one; [12] and in the second [13] we see the Sun (endowed with a human face) half sunk behind the round globe of the Earth (a wavy sea-like sphere) and apparently feeding on it. This has a Blake-like tone and line in the old print, and irresistibly recalls the Miltonic lines in which the Sun receives

> From all his alimental recompense
> In humid exhalation, and at ev'n
> Sups with the Ocean.

Milton may well have seen the pictures and retained the impression.

[11] Chapter 7, p. 139.     [12] P. 136.     [13] P. 138.

In the scale of beings in the Fluddian scheme, angels occupy a relatively high place; souls come below angels; and other creatures below souls; but all creatures are made of varying degrees of that primitive matter, light. Angels are made of subtle matter. We have seen Milton concurring in this. One more precise point is in the lines where the angel says:

> whence the soul
> Reason receives; and reason is her being,
> Discursive or intuitive; discourse
> Is oftest yours, the latter most is ours;
> Diff'ring but in degree, of kind the same.[14]

Fludd has the same idea and the passage is close enough to Milton's:

Quia diversus est modus intelligendi; major in angelis, minor in animalibus . . . Quia anima aliquando est *discursiva*, quatenus scilicet est in corpore humano, angelus vero semper est *intuitivus* et sine discursu.[15]

Let us hear what angels are made of:

. . . essentia simplicissima, et quasi immaterialis, lucida, pura, distincta . . . eorum denique operatio, per quam exercentur, voluntaria est, subita, utilis et honesta, operantur enim sine retardatione aut impedimento.[16]

So Milton's angel:

> And obstacle find none
> Of membrane, joint, or limb, exclusive bars;
> Easier than air with air; if spirits embrace
> Total they mix . . .[17]

And in Book VI they are described as

---

14 *P. L.*, V, 486-90.
15 Tome I, I, IV, 11, p. 123.
16 Tome I, I, IV, 2, p. 110.
17 *P. L.*, VIII, 624-27.

        spirits that live throughout
Vital in every part, not as frail man
In entrails, heart or head, liver or reins

. . . . . . . . . . . .

All heart they live, all head, all eye, all ear,
All intellect, all sense, and as they please,
They limb themselves, and colour, shape or size
Assume, as likes them best, condense or rare.[18]

## With this compare Fludd:

Dæmones ex subtilissimorum cœli spiritualis elementorum materia
componi . . . quorum compositio, si cum creaturis cœlorum in-
feriorum comparetur incorporea dicitur, sed respectu simplicitatis
substantiæ lucidæ cœli Empyrei in quo, um quo et ex cujus ele-
mentis primo die creati sunt, non aliter equam plantæ, herbæ,
carumque semina die tertio cum terra facta fuerunt.[19]

On the subject of men, however, Fludd and Milton do
not agree quite so well; for Fludd, men have souls, material souls, it is true, yet souls, immortal and with all
the ordinary qualities of souls except immateriality.[20]    It
is true that he makes up for what Milton must have considered a lapse from the only doctrine by allowing animals
souls also, which considerably reduces the value of that
given to men.[21]    Even plants and minerals are not without souls for Fludd.    And as all these souls are material,
the question is largely one of vocabulary.    However, to
get a precise relationship with Milton's theory of the soul,
we shall have to go a step further down the evolution of
the doctrine, to the Mortalists.

[18] *Ibid.*, VI, 344-53.
[19] Tome I, I, IV, 1, 2, pp. 108-09.
[20] Vol. III, Tome II, tract. II, sec. I, pars. II, chap. 3, p. 161.  Ref-
erences to Fludd are not always easy, as he occasionally starts a new
numbering of his pages, and he subdivides his sub-divisions of parts in a
most complicated manner.
[21] Tome I, I, VI, 6, p. 177, and IV, 9, p. 119.

What are we to conclude from these general resemblances joined to the few precise points brought forward? Hardly, after all, a direct and precise influence from Fludd on Milton, except, perhaps, in one or two passages more important from the literary than from the philosophical point of view. But Fludd remains as a witness to a movement towards pantheistic materialism in the early seventeenth century. Milton is entirely different from Fludd in his general preoccupations: he cares essentially for a vindication of God's justice and man's liberty; he is turned more towards the political world. But he uses some of the same theories as Fludd, and Fludd's success proves that Milton was no solitary thinker in his own time and country. Besides, we shall see that the Mortalists, who stand quite close to Milton, probably derive their general idea from Fludd.

Many of the ideas in common between the two can be referred to the background of the Kabbalah and Renaissance Neo-Platonism generally; but in their cosmological conceptions the two men come closer together. The idea that matter is the sufficient cause " of all subsequent good " (as Milton puts it) and that everything that exists is only a modification of one universal substance, was gaining ground in European thought. Fludd and Milton are two closely connected links of the chain that was to bring that conception from the reveries of the Renaissance to an age of precise investigation of natural phenomena.

## CHAPTER III

### THE MORTALISTS, 1643–1655

WE come closest of all to Milton's most personal ideas in a group of his immediate contemporaries, the Mortalists.

This group is known to us chiefly by a little pamphlet, *Man's Mortality*, published in 1643 (Amsterdam, printed by John Canne), and republished, with changes, in 1644 (same place and printer) and in 1655 (London, no publisher).[1] The author is generally considered to have been Richard Overton, a London printer and bookseller, and a friend of John Lilburne, the head of the Levellers.[2] Owing to the success of their revolutionary propaganda in the army, Overton and Lilburne frequently got into trouble with the Commonwealth government. Milton could hardly help knowing them, since in March, 1649, it was his task as Secretary to report on their arrest, and he was probably present at a violent scene that took place in Council between them and Cromwell.[3] But if Overton was the principal author, it is likely that he had collaborators. Thomas Edwards, in the first part of his *Gangræna* (1645),[4] says that a certain Clement Wrighter is thought either to be the author or at least to have had a large part

---

[1] This last edition was reissued in 1675. The British Museum possesses copies of all four printings. The edition of 1643 is described by Masson, III, 156.

[2] The title pages of all the editions read "By R. O." Several of the copies in the British Museum bear the pencilled addition, in an old hand-writing, "Richard Overton." On Overton, see the article by C. H. Firth in the *Dictionary of National Biography*.

[3] See Masson, IV, 87.          [4] Pp. 81–82.

in the book on the mortality of the soul.  And in the
second part of the same book (1646)[5] Edwards describes
a meeting of Anabaptists "at the Spitle," where the question of the immortality of the soul was discussed.  A man
called Battie upheld the thesis that the soul was mortal.
Richard Overton seconded, and declared that God had
made man, and the whole of man, from the dust, and that
consequently the whole of man would return to dust.  A
good part of the audience approved.  There would thus
seem to have been a fairly well organized group, that
could command a certain amount of popular support,
back of the writing of *Man's Mortality*.[6]

Milton, who was "among the sectaries and in a world
of discontent" in 1643–1644, must have known the
Mortalists then.[7]  At any rate, they would seem to have
known him and his pamphlet on divorce.  In Chapter VI
of *Man's Mortality*,[8] we find an allusion to "the tyrant
*Mezentius*, that bound living men to dead bodyes."
Shortly before the tract came out, Milton had written,
in the first edition of his *Doctrine and Discipline of
Divorce* (August, 1643): "or as it may happen, a living
soul bound to a dead corpse; a punishment too like that
inflicted by the tyrant Mezentius."[9]  It is only too likely
that Milton was considered as potentially among the sectaries.  But at this date, and for a good while still, there
is no reason to think that he shared the ideas of the

---

[5] P. 17.

[6] That the pamphlet sold is evident from the fact that the edition of 1644
replaced in their proper context passages omitted by accident in 1643 and
printed in that edition *in fine*, which proves that the usual trick of printing
a new title page and sticking it on the unsold copies was not practised in
this case.  In other words, the edition of 1643 was sold out.

[7] Cf. Masson, III, 156, 188, 262–63.

[8] Ed. 1643, p. 44.

[9] *Prose Works*, III, 249.

Mortalists.[10] His views, however, underwent considerable change during his long silence from 1645 to 1649, probably in part as the result of conversations with his new friends, and, as we shall see, there is fairly good ground for suspecting that he collaborated in the edition of 1655. Whoever held the pen, Overton or Wrighter, he was secretary to a group, and Milton was in the group when the London edition came out.

## I. THE EDITION OF 1643–1644 [11]

The title of the pamphlet is perhaps the most important part of it, and indeed, nearly sufficient unto itself:

MANS MORTALLITIE OR A TREATISE Wherein 'tis proved, both Theologically and Phylosophically, that whole Man (as a rationall Creature) is a Compound wholly mortall, contrary to that common distinction of Soule and Body: And that the present going of the Soule into Heaven or Hell is a meer Fiction: And that at the Resurrection is the beginning of our immortallity, and then Actuall Condemnation, and Salvation, and not before. . . .

At the head of the first page, this summary is repeated:

A Treatise proving Man (quatinus Animal rationale) a Compound wholly Mortall.

Chapter I is entitled:

Of Mans Creation, Fall, Restitution, and Resurrection how they disprove the Opinion of the Soul. . . .

From the beginning, we meet with the arguments, quotations, and expressions most familiar to us in Milton:

. . . when God had moulded, formed, and compleatly proportionated *Adam of the Dust of the ground, he breathed in his face the breath of Lives, and Man became a living Soul: Gen.* 2. 7. That

---

10 See above, p. 47.

11 The 1644 edition was only the 1643 edition typographically rearranged and corrected. My citations are from the latter.

is, he gave that lifelesse Body a communicative rationall Facul                    tie
or property of life, in his kind: And so it became a living Crea-
ture, or compleate ἄνθρωπος, of whom was the *Woman*, both innocent and free from sin, and so from *Death* and mortality: for *the
wages of Sin is Death, Rom.* 5. 12. I. *Cor.* 15. 56. Thus Man was
gloriously immortall, yet no longer a Creature incorruptable, then
[ = than] during innocent. . . .[12]

The quotation from Genesis 2:7 is perhaps the most important passage of the Bible for Milton.   In the *De doctrina,* he uses it, as Overton does here, to prove the unity
of man:

... *man became a living soul;* whence it may be inferred . . .
that man is a living being, intrinsically and properly one and individual, not compound and separable. . . .[13]

In the two passages, the Spirit brings about a similar
transformation of matter:

### OVERTON

... he gave that lifelesse Body
a communicative rationall Fac-
ultie. . . .

And so it became a living Creature, or complete anthropos. . . .

### MILTON [14]

... an inspiration of some
divine virtue fitted for the exercise of life and reason, and infused into the organic body. . . .
... for man himself, the whole
man, when finally created, is
called in express terms *a living
soul* . . . the whole man is soul
and the soul man. . . .

In the two passages also the word " animal " is insisted
upon.  Overton writes at the top of his page: " Man
(quatenus animal rationale)," and Milton adds to his
paragraph: " Hence the word used in Genesis to signify
soul is, interpreted by the apostle I Cor. XV, 45, ' animal.' "  Here are then two rather short passages, a page

---

[12] Pp. 1-2.      [13] *Prose Works,* IV, 188.      [14] *Ibid.,* IV, 188.

in each case, which contain several identical ideas and even expressions.

The equivalence of Sin and Death, with the covering quotation, " The wages of sin is death," may be found anywhere.   Both Milton and Overton, however, derive from it the same unorthodox conclusion.   Overton points out humorously the error of those who say that the body alone dies as a consequence of sin:

. . . then the principall or efficient cause deepest in the Transgression was lesse punished, then the instrumentall, the Body being but the Soules instrument whereby it acts and moves: as if a Magistrate should hang the Hatchet, and spare the Man that beate a mans braines out with it. . . .[15]

But for the humorous comparison, which would have been out of place in the *De doctrina,* this is precisely Milton's argument:

. . . what could be more absurd than that the mind, which is the part principally offending, should escape the threatened death, and that the body alone . . . should pay the penalty of sin by undergoing death, though not implicated in the transgression? [16]

And Overton's chapter ends on the words, " let us see how it commensurates with the universallity of Scripture and Reason," [17] of which we find an echo in Milton:

. . . that the spirit of man should be separate from the body . . . is nowhere said in Scripture, and the doctrine is evidently at variance with nature and reason. . . .[18]

In both cases the method of proof is the same: Scripture must be upheld by reason; in any other case, one interprets Scripture at will.

Chapter II — " Scriptures to prove this Mortallity "—

15 Pp. 4–5.                            17 P. 5.
16 *Prose Works,* IV, 271.            18 *Prose Works,* IV, 189.

contains nothing of interest.  The quotations are found in Milton, but that is inevitable in any work on the subject.

Chapter III—"Naturall Reasons to prove it"—is made up in the main of a long scholastic discussion on form and matter, to which a parallel is found in the *De doctrina:*

If all of Man that goeth to his *Manhood* be mortall, where then, or what is this immortall thing the *Soul* they talke of? we have examined all his *parts* and *faculties*, and find even all mortall: It is not sure his *prima materia* though *ingenerable, incorruptible, insensible, indefinite,* &c.  Nor his *Forma prima*, that principle, which first gives essence to a naturall *Body;* the first Active principle, *informing* and figurating the *First Matter, sui appetentem;* for both are generall to the *whole Creation*, whose *Efficient Cause* is onely immediately *God* himselfe, by whose power all things that are made shall be returned to that of which they were made, their *Materia prima*, or created matter: So that, (as *Solomon* saith) *Man has no preheminence above a beast, even one thing befalleth them.*[19]

Milton in the *De doctrina* [20] starts from the argument that "Both are general to the whole creation, whose efficient cause is only immediately God Himself," and changing the aim of the whole structure, uses it to prove the divine origin of matter.  But the basis of the two arguments is the same: (1) God is the efficient cause of all creation, and (2) all creatures originate from the same matter:

. . . there are, as is well known to all . . . four kinds of causes, — *efficient, material, formal* and *final*.  Inasmuch then as God is the primary, and absolute, and sole cause of all things, there can be no doubt but that he comprehends and embraces within himself all the causes above mentioned.  Therefore the material cause must be either God, or nothing: Now nothing is no cause at all. . . . But matter and form, considered as internal causes, constitute the thing

[19] *Man's Mortality*, p. 17.      [20] *Prose Works*, IV, 178-80.

itself. . . . For the original matter of which we speak, is . . . intrinsically good and the chief productive stock of every subsequent good. . . . Matter . . . proceeded incorruptible from God; and even since the fall it remains incorruptible as far as concerns its essence.

Overton had called matter "ingenerable, incorruptible." And Milton established thus his triumphant conclusion: "*restat igitur hoc solum . . . fuisse omnia ex Deo.*"

On the next page of the pamphlet, Overton explains that there is but a difference of degree of qualities between animals and men. We have seen Milton's similar opinion. In the same passage we find Ambrose Parey, the French anatomist, quoted along with Pliny; let us note that another French naturalist, Moulin, will be quoted in 1655.[21] The scientific spirit — a comparatively new birth then — is not therefore completely absent from the beginnings of Miltonic materialism. The Bible alone is not responsible for it, and we feel as though we were returning to normal, modern conditions in recording the fact.

Chapter IV — " Objections from Natural Reasons answered " — is short, and of little significance.

Chapter V — " Objections from Scripture answered " —, on the contrary, is of the highest importance, since it enables us to connect the activities of the group with the influence of Fludd. A long passage, from page 33 to 36, explains that light is the *materia prima* from which all things are made, and that the Sun is the chief repository of that light. We have seen in the previous chapter the expression of Fludd's conception and the parallel passages in Milton. Here are now the connecting links:

The Sun, the most excellent peece of the whole Creation, the Epitome, of God's power, conveyour of life, groweth, strength, and

[21] P. 27.

being to everie Creature . . . it is called by the Learned,[22] *Cor Coeli, Anima et Oculus mundi, Platetarum et Fixarum Choragus, Author generationis.* . . . Therefore, to say God is not *light*, is to say, *he is not.* . . .

Even the retraction theory seems to be known to the Mortalists, and this brings them into connection with the whole movement we have been studying, from the Kabbalah, through Fludd and the Mortalists, to Milton: " for that which we call fire, is nothing but contracted light " and, as we have seen in Fludd, the other elements derive from fire — which is apparent also in Milton's nutriment scheme, as quoted in the last chapter. " This formed light . . . is now the Authour of motion generation and subsistance; so in the beginning the substance or *true light* was the beginner, and by it all *beings* had their beginnings." [23]

The pantheistic scheme is complete on materialistic lines, and it is the same as Fludd's and as Milton's. But we are much nearer Milton here than with Fludd, since the Mortalists are, besides, in complete agreement with Milton over the question of the soul. Cornelius Agrippa is quoted on p. 36, which is a link the more in our argument, since he is one of Fludd's favorite authorities, and one of the chief sponsors of all the theories examined here.

It is natural that Chapter V should try to demonstrate that " soul " and " spirit " in the Bible do not imply a belief in a separate soul. We have also heard Milton on the subject. This notion is sufficiently rare in the seventeenth century to be in itself a proof of connection. Particularly, the text, " the spirit shall return to God," for

---

[22] This probably means by Fludd, since he obviously is the one of the learned nearest at hand and in fullest harmony with the author.

[23] *Man's Mortality*, p. 36.

the interpretation of which Milton had to bring Euripides
to the rescue, is said to mean: "shall return to dust," or
Nature, even as Milton will say.[24]  I must admit that I
cannot but see a complete lack of intellectual honesty in
this interpretation of the word "God"; and a proof of
complicity in guilt between Overton and Milton.

Chapter VI—"Of procreation, how from thence this
Mortality is proved"—gives us one of Milton's "noblest" ideas:

As the whole Tree is potentially in the seed, . . . so in the seed
of mankind, is whole man potentially, . . . life and limbes, . . .
soul and body.[25]

So Milton, in the *De doctrina:*

If the soul be equally diffused throughout any given whole, and
throughout every part of that whole,[26] how can the human seed, the
noblest and most intimate part of all the body, be imagined destitute
and devoid of the soul of the parents. . . ?[27]

And both come to the conclusion that God lets nature
do her work and does not interfere, by creating a soul,
at each birth.  And both add that the birth of animals
is just as the birth of men.  "Fish, Birds, and Beasts each
in their kind," says Overton.[28]  And Milton:

> Let the waters generate
> Reptile with spawn abundant, living soul,
> And let fowl fly above the earth. . . .
> Cattle and creeping things, and beasts of the earth
> Each in their kind. . . .

[24] See above, pp. 146–47.
[25] *Man's Mortality*, p. 41.
[26] Overton, to illustrate the point, proposes, somewhat profanely (p. 15):
"they may as well say, the *Popes* Soule is in his GREAT TOE when men
kisse it, as say, the Soul liveth, when the Body dyeth."
[27] *Prose Works*, IV, 192–93.
[28] P. 46.

And animals were in their origin as immortal as men, and shall be raised from the dead also:

> For all other *Creatures* as well as man shall be raised and delivered from Death at the Resurrection. . . . Death comming upon all the Creatures by the sinne of Adam . . . the death of the Beasts . . . was part of the Curse. . . .[29]

We have seen the Miltonic texts: "no created thing can be finally annihilated." [30]

The last chapter (VII).—"Testimonies of Scripture to prove that whole man is generated, and propagated by Nature"—contains the texts which are necessarily used by Milton in the *De doctrina,* and is of small interest.

Masson [31] points out that there is but little reference in the whole pamphlet to the promised immortality after judgment. He adds that Overton seems to have but little belief in it. After going through the text, that is also my opinion. Besides the formula in the title and a few lines at the end, there are only very vague and inconclusive allusions to " New Heavens and a new earth " and to "our only hope being in Christ," which seem a mere concession to contemporary prejudice in favor of immortality.[32] On this point, an examination of the 1655 edition will enable us to connect Milton even more intimately with the group.

What are we to conclude from all this (reserving the last point)? It seems to me necessary to admit that Milton knew the pamphlet *Man's Mortality,* discussed it with

---

[29] *Man's Mortality,* p. 50.

[30] *Treatise,* in *Prose Works,* IV, 181, and *Paradise Lost,* as quoted above, p. 145.

[31] III, 157. Masson had read the pamphlet, but was not sufficiently acquainted with Milton's philosophy to catch the intimate relationship between the two systems; so he passes it over lightly.

[32] The argument about animals being immortal also may be considered as not very decisive, and even perhaps meant to ridicule the idea.

the authors, who were among his friends, and absorbed the very substance of it.  It is impossible to believe that men who were acquainted, who brought their whole spirit into propaganda work, and who held in common so many ideas that were anathema, should not have worked together.  The analysis of the 1655 edition confirms this hypothesis.

## II. The 1655 (London) Edition.

We have seen how little the first pamphlet insisted on resurrection.  Now, Milton, while adopting the ideas of the Mortalists, kept his own intensely religious spirit, and particularly his absorbing thirst for justice.  To him, to his whole scheme of thought, for abstract and for sentimental reasons, immortality was necessary.  In 1655 he was completely liberated from dogma, and accepted all his friends' ideas; but as compensation — and can we imagine Milton having no influence over any group he was connected with? — he lifted their whole conception into a more religious atmosphere.  He gives to the second pamphlet the elevated tone that was somewhat lacking in the first.

As a consequence, Chapter III of 1644 becomes Chapter I of 1655, and eight pages (20 to 27) are added on the subject:

That which is finite and mortal ceaseth from the time of the grave till the time of the resurrection.

Page 27 has it:

Therefore, well saies Tertullian, in his book *de Anima*, that the Soul and the Body of man are both one; which, saith Saint Jerome, in his Epistle to Marcellina, and Anapsychia, was the opinion of the greatest part of the western Churches.  And Saint Augustine, in his four books *of the Original of Souls*, leaves the question undecided; neither dares he rashly determine anything.

The same collection of authorities, in the same order — Tertullian, Jerome, the Western Church, and Augustine in a doubting mood — is found in Chapter VII of the *De doctrina*, to prove the similar doctrine that the soul goes from father to son at generation because the soul is one with the body:

> . . . was considered as the more probable opinion by Tertullian and Apollinarius, as well as by Augustine, and the whole western church in the time of Jerome, as he himself testifies, Tom. 11, Epist. 82 . . . Augustine was led to confess that he could neither discover by study, nor prayer, nor any process of reasoning, how the doctrine of original sin could be defended on the supposition of the creation of souls.[33]

This Miltonic passage, in an addition which is in the Miltonic spirit, seems to me to leave no room for doubt. Milton's knowledge and intelligence have left a mark here.  Perhaps his style also, for the phrase "neither dares he rashly determine anything" at the end of the sentence, and a purely rhetorical repetition, is an example of a peculiarly Miltonic trick of composition.

On page 40, another addition is a quotation from Ames, whom we know to have been a favorite theologian of Milton's orthodox times.[34]

As a Post-Script, we find an amusing trait which may well be Miltonic also.  I have shown that there was much of the nationalist in Milton; he claimed Druidic sources for English civilization, and even for universal

[33] *Prose Works*, IV, 189-90, 193.  The reference is to the epistle to Marcellina and Anapsychia which is quoted in the pamphlet.
[34] *Cf.* Sumner in his preface to the *De doctrina*, in *Prose Works*, IV, xviii.

civilization (in a humorous mood, let us hope).[35]   Here, he claims further (if it be he) the honors for Great Britain of having invented the theory of immortality. He explains that in ancient chronicles (he was reading them at the time for his *History*) it is recorded that " King Druis [hence the name druids] to encourage his subjects to fight, invented immortality of the soul." And yet Milton's patriotism does not go so far as to adopt the theory.

The small volume ends on the ingenious couplet (and can this be another Miltonic addition?):

> Qualis in novissimo vitæ die quisque moritur,
> Talis in novissimo mundi die judicabitur.

Our last three chapters have placed Milton in his own times and among his countrymen. We cannot undertake here to trace further back the origin of his ideas, of the ideas of the group and tradition he belonged to. We have seen the development of certain sixteenth-century conceptions that originated partly in the Kabbalah, were further developed by Fludd into a immensely complicated but more coherent system, were brought back to earth and plain common-sense by the Mortalists, and finally — this being the goal we wanted to reach — were elevated by Milton into the permanent sphere of supreme artistic beauty.

[35] *Prose Works*, II, 90.  There have, however, been many who held the opinion seriously.

# CONCLUSION

IT is of interest to note that the next great step taken by European thought, the pantheism of Spinoza, only marks a further stage of evolution of the ideas we have been studying in England. There has been a good deal of controversy as to whether or not Spinoza derived his ideas from the Kabbalah. There are intellectual worlds between the two; but when the history of European thought in the seventeenth century is properly investigated, it will be seen that throughout Europe there was in progress an evolution of thought of which the English line from Fludd to Milton is only one manifestation.[1] And there is no doubt that Spinoza takes his proper place—one of the very highest—at the end of that evolution. The froth of the Renaissance was being analyzed and the results confronted with the findings of a scientific century; but a kernel of great ideas remained alive and fruitful.

It is possible, and even probable, that Milton had occasion in his later life to discuss Spinoza's ideas. They had a common friend, Oldenburg, a frequent correspondent of both. In 1661, Oldenburg had a memorable conversation with Spinoza on God, thought and extension, and the nature of the union of body and soul.[2] Spinoza sent Oldenburg a long letter on the subject—probably

[1] In France, Jean d'Espagnet, a Bordeaux magistrate (*Enchiridion*, 1647), represents Fludd's stage of evolution in a much more concise and literary form.
[2] Oldenburg to Spinoza, Aug. 26, 1661. See *The Chief Works of . . . Spinoza* (London, 1912), II, 275.

the most interesting letter of his that has survived. He explains therein his conception of the One Substance, which
cannot have been created and is infinite and perfect.[3]  It
seems to me probable that Oldenburg, who was then in
London and visited Milton, showed the poet this interesting letter; if so, Milton must certainly have been struck
by the resemblances between his conception of substance
and Spinoza's.

Milton had but little of the scientific spirit: he was essentially a great rhetorician in the service of a great
moralist; but he was deeply interested in science; he
admired Bacon; Galileo was one of his heroes.  Through
Oldenburg, he was in connection with Boyle and the
founders of the Royal Society.

But Milton has a greater value than that of a representative of his own time; his thinking occasionally
reaches a depth that makes it permanently valid.  What
do we mean by that word " depth " ?  It seems to me that
we apply it to whatever, in works that are now antiquated
in thought and feeling, strikes us, men of today, as new
and original, as carrying still a revelation for us.  In the
middle of Plato's theosophy, which seems to us so puerile;
of the Hindoo mythology, which seems to us so artificial;
of Pascal's religion — whatever may be our own religious
opinions — we come upon phrases and ideas that still
bring to us the sensation of a superior power of thought,
and shreds of truth otherwise hidden from us.  Above all
systems and modes of thought, such ideas remain eternally
true, new, and surprising for mankind.  They give life to
books which, without them, would have been forgotten
long ago, even as, for instance, Fludd is forgotten because that power is not in him.  But that power is in

[3] *Ibid.*, II, 276–79.

Milton. His work is full of phrases like these, which strike and penetrate our minds:

> While other animals inactive range,
> And of their doings God takes no account.

Of her, who sees when thou art seen most weak.

> Evil into the mind of God or man
> May come and go.

Even today, man can use such splendid forms and moulds of thought as these, pour his mind into them, and obtain results. For Milton has not only constructed a cosmology: he has reached deeper; he has looked for ultimate reality within the heart of man, and placed the laws of destiny in man's soul and will.

The lesson that emerges from Milton's poems is the same as the lesson of the magnificent series of novels of that modern among the moderns, George Meredith: man's destiny is but the translation into outward events of his inner history; his weaknesses bring catastrophe; his qualities, victory; the God of this world is an internal God; He is the inevitable Force that expresses in outward facts the tendencies of our souls. Meredith said — and Milton might have said:

> Forgetful is green Earth, the Gods alone
> Remember everlastingly: they strike
> Remorselessly, and ever like for like.
> By their great memories the Gods are known.[4]

And:

... the Fates are within us. Those which are the forces of the outer world are as shadows to the power we have created within us. ... It is true that our destiny is of our own weaving.[5]

[4] *Odes in Contribution to the Song of French History:* "France, December, 1870."     [5] *Vittoria*, Chap. XLV.

Meredith's ideal of marriage, too, is the same as Milton's:

> . . . the senses running their live sap, and the minds companioned, and the spirits made one by the whole natured conjunction . . . between the ascetic rocks and the sensual whirlpools.[6]

Their conceptions of woman are not so different as might appear: Meredith's women, like Diana, generally find their leader in a man; and that is all Milton demands; and Milton admits them to all the privileges Meredith claims for them. It was Milton who said, and Meredith who might have wished to have said:

> . . . smiles from reason flow
> . . . and delight to reason joined:[7]

essential definitions of the Comic Spirit as Meredith conceives it in his *Essay on Comedy:* the Comic Spirit that flows from intellectual relationship between the sexes, since it is Adam who proposes this ideal to Eve.

Human thought has not left Milton behind, and has still to revere in him, as well as the marvellous poet, the profound thinker. His contact with Spinoza gives us the measure of his strength; his contact with Meredith, that of his lasting value. Those two great minds, so different one from the other, will serve as witnesses to the permanent worth of Milton the thinker.

[6] *Diana of the Crossways,* Chap. XXXVII.
[7] *Paradise Lost,* IX, 239, 243.

# APPENDICES

# APPENDIX A

## MILTON'S BLINDNESS

W E possess a considerable number of facts that throw light on Milton's health. Unfortunately, the science of Milton's time was not sufficiently advanced to permit of entirely conclusive inferences from the existing documents. We propose, however, to examine the various hypotheses which might explain the known facts, and by the elimination of theories contradicted by our texts to try to reach at least a reasonably probable conclusion.

Let us listen first to Milton himself.

On the 28th of September, 1654 — he had been blind since 1651 — the poet addressed to his friend Leonard Philaras, an Athenian then in Paris, who had offered to lay his case before the celebrated Parisian oculist, Dr. Thévenot, a letter in which he described as follows the progress and symptoms of his disease:

It is now, I think, about ten years since I perceived my vision to grow weak and dull; and at the same time I was troubled with pain in my kidneys and bowels, accompanied with flatulency. In the morning, if I began to read, as was my custom, my eyes instantly ached intensely, but were refreshed after a little corporeal exercise. The candle which I looked at, seemed as it were encircled with a rainbow. Not long after the sight in the left part of the

---

[1] This appendix represents the greater portion of an article entitled " Milton devant la médecine," published in collaboration with M. Camille Cabannes, Professor of Ophthalmology in the Faculty of Medicine of Bordeaux, in the *Revue anglo-américaine*, I (1923), 120-34. The translation has been revised, from the point of view of terminology, by Dr. Thomas J. Williams, of Chicago, Illinois, who, however, should not be held responsible for the opinions expressed.

left eye (which I lost some years before the other) became quite obscured; and prevented me from discerning any object on that side. The sight in my other eye has now been gradually and sensibly vanishing away for about three years; some months before it had entirely perished, though I stood motionless, everything which I looked at seemed in motion to and fro. A stiff cloudy vapour seemed to have settled on my forehead and temples, which usually occasions a sort of somnolent pressure upon my eyes, and particularly from dinner till the evening. . . . I ought not to omit that while I had any sight left, as soon as I lay down on my bed and turned on either side, a flood of light used to gush from my closed eyelids. Then, as my sight became daily more impaired, the colours became more faint, and were emitted with a certain inward crackling sound; but at present, every species of illumination being, as it were, extinguished, there is diffused around me nothing but darkness, or darkness mingled and streaked with an ashy brown. Yet the darkness in which I am perpetually immersed, seems always, both by night and day, to approach nearer to white than black; and when the eye is rolling in its socket, it admits a little particle of light, as through a chink. And though your physician may kindle a small ray of hope, yet I make up my mind to the malady as quite incurable; and I often reflect, that as the wise man admonishes, days of darkness are destined to each of us, the darkness which I experience, less oppressive than that of the tomb is, owing to the singular goodness of the Deity, passed amid the pursuits of literature and the cheering salutations of friendship. . . . And, my dear Philaras, whatever may be the event, I wish you adieu with no less courage and composure than if I had the eyes of a lynx.[2]

We have here a precious document, written for a friend, addressed ultimately to a physician, and composed with all possible care; intended only for friends, it furnishes entirely sincere proof of the strength of mind which was Milton's in the early years of his affliction. Let us now observe the poet face to face with his enemies, justifying himself in the *Defensio secunda pro populo Anglicano* against the accusations of his political adversaries, who had called his blindness a punishment of God for his pri-

[2] *Prose Works*, III, 507-08.

vate vices and public crimes.  To these calumnies Milton replied with a firmness and nobility of soul which yet did not exclude all traces of humor:

I certainly never supposed that I should have been obliged to enter into a competition for beauty with the Cyclops. . . . It is of no moment to say anything of personal appearance, yet lest (as the Spanish vulgar, implicitly confiding in the relations of their priests, believe of heretics) any one, from the representations of my enemies, should be led to imagine that I have either the head of a dog, or the horn of a rhinoceros, I will say something on the subject. . . . I do not believe that I was ever once noted for deformity, by any one who ever saw me; but the praise of beauty I am not anxious to obtain.  My stature certainly is not tall; but it rather approaches the middle than the diminutive. . . . Nor, though very thin, was I ever deficient in courage or in strength; and I was wont constantly to exercise myself in the use of the broadsword, as long as it comported with my habit and my years.  Armed with this weapon, as I usually was, I should have thought myself quite a match for any one, though much stronger than myself. . . . At this moment I have the same courage, the same strength, though not the same eyes; yet so little do they betray any external appearance of injury, that they are as unclouded and bright as the eyes of those who most distinctly see.  In this instance alone I am a dissembler against my will. . . . It is not so wretched to be blind, as it is not to be capable of enduring blindness. . . . I call thee, O God, the searcher of hearts, to witness, that I am not conscious, either in the more early or in the later periods of my life, of having committed any enormity, which might deservedly have marked me out as a fit object for such a calamitous visitation.  But since my enemies boast that this affliction is only a retribution for the transgressions of my pen, I again invoke the Almighty to witness, that I never, at any time, wrote anything which I did not think agreeable to truth, to justice, and to piety. . . . Thus, therefore, when I was publicly solicited to write a reply to the Defence of the royal cause, when I had to contend with the pressure of sickness, and with the apprehension of soon losing the sight of my remaining eye, and when my medical attendants clearly announced, that if I did engage in the work, it would be irreparably lost, their premonitions caused no hesitation and inspired no dismay  . . my resolution was unshaken, though the alternative was either the loss of my sight, or the desertion of my duty. . . . I resolved, therefore, to make the short interval of sight, which was left me to enjoy, as beneficial as possible to the public interest.[3]

And it was indeed deliberately that Milton sacrificed his eyesight, which reasonable care might have enabled him to keep much longer, in order to write the *Defence of the English People*. He derived no profit from the task except fame, and the fame of a pamphleteer was not that which he had aspired to from his early youth, when he had promised himself to become one of the great poets of humanity. We may agree with him, then, without reservation, when he declares that he sacrificed himself to what he believed to be for the public good. To the appeal of the leaders of the Republic he responded with undeniable heroism, fully conscious of his danger.

In this same *Defensio secunda*, Milton adds several details of importance for our subject:

My father destined me from a child to the pursuits of literature; and my appetite for knowledge was so voracious, that, from twelve years of age, I hardly ever left my studies, or went to bed before midnight. This primarily led to my loss of sight. My eyes were naturally weak, and I was subject to frequent head-aches; which, however, could not chill the ardour of my curiosity, or retard the progress of my improvement.[4]

Milton's biographers are agreed on this point. A last quotation, taken from the invocation to light at the beginning of Book III of *Paradise Lost*, shows us Milton's attitude unchanged at the end of his life:

> . . . in my flight
> Through utter and through middle darkness borne,
> With other notes than to th' Orphean lyre
> I sung of chaos and eternal night . . .

[3] *Prose Works*, I, 235-38.      [4] *Ibid.*, I, 254.

> . . . thee I revisit safe,
> And feel thy sovran vital lamp; but thou
> Revisit'st not these eyes, that roll in vain
> To find thy piercing ray, and find no dawn;
> So thick a drop serene hath quenched their orbs,
> Or dim suffusion veiled. . . .
>                     . . . Thus with the year
> Seasons return, but not to me returns
> Day or the sweet approach of even or morn,
> Or sight of vernal bloom, or summer's rose,
> Or flocks, or herds, or human face divine;
> But cloud instead, and ever-during dark
> Surrounds me, from the cheerful ways of men
> Cut off. . . .
> So much the rather thou, Celestial Light,
> Shine inward, and the mind through all her powers
> Irradiate, there plant eyes, all mist from thence
> Purge and disperse, that I may see and tell
> Of things invisible to mortal sight.[5]

And the poet, speaking to his Muse, represents himself as full of confidence and strength:

> On evil days though fallen, and evil tongues;
> In darkness, and with dangers compassed round,
> And solitude; yet not alone, while thou
> Visit'st my slumbers nightly, or when morn
> Purples the east. . . .[6]

Such was the man. Let us now attempt to arrive at plausible conclusions on the subject of the disease which brought about his loss of sight. The important fact to start with, in our opinion, is Milton's perception of colors. In a useful article published in *Modern Language Notes* for December, 1894,[7] Mr. V. P. Squires presents statistics which seem to us decisive on this point. Milton mentions

---

[5] *Paradise Lost*, III, 15–55.
[6] *Ibid.*, VII, 26–30.
[7] IX, 454–74. See particularly section VII, pp. 465–66.

in his works 29 different shades of color; he could, therefore, distinguish them. Of these 29 colors, those named
most frequently are: gold, 47 times; green, 43 times; red
and its varieties, 19 times; violet, 13 times; gray, 12
times; blue, 13 times; the other shades recur much less
often. Now, these are the normal colors of nature: the
gold of the sun, the red, gold, and violet of sunrise and sunset, the green of vegetation, the blue of the sky, the gray
of somber days, of the earth, and of cities. Milton, therefore, saw the colors about him in a normal manner. He
also saw colors at a distance; we need cite only a description of a sunset and moonrise, which, written at a time
when literature made little of " picturesque " effects, is
a sufficient proof:

> . . . the sun now fall'n
> Beneath the Azores; whether the prime orb,
> Incredible how swift, had thither roll'd
> Diurnal, or this less voluble earth
> By shorter flight to the east, had left him there
> Arraying with reflected purple and gold
> The clouds that on his western throne attend:
> Now came still evening on, and twilight gray
> Had in her sober livery all things clad;
> Silence accompanied, for beast and bird,
> They to their grassy couch, these to their nests
> Were slunk, all but the wakeful nightingale;
> She all night long her amorous descant sung;
> Silence was pleas'd: now glow'd the firmament
> With living sapphires; Hesperus, that led
> The starry host, rode brightest, till the moon
> Rising in clouded majesty at length,
> Apparent queen, unveiled her peerless light,
> And o'er the dark her silver mantle threw.[8]

This ability to see colors both precisely and at a distance tells strongly against the hypothesis of myopia, at

---

[8] *Paradise Lost*, IV, 591–609.

least of a pernicious myopia sufficiently accentuated to lead ultimately to a detachment of the retina. Milton, it is true, tells us that his eyes had been " naturally weak " since his twelfth year; and his first biographer remarks that " his Eyes were none of the quickest." [9] It is possible, of course, to interpret this as myopia; but myopia of the aggravated type that results in blindness does not ordinarily allow its victims to distinguish so well the numerous shades of color which Milton mentions.

Equally out of the question are congenital nystagmus, congenital cataract, and astigmatism, since Milton could see colors precisely and at a distance. We may also discard the hypothesis of congenital retinitis pigmentosa since there is no indication of hemeralopia. Without being necessarily nyctalopic, Milton does not complain of being unable to see at twilight or dawn; these, indeed, were his favorite hours for work. He studied, no doubt, by the light of candles, but even so, he could have experienced no difficulty in reading at these times of the day.

Thanks to the letter to Philaras, we know of six symptoms which allow us to go beyond this purely negative method. The first three are: (1) the gradual modification of his sight, which he lost first in the left eye and then, after several years, entirely, the disease having first attacked the whole of the left eye and then the right; (2) the rainbow iris around the candle; and (3) the progressive loss of his color vision. These three symptoms support the hypothesis of chronic glaucoma with atrophy of the optic nerve.

But we have to do not merely with a lesion of the optic nerve; the three other clearly marked symptoms indicate

[9] See *The English Historical Review*, XVII (1902), 108.

in addition a lesion of the retina itself. They are: (4) the lights which he saw in the night when he turned in his bed; (5) the fluctuation of objects before his eyes; and (6) during the period of blindness, the fact that a ray of light was perceptible when he turned his eye in its socket.

All this might indicate a detachment of the retina. We do not think so, partly because retinal detachment in both eyes is not common, partly because we have eliminated the hypothesis of myopia which might have caused it, and partly because we have no reason to suspect a traumatic retinal detachment. Furthermore, these last three symptoms, which appeared only at an advanced stage of his malady (the last after he had become blind), are encountered in the very last period of chronic progressive inflammatory lesions of the retina and the optic nerve.

We arrive, therefore, at this plausible diagnosis: weakness of the eyes from infancy (we shall come back to this); then, as the result of early overuse of his eyes in bad light, inflammatory and atrophic lesions of the optic nerve and the retina, probably complicated by secondary glaucoma. Now, putting aside the possibilities which we have rejected above, this points to a very bad general condition, which, in view of the peculiar effect on the visual organs, can be only a condition of hereditary syphilis, the effects of which are manifested from infancy (whence the "weakness" referred to above) and which ends in complete blindness. Hereditary syphilis is known as a general cause of eye troubles which follow a course similar to that taken by Milton's.

If we examine now what we know concerning the

general health of Milton himself and of his family, we shall find, we believe, full confirmation of this hypothesis.

Milton tells us in a passage already cited that he was small and thin and subject to digestive troubles; his biographers remark that all his life he was in the hands of physicians; a victim of arthritis, which enlarged the joints of his fingers, he died in the end of gout after sufferings of which the echo is heard in *Samson Agonistes,* when the chorus complains bitterly that the virtuous sons have to bear the consequences and

> The punishment of dissolute days,

as the result of ancestral sins.

The history of his family is perhaps more illuminating still. We know that his mother also had weak sight. His first daughter, Anne, born in July, 1646, apparently in good physical condition, soon, we are told, became ill and deformed, although her features remained attractive. Concerning his second daughter, Mary, born in October, 1648, we have no medical knowledge. His son, John, born in March, 1650, died shortly afterwards. His daughter Deborah, born in May, 1652, seems to have had a good constitution, but we shall presently see something of her descendants. Milton's wife died in July, 1652; he remarried in 1656; in October, 1657, he had a daughter, Catherine, who died in March, 1658, his second wife having died in February of the same year. The first child of his sister Anne lived only a short time. His brother Christopher lost three children either at birth or in infancy. Among the immediate descendants of Milton, his first daughter, Anne, who was an invalid, died at the birth of her first child, who died also. His third daughter,

Deborah, had ten children, the greater number of whom died in early infancy, two only surviving their mother.

Is there any meaning in this series of catastrophes? No doubt the state of medicine and hygiene in the seventeenth century will explain many things. Nevertheless, if we keep in mind the weakness of Milton's mother's eyes, the bad constitution of his eldest daughter, the fact that of the three branches of the family which we know not one was spared, and the rapid extinction of his own descendants in spite of the large number of children, and add to all this the poor constitution of Milton himself, naturally the member of the family concerning whom our information is least defective, it seems to us that the hypothesis of hereditary syphilis is borne out in a very evident manner by all these facts.

Another hypothesis which might explain the large infant mortality is that of hereditary tuberculosis. This hypothesis seems to us infinitely less probable than the other, for it takes no account of Milton's gradual loss of sight and is, therefore, of no use in the solution of our main problem.

We conclude, then, after considering the whole body of available documents, that Milton's blindness was due to retinitis, complicated perhaps by glaucomatous troubles developed from eyestrain as a result of a generally bad state of health, probably attributable to hereditary syphilis.

The impression produced on a physician by the portraits of Milton, with his Olympian brow (frontal prominences very marked) and his long, narrow face, is all in favor of the idea of hereditary syphilis.[10]

[10] See, in particular, the youthful portrait reproduced as the frontispiece of vol. I of the Bohn edition of the *Prose Works*.

Certain writers have tried to establish a relation between genius and a syphilitic heredity. We shall not go so far. It is sufficient to point out that our hypothesis does not lessen the genius of the poet. It is a matter of general observation that, from the point of view of the intellectual faculties, there are two categories of hereditary syphilitics: some are degenerates, unintelligent or even idiotic; some others, on the contrary, are endowed with a precocious and supernormal intelligence. Milton evidently belonged to this last category. It appears to us, moreover, that Milton's physicians did not deceive him when they warned him against overworking his eyes. It was clearly the excessive effort which he imposed on his eyesight all his life which brought on his blindness. It was above all the intense eyestrain involved in the composition of the *Defensio pro populo Anglicano,* at a time when he was half blind, that led to his total loss of sight. In all this his physicians were right; and yet, for us, an atmosphere of half-comic pathos surrounds the activity of these physicians when we read what Milton's first biographer, perhaps a physician himself, tells us of their methods and their ideas:

While he was thus employ'd his Eyesight totally faild him; not through any immediat or sudden Judgment, as his Adversaries insultingly affirm'd; but from a weakness which his hard nightly study in his youth had first occasion'd, and which by degrees had for some time before depriv'd him of the use of one Eye: And the Issues and Seatons, made use of to save or retrieve that, were thought by drawing away the Spirits, which should have supply'd the Optic Vessells, to have hasten'd the loss of the other. He was indeed advis'd by his Physitians of the danger, in his condition, attending so great intentness as the work requir'd. But hee, who was resolute in going through with what upon good consideration hee at any time design'd, and to whom the love of Truth and his

Country was dearer than all things, would not for any danger de-
cline thir defense.[11]

The conclusion of the anonymous biographer is also
ours.  Knowing with what a miserable physical organism
his ancestors had endowed him, we understand Milton
better, and our admiration for the energy of his will cannot but be increased as a result of this study.  Perhaps
we know now why Milton, once he had taken his degrees
at the university, remained for six years in his father's
house in the country without adopting a profession.  Perhaps we know why, in spite of all the ardor of his patriotism and of his Parlimentarian convictions, he did not enter
the army but remained at home to educate a few pupils
and to battle with his pen during the Civil War.  And if
our hypotheses are correct, Milton, had he taken care of
himself and listened to the advice of his physicians, would
have been able to keep his sight several years longer.

Not only did he contend all his life against an organism
undermined from birth; not only did he impose on this
body the labor and study necessary to the realization of a
high spiritual and artistic ambition, and, during more than
sixty years, twenty-two of which were years of total blindness, lead by his will alone the life which he wished to
lead, so that in the end all his aims were accomplished
in spite of the illness which drained his strength; but more
than that, placed at a critical moment before a necessary
sacrifice, he did not hesitate. He knew that he was the one
man in all England in the Parliamentary party who was
capable of replying to Salmasius and of vindicating the
honor of the Republic; he knew also that in accepting the
task he abandoned all hope of preserving his sight.  He

[11] *English Historical Review,* XVII (1902), 106.

accepted the task. His heroism was of good alloy, and was not built on illusions: he was not deceived in believing himself capable of replying worthily to Salmasius any more than in thinking that he would lose what remained of his sight. It is because of this that he retains his place among the heroes, whatever may be our opinion of the cause for which he sacrificed himself, and that he continues to deserve our admiration, not only as a great poet, one of the most powerful artists of all time, but also as a great man, one of the strongest wills, the most enlightened consciences that humanity has produced.

# APPENDIX B

A COMPLETELY new conception of Milton has been brought forward since 1917. It may be summed up, in the main, by saying that it considers Milton as a Renaissance thinker and artist, and no longer as a Puritan. In the elaboration of this new view two groups have been chiefly at work: an American group, by far the more numerous; and a European group, centering mainly in Germany and starting from the work of Mr. S. B. Liljegren, of the University of Lund, Sweden. The edition of the sonnets published in 1921 by Professor John S. Smart of the University of Glasgow,[2] and my own *Pensée de Milton* (Paris, 1920) stand outside both of these groups.

## I. THE AMERICAN GROUP [3]

1. EDWARD CHAUNCEY BALDWIN. A note on *Paradise Lost* IX. In *M. L. N.*, February, 1917, XXXII, 119–21.

[1] In 1916 Mr. Elbert N. S. Thompson published his very useful *John Milton: topical bibliography* (New Haven, Yale University Press). This appendix is an attempt to continue his work down to the present moment (June, 1924). A great part of the material which it contains originally appeared in an article entitled " La conception nouvelle de Milton," which I contributed to the *Revue germanique* for April–June, 1923 (XIV, 113–41).

[2] *The Sonnets of Milton, with an introduction and notes*, Glasgow, Maclehose, Jackson and Co., 1921. This is a most important work from the biographical point of view. Prof. Smart has in preparation historical work of the highest interest on Milton, and intends " to get Milton completely and resolutely demassonised."

[3] The following abbreviations have been used: *J. E. G. P. = Journal of English and Germanic Philology; M. L. N. = Modern Language Notes; M. L. R. = Modern Language Review; M. P. = Modern Philology; P. M. L. A.= Publications of the Modern Language Association; S. P. = Studies in Philology.*

2. JAMES HOLLY HANFORD. The dramatic element in *Paradise Lost*. In *S. P.*, April, 1917, XIV, 178–95.

A criticism of Sir Walter Raleigh's phrase, "Milton is an epic, not a dramatic poet"; shows the truth and depth of the human drama between Adam and Eve. Very important.

3. EDWIN GREENLAW. "A better teacher than Aquinas." In *S. P.*, April, 1917, XIV, 196–217.

Starts from the text of the *Areopagitica*, and analyzes it by comparing it with the episode of Guyon in the *Faerie Queen;* finds there an anticipation of Milton's theories on man's freedom, on destiny as a consequence of man's moral state, on reason and passion; shows the influence on Milton's thought of Renaissance Neo-Platonism. Does not sufficiently insist on the conception of the " goodness " of matter, which separates Milton and the Renaissance from ancient Neo-Platonism.. A very important article.

4. ELBERT N. S. THOMPSON. A forerunner of Milton. In *M. L. N.*, December, 1917, XXXII, 479–82.

On Henry More and astronomy.

5. JOHN ERSKINE. The theme of death in *Paradise Lost*. In *P. L. M. A.*, December, 1917, XXXII, 573–82.

6. R. E. NEIL DODGE. Theology in *Paradise Lost*. In *University of Wisconsin Studies in language and literature*, 1918, No. 2, pp. 9–21.

7. EDWARD CHAUNCEY BALDWIN. A note on *Il Penseroso*. In *M. L. N.*, March, 1918, XXXIII, 184–85.

On Milton and Hermes Trismegistus. An important short note.

8. EDWARD CHAUNCEY BALDWIN. Milton and *Ezekiel*. In *M. L. N.*, April, 1918, XXXIII, 211–15.

9. ROBERT L. RAMSAY. Morality themes in Milton's poetry. In *S. P.*, April, 1918, XV, 123–58.

Shows Milton's emancipation from Platonism in *Comus* and the cause thereof: his belief in the goodness of matter. A little of the moralities left in Milton.

10. ELBERT N. S. THOMPSON. Milton's *Of Education*. In *S. P.*, April, 1918, XV, 159–75.

11. JAMES HOLLY HANFORD. The temptation motive in Milton. In *S. P.*, April, 1918, XV, 176–94.

Shows the Puritan and Christian element in Milton in his liability to succumb before passion.

12. RONALD S. CRANE. Imitation of Spenser and Milton in the early eighteenth century: a new document. In *S. P.*, April, 1918, XV, 195–206.

13. ELMER EDGAR STOLL. Was Paradise well lost? In *P. M. L. A.*, September, 1918, XXXIII, 429–35.
A reply to No. 5.

14. ALLAN H. GILBERT. A geographical dictionary of Milton. New Haven, Yale University Press, 1919.

15. ALLAN H. GILBERT. A parallel between Milton and Seneca. In *M. L. N.*, February, 1919, XXXIV, 120–21.
Points out the resemblance between "Nor love thy life, nor hate" (*P. L.*, XI, 549) and "In utrumque enim monendi ac firmandi sumus, et ne nimis amemus vitam et ne nimis oderimus" (Seneca, *Epist.*, XXIV, 24).

16. JAMES HOLLY HANFORD. Milton and the return to humanism. In *S. P.*, April, 1919, XVI, 126–47.
A manifesto of the new conception of Milton: "proposes a reinterpretation and a revaluation of the poem in terms of humanism . . . to see Milton's philosophy as a whole . . . to set him in his right relation, not to Puritanism alone, but to the whole Renaissance . . . [to] realize the significance of his work as a poetic criticism of life." Very important.

17. ELBERT N. S. THOMPSON. Milton's knowledge of geography. In *S. P.*, April, 1919, XVI, 148–71.

18. ALLAN H. GILBERT. The Cambridge manuscript and Milton's plans for an epic. In *S. P.*, April, 1919, XVI, 172–76.

19. ALLAN H. GILBERT. Pierre Davity: his *Geography* and its use by Milton. In the *Geographical Review*, May, 1919, VII, 322–38.

20. DAVID HARRISON STEVENS. The order of Milton's sonnets. In *M. P.*, May, 1919, XVII, 25–33.

21. GEORGE SHERBURN. The early popularity of Milton's minor poems. In *M. P.*, September, 1919, and January, 1920, XVII, 259–78, 515–40.

22. EDWARD CHAUNCEY BALDWIN. Milton and the Psalms. In *M. P.*, December, 1919, XVII, 457–63.

23. HARRY GLICKSMAN. The sources of Milton's *History of Britain*.

In *University of Wisconsin Studies in language and literature*, 1920, No. 11, pp. 105–44.

Very important and thorough.

24. ALLAN H. GILBERT. Milton on the position of women. In *M. L. R.*, January and July, 1920, XV, 7–27, 240–64.

Very important; the most considerable work that has appeared on the subject. It ought to destroy forever the legend of Milton's contempt for women. Comes to the same conclusions as the section devoted to the subject in Part II of the present work.

25. HARRY GLICKSMAN. Lowell on Milton's *Areopagitica*. In *M. L. N.*, March, 1920, XXXV, 185–86.

26. ELBERT N. S. THOMPSON. War journalism three hundred years ago. In *P. M. L. A.*, March, 1920, XXXV, 93–115.

On Milton as press censor.

27. HARRY GLICKSMAN. The editions of Milton's *History of Britain*. In *P. M. L. A.*, March, 1920, XXXV, 116–22.

28. ALLAN H. GILBERT. Milton and the mysteries. In *S. P.*, April, 1920, XVII, 147–69.

Comes, in the main, to a negative conclusion on the subject of influence.

29. EDWARD CHAUNCEY BALDWIN. Milton and Plato's *Timæus*. In *P. M. L. A.*, June, 1920, XXXV, 210–17.

Insists on the main difference: for Milton, matter is good.

30. WILLIAM HALLER. Order and progress in *Paradise Lost*. In *P. M. L. A.*, June, 1920, XXXV, 218–25.

Continues the discussion begun in Nos. 5 and 13, with little result.

31. ALWIN THALER. Milton in the theatre. In *S. P.*, July, 1920, XVII, 269–308.

32. JAMES HOLLY HANFORD. The date of Milton's *De doctrina Christiana*. In *S. P.*, July, 1920, XVII, 309–19.

See my note, p. 111, above.

33. EDWIN GREENLAW. Spenser's influence on *Paradise Lost*. In *S. P.*, July, 1920, XVII, 320–59.

Perhaps the most important single piece of work of the American group. Shows the intimate relationship in thought between Spenser and Milton, and its origin in the influence of Renaissance philosophy: Copernicus, Bacon, Galileo, Bruno. A decisive demonstration in favor of the new conception of Milton.

34. JAMES WADDELL TUPPER. The dramatic structure of *Samson Agonistes*. In *P. M. L. A.*, September, 1920, XXXV, 375–89.

35. ELBERT N. S. THOMPSON. Milton's part in *Theatrum poetarum*. In *M. L. N.*, January, 1921, XXXVI, 18–21.

36. JAMES HOLLY HANFORD. The arrangement and dates of Milton's sonnets. In *M. P.*, January, 1921, XVIII, 475–83.
A sequel to No. 20.

37. JAMES HOLLY HANFORD. Milton and Ochino. In *M. L. N.*, February, 1921, XXXVI, 121–22.

38. C. A. MOORE. The conclusion of *Paradise Lost*. In *P. M. L. A.*, March, 1921, XXXVI, 1–34.
Continues the discussion begun in Nos. 5, 13, and 30. The whole controversy seems to me to be rather barren.

39. ELBERT N. S. THOMPSON. Mysticism in seventeenth-century English literature. In *S. P.*, April, 1921, XVIII, 170–231.

40. JAMES HOLLY HANFORD. Milton and the art of war. In *S. P.*, April, 1921, XVIII, 232–66.

41. P. F. SHERWIN. Detached similes in Milton's epics. In *M. L. N.*, June, 1921, XXXVI, 341–48.

42. EDWARD CHAUNCEY BALDWIN. The Authorized Version's influence upon Milton's diction. In *M. L. N.*, June, 1921, XXXVI, 376–77.

43. JAMES HOLLY HANFORD. The chronology of Milton's private studies. In *P. M. L. A.*, June, 1921, XXXVI, 251–314.
Perhaps the most scholarly and useful instrument of work in Miltonic research; indispensable to a proper study of Milton. An analytical study of his *Commonplace Book*. I have used it (see pp. 254 and 273, above) in confirmation of my hypothesis on Azazel and of my remarks on Augustine.

44. PAULL FRANKLIN BAUM. *Samson Agonistes* again. In *P. M. L. A.*, September, 1921, XXXVI, 354–71.
A reply to No. 34.

45. JOHN A. HIMES. Further interpretations of Milton. In *M. L. N.*, November, 1921, XXXVI, 414–19.

46. RAYMOND DEXTER HAVENS. The influence of Milton on English poetry. Cambridge, Harvard University Press, 1922.

A considerable work, of thorough scholarship, well indexed, and of the greatest utility for a knowledge of eighteenth-century, English literature. Does not perhaps take sufficiently into consideration the work of the modern school on Milton, and seems to me too narrow in its conception of " influence," with the result that he ends in finding little of importance as a consequence of Milton's popularity. Undoubtedly, however, a remarkable and useful contribution to literary history.

47. MURRY W. BUNDY. Milton's view of education in *Paradise Lost*. In *J. E. G. P.*, January, 1922, XXI, 127–52.

48. E. K. RAND. *J* and *I* in Milton's Latin script. In *M. P.*, February, 1922, XIX, 315–19.

49. E. K. RAND. Milton in rustication. In *S. P.*, April, 1922, XIX, 109–35.

50. ALLAN H. GILBERT. Milton and Galileo. In *S. P.*, April, 1922, XIX, 152–85.

51. JESSE FLOYD MACK. The evolution of Milton's political thinking. In the *Sewanee Review*, April–June, 1922, XXX, 193–205.

52. JAMES HOLLY HANFORD. The evening star in Milton. In *M. L. N.*, November, 1922, XXXVII, 444–45.

53. HARRY GLICKSMAN. A comment on Milton's *History of Britain*. In *M. L. N.*, December, 1922, XXXVII, 474–76.

54. WARREN H. LOWENHAUPT. The writing of Milton's *Eikonoklastes*. In *S. P.*, January, 1923, XX, 29–51.

An important piece of historical research, proving the indebtedness of Milton's *Eikonoklastes* to a previous *Eikon Alethine*.

55. ALLAN H. GILBERT. The problem of evil in *Paradise Lost*. In *J. E. G. P.*, April, 1923, XXII, 175–94.

56. JAMES HOLLY HANFORD. The Rosenbach Milton documents. In *P. M. L. A.*, June, 1923, XXXVIII, 290–96.

57. ALLAN H. GILBERT. Milton's textbook of astronomy. In *P. M. L. A.*, June, 1923, XXXVIII, 297–307.

58. ALLAN H. GILBERT. The outside shell of Milton's world. In *S. P.*, October, 1923, XX, 444–47.

59. MARTIN A. LARSON. The influence of Milton's divorce tracts on Farquhar's *Beaux Stratagem.* In *P. M. L. A.,* March, 1924, XXXIX, 174–78.

60. LOUIS I. BREDVOLD. Milton and Bodin's *Heptaplomeres.* In *S. P.,* April, 1924, XXI, 399–402.

## II. EUROPEAN CRITICS [4]

61. S. B. LILJEGREN. Studies in Milton. Lund [Sweden], Gleerup, 1918.

One of the most important and striking works which the new movement has produced. A first part seeks to show that Milton's character partook of the curious combination of elements — Machiavellism allied with Stoicism — which resulted in the seventeenth century from the fusion of the Renaissance with Calvinism; it concludes with a formula with which I am in entire accord: " The force of Milton's inspiration was supplied by the passions dominating his soul and his surroundings." Then follow two historical studies, characterized by solid erudition and a remarkable power of analysis, on " Milton and Galileo " and " Milton and the Pamela Prayer." The total result of the book is to throw into stronger relief than ever before the Renaissance traits in Milton the man.

62. WALTHER FISCHER. In *E. S.,* 1918, LII, 390–96.

Review of No. 61. Maintains the older conception of Milton as a more or less liberal Calvinist; recognizes that Liljegren seems to have proved the interpolation of the Pamela Prayer; suggests that the inquiry be carried farther.

63. GUSTAV HÜBENER. In *Deutsche Literaturzeitung,* February 22, 1919, XL, 150–51.

Review of No. 61. Concludes: " Es ist schwer, sich hier der Bündigkeit der sorfältigen Beweisführung zu entziehen . . . aber hier wie in der Galileifrage bleibe die letzte Instanz durch keine nachweisbare Tatsache ausgeschlossen: das Vertrauen zu Miltons Persönlichkeit."

64. S. B. LILJEGREN. Bemerkungen zur Biographie Miltons. In *E. S.,* 1920, LIV, 358–66.

A reply to the preceding criticisms. A few phrases to note: " Milton war kein Mystiker. . . . Es scheint mir, als ob ihm Gott trotz allem zur algebraischen Formel werde, die [Milton] zu Hilfe nimmt, um eine Lösung eines schwierigen mathematischen Problems zu erzielen. . . . Zu allen Zeiten hat Milton die Bibel korrigiert und rundweg erklärt, Gott könne so oder so nicht gemeint haben, wenn etwa die wörtliche Interpretation Miltons Wünschen widersprochen."

[4] In this section of the bibliography, *B. A.* stands for the *Beiblatt zur Anglia* and *E. S.* for *Englische Studien.*

65. A. STERN. In *Literaturblatt für germanische und romanische Philologie*, 1920, XLI, 242–46.

A criticism of Liljegren (No. 61): thinks the question of the visit to Galileo remains unsettled; is inclined to think that Liljegren is right on the question of the Pamela Prayer.

66. HEINRICH MUTSCHMANN. Der andere Milton. Bonn und Leipzig, Kurt Schroeder Verlag, 1920.

67. HEINRICH MUTSCHMANN. Milton und das Licht. Die Geschichte einer Seelenkrankung. Halle, Niemeyer, 1920.

The starting-point of these two works is the new conception of Milton's personal character outlined by Prof. Liljegren. Herr Mutschmann has taken the latter's conclusions and pushed them to an unexpected and, as it seems to me, altogether illegitimate extreme. The spirit of system has taken possession of him in a truly diabolical manner; all that we know of Milton is cited, falsified, and exploited by him in order to prove that Milton was a monster who had committed the most shameful offenses and who was prevented by his cowardice alone from developing into a great criminal. Concerning the theory of albinism on which Mutschmann bases his conclusions as to Milton's character, I have expressed myself at length in No. 88 (see especially pp. 125–28), and need add nothing here. Of somewhat greater value — though here also the spirit of system is at work — are the pages in which Mutschmann endeavors to show that Milton was a Neo-Stoic. It is inevitable that he should not entirely succeed, for to limit the influences upon Milton to one period or to one school is impossible. The basis of his thought was the pantheistic materialism and the individualism of the Renaissance, which he drew from the cultivated *milieu* of his time and which was the natural expression of his own personality. He justified himself by an eclecticism in which appear in nearly equal proportions the Kabbalah, Neo-Platonism, Stoicism, and other systems still. But from each of these systems he rejected essential elements, so that we cannot say that he was a Kabbalist, a Neo-Platonist or a Neo-Stoic.

68. GUSTAV HÜBENER. Milton — der Albino. In *E. S.*, 1920, LIV, 473–77.

Attacks the theories of Herr Mutschmann.

69. A. STERN. In *Frankfurter Zeitung*, May 23, 1920, Literaturblatt.

An ironical discussion of the theories of Herr Mutschmann by a veteran German Miltonist.

70. HEINRICH MUTSCHMANN. Der Albino als Dichter. In *Kölnische Zeitung*, December, 19, 1920.

Explains his theories and appeals to specialists in medicine for aid.

71. WALTHER FISCHER. In *Literaturblatt für germanische und romanische Philologie*, 1921, XLII, 174–83.

A long review of Nos. 66 and 67; combats Mutschmann on all his main points. Mutschmann replies with considerable skill (pp. 429–30) and Fischer again returns to the attack (pp. 431–32): the point of this supplementary discussion is whether or not the term " aubrun," which Aubrey used to describe the color of Milton's hair, meant " white " in the seventeenth century.

72. S. B. LILJEGREN.  A fresh Milton-Powell document.  In *E. S.*, 1921, LV, 40–45.

Publishes for the first time the petition of Anne Powell (Milton's mother-in-law) to the Council of State asking the restoration of the property of her husband which had been confiscated and sold after the siege of Oxford.

73. GUSTAV HÜBENER.  Milton's Satan.  In *E. S.*, 1921, LV, 136–39.

Studies the rôle of resentment in the character of Satan.

74. HEINRICH MUTSCHMANN.  Zur Milton-Frage.  In *E. S.*, 1921, LV, 140–46.

Replies to his critics, particularly Herr Hübener.

75. RUDOLF METZ.  Nochmal der andere Milton.  In *E. S.*, 1921, LV, 313–18.

A new attack on Herr Mutschmann.

76. GUSTAV HÜBENER.  Erwiderung.  In *E. S.*, 1921, LV, 318–19.

A reply to No. 74, attacking especially this time the theory of Milton's albinism.

77. HEINRICH MUTSCHMANN.  Nochmals zur Milton-Frage.  In *E. S.*, 1921, LV, 479–80.

A reply to his adversaries with No. 76 as a starting-point.

78. HEINRICH MUTSCHMANN.  Toland und Milton.  In *B. A.*, April, 1921, XXXII, 87–90.

79. S. B. LILJEGREN.  In *B. A.*, June, 1921, XXXII, 121–25.

A hostile review of the theories of Herr Mutschmann.

80. HEINRICH MUTSCHMANN.  Zur Psychologie des Verfassers der " Nachtgedanken."  In *B. A.*, January, 1922, XXXIII, 12–23.

Applies his theories to Edward Young; accuses W. Thomas (*Le poète Edward Young*, Paris, 1901) of having gone too far in idealizing his character.

81. S. B. LILJEGREN.  Ethisches und Literaturanalytisches zur Milton-Frage.  In *E. S.*, 1922, LVI, 59–68.

Replies to No. 73; raises anew the question of the character of Milton and of the expression of this character in Satan; stresses the harmony between his views and those of *La pensée de Milton*.

82. F. A. POMPEN.   Recent theories about Milton's personality. In *Neophilologus*, July, 1922, VII, 272–79.

83. WALTHER FISCHER.   Der alte und der neue Milton.   In *Germanisch-romanische Monatsschrift*, September–October, 1922, X, 292–305.

84. S. B. LILJEGREN.   Die englischen Quellen der Philosophie Miltons und verwandtes Denken.   In *B. A.*, October, 1922, XXXIII, 196–206.

A discussion of Milton's " mortalism " and its relations to seventeenth-century thought.

85. S. B. LILJEGREN.   Milton's philosophy in the light of recent research.   In the *Scandinavian Scientific Review*, 1923, II, 114–23.

Sums up the theses proposed in *La pensée de Milton* together with what has been done since on the philosophy of Milton.

86. HEINRICH MUTSCHMANN.   Miltons Selbstdarstellung in *L'Allegro* und *Il Penseroso*.   In *B. A.*, 1923, XXXIV, 338–42.

87. S. B. LILJEGREN.   La pensée de Milton et Giordano Bruno. In *Revue de littérature comparée*, October–December, 1923, III, 516–40.

88. D. SAURAT AND C. CABANNES.   Milton devant la médicine.   In *Revue anglo-américaine*, December, 1923, I, 120–34.

See Appendix A, above. A portion of the article, containing a criticism of the theories of Herr Mutschmann (pp. 125–28), has been omitted from this translation.

89. S. B. LILJEGREN.   Milton's personality.   In *Neophilologus*, January, 1924, IX, 119–21.

Supplements and corrects No. 82; brings out some of the implications of his own and my researches into the character of Milton.

90. J. H. HARDER.   Milton, Puritan or Calvinist?   In *Neophilologus*, April, 1924, IX, 199–203.

91. S. B. LILJEGREN.   Milton Wahl des Berufs.   In *B. A.*, May, 1924, XXXV, 158–60.

A criticism of H. Schöffler, *Protestantismus und Literatur* (Leipzig, 1922), pp. 39–44, on the question of the motives which led Milton to abandon his intention of entering the church.

92. J. VELDKAMP. Calvinism and pride. In *Neophilologus*, July, 1924, IX, 281–83.

A reply to No. 89.

93. WALTHER FISCHER. Defoe und Milton. In *E. S.*, 1924, LVIII, 213–27

# INDEX

# INDEX

Absolute, Milton's conception of the, 113–16.

Absolutism, relation of Milton's views to nineteenth-century, 199–200.

Adam, 56, 128, 129, 130, 132, 140, 143, 145, 150, 152, 153, 154, 160, 161, 163, 166, 167, 169, 170, 174, 175, 177, 178, 221, 228, 231, 232, 252, 258, 261, 262, 271, 275, 277, 296.

*Adam, Life of,* 261 n.

Æschylus, 112.

Agatha, Council of, 267.

Agrippa, Cornelius, 281, 317.

Aims of Creation, 131–33.

Albinism, Milton's alleged, 349, 350, 351.

Alfaric, P., 273.

Allegory in *Paradise Lost,* 212; in *Paradise Regained,* 233–34.

Ambrose, Saint, 267.

Ames, William, 321.

Anabaptists, 311.

Angels, Fall of the, 253–58, 263, 270.

*Animadversions upon the Remonstrant's Defence,* 30, 44; quoted, 40–41, 266.

Apollinaris, Saint, 269.

*Apology for Smectymnuus,* 9, 30, 41, 44–47, 253, 261, 266, 282 n.

Aquinas, Saint Thomas, 75, 206.

*Arcades,* 12, 14.

*Areopagitica,* 30, 32, 67; quoted, 24, 73–78, 124–25, 183, 184, 185, 205, 206, 236, 253, 267, 292, 321–22.

Arianism, 34, 117.

Armageddon, 196.

Arminianism, 22.

Arminius, 75.

Athanasius, Saint, 267.

Augustine, Saint, 65, 152, 167, 212, 249, 250, 257, 265, 266, 267, 269, 321; influence on Milton, 273–79.

Authorities, Milton's contempt for, 40–41, 68.

Azazel, 254–56, 346.

Bacon, Lord, 324, 345.

Bailey, John, 250.

Baldwin, E. C., 342, 343, 344, 345, 346.

Battie (an Anabaptist), 311.

Baum, P. F., 346.

Beeching, H. C., 126 n.

Beelzebub, 216.

Being, God's plan of, 125–31; diagram of, 172.

Belial, 215, 234.

Bible, Milton and the, 21, 61–62, 64, 67, 121, 122, 147–48, 182, 205–06, 247, 253; quoted, 42 n, 155, 166, 251, 252, 253, 255, 256, 259, 260, 261, 262, 263, 269, 272, 285, 313.

Bishops, Milton's pamphlets against the, 32–49, 72, 73; the tyranny of, 42.

Blake, William, v, vi, 114, 130, 178, 207, 209–10, 211, 237, 299, 306.

*Blake and Milton* (Saurat), v, 299 n.

"Blind mouths," 20, 72.

Blindness, Milton's, 88, 240; probable causes of, 329–41.

Body and soul, unity of in Milton's thought, 57–58, 143–48.

Books, Milton's praise of, 74, 235.

Bousset, W., 252 n, 253 n, 261 n, 262 n.

Boyle, Robert, 324.

Bradshaw, John, 93.

Bredvold, L. I., 348.

Bridgewater, Earl of, 12.

Bruno, Giordano, v, 345, 351.

Bucer, Martin, 63.

Bundy, M. W., 347.

Byron, Lord, xvi.

Byzantine historians in Milton's library, 254.

Cabannes, Camille, 329 n, 351.

Calvin, John, 4, 40–41, 250, 262.

Calvinism, 22, 125, 348, 352.

Cambridge, University of, 6, 43.

355

356 INDEX

Canne, John, 310.
Catholicism, Milton's hatred of, 11,
62, 95–96, 176, 184.
Censorship, Milton's opposition to,
73, 183–85.
Chaos, Milton on the origin of,
285.
Chappell, William, 6.
Charles I, 23, 81, 99, 189.
Charles, R. M., 252 n, 256, 261 n.
Chastity, Milton on, 9, 12, 16–18,
45–46, 50–51, 55–58.
Chillingworth, William, 23.
Christ, 171; as Divine Reason, 106,
173–74, 177, 200, 210, 211; as
the Greater Man, 172, 174–80; as
the manifested God, 173; his ap-
proaching reign on earth, 39, 196;
in *Paradise Regained*, 234; not
mentioned in *Samson Agonistes*,
238; Augustine's conception of,
277. *See* Son, the.
Church, Milton on the, 11, 35, 92,
95.
Civil War, Milton's rôle in the, xvi,
80.
Clement of Alexandria, 265, 266.
Clergy, Milton's attitude toward the,
35–36, 92, 95, 96, 114.
Climate, Milton's complaints of the
English, 74.
*Colasterion*, 30; quoted, 68–69.
Color perception in Milton, 333–34.
*Commonplace Book* (Milton's), 346.
Commonwealth, the, 20, 72, 81; Mil-
ton a servant of, 86–94.
Communion of the Saints, 132, 182,
200.
*Comus*, 8, 9, 12, 15, 16, 17, 18, 19,
39, 46, 343.
*Considerations touching the likeliest
Means to remove Hirelings out
of the Church*, 31, 268; quoted,
96–99.
Copernicus, 345.
Cordovero, 281.
Cosmology, Milton's, 134–48.
Councils, Milton's contempt for the
decisions of, 266, 267.
Crane, R. S., 344.
Creation, 199; the aims of, 131–33;
brought about through the Son,
118, 134, 136; of man, 277.

Cromwell, Oliver, 22, 32, 33, 63, 73,
81, 90, 92, 93, 94, 95, 104, 188,
189, 190.
Crucifixion, 177, 178; Augustine on
the, 278.
Cyprian, Saint, 265.

Dalila, 236, 242.
Dante, 28, 171.
Davity, Pierre, 344.
Death, Milton on, 143–47, 199. *See*
Mortalism *and* Mortalists.
*De civitate Dei*, quoted, 152, 274–
79. *See* Augustine, Saint.
Decree of God, 125–31.
*De doctrina Christiana*, 46, 49, 67,
203–04, 210, 259, 274, 286; date
of, 111 n, 345; plan of, 112;
dogma in, 219; quoted, 113, 114,
115, 116, 117, 118, 119, 120, 121,
122, 125, 127, 129, 130, 132, 134,
135, 136, 137, 138, 139, 140, 141,
142, 143, 144, 146, 147, 148, 150,
158, 159, 173, 174, 175, 177, 180,
181, 182, 196, 197, 203, 204, 205,
206, 209, 247, 253, 257, 263, 268–
69, 290, 293–94, 313, 314, 315,
316, 318, 319, 321.
*Defensio pro populo Anglicano*, 31,
88–92, 228; quoted, 187, 189,
267–68, 339–40.
*Defensio pro se*, 31, 94.
*Defensio Regia pro Carolo I*, 88.
*Defensio secunda*, 31, 72, 73, 90;
quoted, 92–94, 106, 151, 185–87,
188, 189–91, 193–95, 330–32.
Defoe, Daniel, 352.
Demiurge, the Son as a, 120, 290;
in the *Zohar*, 290.
Deodati, Charles, 7, 9, 11, 12 n.
Derby, Countess of, 12.
Desire, legitimacy of, 105, 137, 155,
158, 160. *See* Sensuality.
Destiny, Milton's conception of, 81,
104–05, 107, 179–80, 192–97, 242.
*See* History.
*Detraction which followed upon my
writing certain Treatises, On the*,
71.
Diderot, Denis, 78.
Disestablishment of the Church, 92,
95.
*Divina Commedia*, 28.

Divine right of kings, Milton's rejection of, 89.
Divinity of matter. *See* Matter.
Divorce pamphlets, Milton's, xv, 30, 49–70, 73, 156, 158 n, 159 n, 166, 295.
" Divorcers," sect of, 69.
*Doctrine and Discipline of Divorce*, 30, 68, 73; quoted, 50–54, 58–63, 266, 311.
Dodge, R. E. N., 343.
Dogma, Milton's attitude toward, 203–10; few traces of in the *De doctrina*, 203; completely absent from *Samson*, 236–39; Satan's criticism of, 217–19.
" Double vision," Milton's, 178.
Druidic sources of English civilization, 321–22.
Dualism, Milton's attitude toward, 58, 80, 92 n, 105, 141.
Duality of man's nature, 149–55, 198, 277.

Economic factors, Milton's neglect of, 103 n.
*Education, Of*, xv–xvi, 30, 32, 78–79, 282 n.
Edwards, Thomas, 310–11.
Egotism, Milton's, 78, 79. *See* Pride.
*Eikon Alethine*, 347.
*Eikon Basilike*, 86, 227.
*Eikonoklastes*, 29, 30, 347; quoted, 86–88, 190.
Eleazer of Worms, 284 n.
Elect, Milton's conception of the, 172, 174, 180, 191, 199, 200, 211, 215, 277, 297.
Elegies, Milton's Latin, 7–9.
Eliberis, Council of, 267.
England, Milton's idea of, 32, 34, 37, 59–60, 76.
Enoch, Book of, 252 n, 254–58, 261, 274.
En-Sof, conception of in the *Zohar*, 289.
Epiphanius, Saint, 267, 270.
Erskine, John, 343.
Esdras, 259.
d'Espagnet, Jean, 323.
Ethics, Milton's theories of, 149–71.
Euripides, 146, 206, 318.

Eve, 144, 152, 153, 160, 161, 169, 176, 228, 232, 234, 259, 261, 263, 270, 271, 275, 283, 285.
Evil, the problem of, in Milton, 19–20, 32, 56, 82, 149–55, 259; in Hebrew speculation, 262.

*Faerie Queene*, 218 n, 343.
Fall, the, Milton's conception of, xvii, 18–19, 46, 49–70, 57, 58, 67, 69, 82, 129, 149, 164, 170, 171, 200, 233; as the triumph of passion over reason, 150–52, 198; as sensuality, 55, 152–55; in *Samson Agonistes*, 236; of Satan, 129, 154; in Hebrew speculation, 251–53, 262; in Paul, 259–61; in the writings of the Fathers, 264–79. *See* Angels, Fall of the.
Family, medical history of Milton's, 337–38.
Fathers of the Church, Milton's attitude toward the, 35, 40, 68, 264–73.
deFaye, E., 251 n, 270.
Fehr, B., vi n.
Fichte, J. G., 123.
Fifth Monarchy, the, 24, 283.
Firth, C. H., 310 n.
Fischer, W., 348, 349, 350, 351, 352.
Fludd, Robert, vi, vii, 280, 281, 283 n, 322, 323; influence on Milton, 301–09; on the Mortalists, 316–17.
Freedom. *See* Liberty.
Free will, doctrine of, 12, 23, 62, 75, 81, 82, 124, 125, 192, 198, 270, 277, 286, 289, 292.

Galileo, xvi, 324, 345, 348.
*Gangræna* (Thomas Edwards), 310–11.
Garnett, Richard, 1–2.
Gassendi, 301.
Gauden, Dr. John, 228.
Gilbert, A. H., 344, 345, 347.
Glicksman, H., 344, 345, 347.
Gnostics, the, 267, 270.
God, Milton's conception of, 34, 37, 49, 81, 105, 113–33, 136, 236, 238–39.
Goethe, J. W., 230, 300.
Goodness of the natural instincts,

16, 294; of matter, 105. *See* Matter.
Government, origin of in the Fall, 82, 188; derives its powers from the people, 82, 89, 189; a necessary evil, 62, 188.
Greater Man, Christ as the, 172, 174-80, 199, 277, 297.
Greenlaw, E., vi, 218 n, 286 n, 343, 345.
Gregory, Saint, 263.
Grotius, Hugo, 68.
Guignebert, Charles, 251 n.
Gunkel, H., 263 n.
Gunpowder, use of by rebel angels, 208.
Guyon (in the *Faerie Queene*), 343.

Hales, John, 23.
Hall, Bishop, 32, 40, 44.
Haller, W., 345.
*Hamlet*, 268.
Hanford, J. H., vi, 111 n, 254, 273, 343, 344, 345, 346, 347.
Harder, J. H., 351.
Harrison, Col. Thomas, 216.
Hartlib, Samuel, 78.
Havens, R. D., 347.
Hebrew sources of the myth of the Fall, 251-58.
Hebrews, the, disbelief in the existence of the soul, 142; attitude toward polygamy, 182.
Hegel, G. W. F., 123.
Hell, 175.
Henry VIII, 33.
Herbert of Cherbury, 207.
Heretical ideas in Satan's speeches, 217-19.
Hermes Trismegistus, 343.
Hermetism, 301.
Hilarius, Saint, 272.
Himes, J. A., 346.
History, Milton's conception of God in, 80, 130.
*History of Britain*, 195, 322, 344, 345.
Hobbes, Thomas, 207.
Holy Spirit, unimportance of in Milton's system, 134-35, 177, 239.
Homer, 4.
Hooker, Richard, 272.
Horton, 10, 12.
House of Lords, 73.

Hübener, G., 348, 349, 350.
Hugo, Victor, xvi, 112, 300.
Human nature, Milton's conception of, xvi, 16, 70. *See* Ethics.
*Humble Remonstrance* (Bishop Hall), 32, 40.
Huxley, Thomas, 249.

*Il Penseroso*, 12, 14.
Immortality, Milton's views on, 138, 143, 277. *See* Mortalism *and* Mortalists.
*In Adventum Veris*, 8.
Independents, the, 73, 81; Milton's relations with, 30.
Infernal Council, the, 226, 228.
Inspiration, Milton's ideas on, 206. *See* Bible.
Instincts, goodness of the natural, 16, 294.
Intellectual liberty. *See* Liberty.
Irenæus, Saint, 255, 264, 265, 267, 270.
Irony, God's, 127 n, 229-32.
Italian sonnets, Milton's, 7.
Italy, Milton's travels in, 13, 20; his judgment of, 75-76, 185.

Jerome, Saint, 265, 266, 267, 272, 321.
Johnson, Samuel, 217, 282 n.
Jonathan the Targoum, 253, 255.
*Judgment of Martin Bucer concerning Divorce*, 63.
Justin Martyr, 265, 266.

Kabbalah, the, influence on Milton, vi, 280, 281-300, 309, 317, 322, 323, 349; Fludd's relations to, 301.
Kant, Immanuel, 123, 147.
Karppe, S., 285, 290 n, 291 n, 292 n, 293, 296 n.
Kings, Milton's attitude toward. *See* Monarchy *and* Tyranny.
Kircher, Father, 281.
Koran, 262 n.

Lactantius, 265, 267, 271, 272.
*L'Allegro*, 12, 14.
Lamartine, 300.
Landor, W. S., 235.
Larson, M. A., 348.
Latin poems, Milton's, 6-9, 15.

Laud, Archbishop, 22.
Law, Milton's rejection of the moral, 181–82.
Liber, M., 251 n.
Liberty, Milton's passion for, xvi, 3, 11, 47; his general conception of, 90, 181–92; intellectual, 3, 188–89; moral, 181–82; political, 185–92; priests, enemies of, 78; established by Christ, 95.
Light, Milton's invocation to, 222–23; probable source in Fludd, 302–05.
Lilburne, John, 310.
Lilith, 285.
Liljegren, S. B., v, vi, 87 n, 342, 348, 349, 350, 351.
Lods, A., 251 n, 256 n.
Long Parliament, 20, 23, 72.
Loria, 281.
Love, Milton's conception of, 45–46; among the angels, 144, 294.
Lowenhaupt, W. H., 347.
Lower classes, the, Milton's attitude toward. See People.
Lust as the Fall, 46. See Sensuality.
Lycidas, 12, 14, 19.

Mack, J. F., 347.
Man as part of God, 185.
Man's Mortality, 111 n, 310–22.
Marriage, Milton on, 46, 49–70, 159, 160; Paul on, 260–61; the Fathers on, 266.
Marston Moor, 73.
Mary, the Virgin, 175–76, 265.
Masson, David, xvi, 3, 4, 5, 6, 9, 11, 12, 24, 32, 121, 206, 216, 252, 310 n, 311, 319 n, 342 n.
Materialism in Milton, 140, 175, 280, 302; in Fludd, 302.
Mathematics, Milton's interest in, 12.
Matrona, the, 285, 297.
Matter, Milton's belief in the divinity of, 16, 46, 105, 106, 114, 136–43, 193, 198, 276, 279, 280 n, 288, 309, 315, 343, 345; Origen on, 270; Augustine on, 276; Satan's heretical views on, 218.
Mephistopheles, 230.
Meredith, George, 54, 325–26.
Metz, R., 350.
Mezentius, 53, 311.
Michael, 150.

Millenarians, the, 24; Milton's relations to, 283.
Milton, Christopher, 5.
Milton, John (father of the poet), 3–5, 10.
Milton, John, unity of his private, political and literary life, xiv–xvii; his pride and egotism, xv, xvi, xvii, 1, 5, 6, 9, 27, 47, 49, 52, 78, 79, 105, 106, 203–04, 214, 220, 238; his family, 1–5; little of religious fanaticism in him or his family, 2–5; his grandfather, 3; his father, 3–5; early recognition of his genius, 5–6; at Cambridge, 6; friendship with Deodati, 6–7; his susceptibility to women, 7–8; his poetical plans, 10; at Horton, 10–12; travels in Italy, 13; his motives in giving up poetry for politics, 24–28; his marriage with Mary Powell, 49–55; their separation, 50; his reconciliation with her, 69; his disillusionment, 70; his services to the Commonwealth, 85–94; his return to literature, 94–95; his personal peril after the Restoration, 104; his blindness, 329–41.
poems. See Arcades, Comus, Elegies, Il Penseroso, Italian sonnets, In Adventum Veris, L'Allegro, Latin poems, Lycidas, Paradise Lost, Paradise Regained, Prolusiones, Samson Agonistes, Sonnets.
prose works. See Animadversions upon the Remonstrant's Defence, Apology for Smectymnuus, Areopagitica, Colasterion, Commonplace Book, Considerations touching the likeliest Means to remove Hirelings out of the Church, De doctrina Christiana, Defensio pro populo Anglicano, Defensio pro se, Defensio secunda, Divorce pamphlets, Doctrine and Discipline of Divorce, Education, Eikonoklastes, History of Britain, Judgment of Martin Bucer concerning Divorce, Pamphlets, Prelatical Episcopacy, Ready and easy Way to establish a free

Commonwealth, Reason of Church Government, Reformation in England, Tenure of Kings and Magistrates, Tetrachordon, Treatise of Civil Power in Ecclesiastical Causes, True Religion, Heresy, Schism, Toleration.

ideas. See Absolute, Aims of Creation, Being, Body and soul, Calvinism, Catholicism, Censorship, Chastity, Christ, Church, Clergy, Cosmology, Creation, Death, Decree of God, Demiurge, Desire, Destiny, Dogma, Dualism, Duality of man's nature, Elect, Ethics, Evil, Fall, Free Will, God, Goodness of natural instincts, Government, Greater Man, History, Holy Spirit, Human nature, Immortality, Liberty, Love, Marriage, Materialism, Matter, Monarchy, Mortalism, Nature, Necessity, Normal human nature, Ontology, Pantheism, Passion, People, Political ideas, Predestination, Priests, Psychology, Reason and passion, Religion, "Retraction," Scale of beings, Sensuality, Sin, Son, Toleration, Trinity, Unity, Woman.

sources and background. See Augustine, Azazel, Bible, Enoch, Fathers of the Church, Fludd, Gnostics, Hebrew sources of the myth of the Fall, Kabbalah, Man's Mortality, Mortalists, Neo-Platonism, Neo-Stoicism, Occultism, Originality of Milton's thought, Paul, Plato, Puritanism, Reason and passion, Spenser, Walton's Bible, Zohar.

Monachus, Georgius, 254.

Monarchy, Milton's attitude toward, 36, 44, 47, 78, 83, 151.

Moore, C. A., 346.

Moral liberty. See Liberty.

More, Alexander, 227.

More, Henry, 281, 343.

Mortalism, Milton's, vi, 141, 156, 174, 282 n, 351; sources of, 310–22.

Mortalists, the, vi, vii, 280, 308, 309, 310–22.

Moulin, 316.

Music, love for in the Milton family, 4, 12.

Mutschmann, H., 349, 350, 351.

Mysticism, Milton's freedom from, 80, 233.

Nature, Milton's feeling for, 8, 15–16; disorder of, after the Fall, 145.

Necessity, God not subject to, 118, 140.

Neocæsaria, Council of, 267.

Neo-Platonism, v, 280 n, 301, 309, 343.

Neo-Stoicism, 349.

New Forcers of Conscience under the Long Parliament, On the, 72.

Newman, J. H., 184.

Newton, Bishop, 255; quoted, 116.

Nietzsche, F., 300.

Normal human nature, Milton's conception of, 58, 67, 155–59, 198.

Occultism, Milton's relations to, 132. See Kabbalah and Fludd, Robert.

Ochino, 346.

Oldenburg, H., 323–24.

Old Testament, Milton's attitude toward the, 121.

Omnipresence as an attribute of God, 114.

Onkelos, 253.

Ontology, Milton's, 113–33.

Ophites, 270.

Orage, A. R., v.

Origen, 255, 265, 266, 267, 270.

Originality of Milton's thought, v, 56 n, 151 n, 247, 276, 298–99.

Original sin, doctrine of not in Samson Agonistes, 237–38.

Orthodoxy, Milton's rejection of, 105.

Overton, Richard, 93, 310–22.

Oxford University, 4.

"Pamela Prayer," the, 348.

Pamphlets, Milton's, character of, 23, 28, 29, 48; classification of, 30–31; historical matter in, 33.

Pantheism in Milton, 16, 46, 113, 115, 140, 149, 208, 239, 286, 289, 290,

302; in the *Zohar*, 282 n, 290, 293; in Fludd, 302; in *Man's Mortality*, 317.

Pantheistic materialism in the seventeenth century, 309.

*Paradise Lost*, 19, 24, 28, 29, 34, 39, 46, 49, 56, 66, 67, 69, 74, 88, 95, 104, 211, 212, 213–32, 268; anticipations of in Milton's early work, 10; God in, 122; theological discussions in, 128; largely a political poem, 195; non-dogmatic elements in, 208; artistic construction of, 213; Milton's personality in, 213–29; Milton the hero of, 220; compared with *Samson Agonistes*, 236.

quoted, *Book I:* 175, 180, 214–16, 222, 225–26, 254–56, 273; *Book II:* 144, 155, 216, 226–27, 286; *Book III:* 119, 120, 123, 125, 128–29, 178, 180, 208, 222–23, 227, 287 n, 289, 302–04, 332–33; *Book IV:* 16, 129, 157–58, 160, 161, 162, 175, 190, 217, 218–19, 227, 263 n, 334; *Book V:* 119, 125, 129, 133, 138, 139, 140, 143, 149, 175, 208, 218, 230, 257–58, 305, 307; *Book VI:* 120, 209, 308; *Book VII:* vi, 8, 115, 118, 120, 122, 124, 126, 127, 132, 135, 142, 223–24, 272, 286, 287–88, 293 n, 333; *Book VIII:* 119, 144, 150–51, 154, 156, 157, 161, 162, 163, 164, 169–70, 230–31, 294, 296, 307; *Book IX:* 145, 150, 152, 153, 154, 160, 171, 218, 224, 283–84, 295, 296; *Book X:* 120, 130, 140, 144–45, 164, 219, 228–29, 275; *Book XI:* 164–65, 177, 232, 256, 257; *Book XII:* 131, 150, 175, 182, 189, 231, 253, 277, 278, 296.

*Paradise Regained*, 24, 178, 204, 233–36; theme of, 171; freedom of from dogma, 207, 237; quoted, *Book I:* 176, 234; *Book II:* 234–35, 257; *Book III:* 191–92; *Book IV:* 133, 176–77, 235.

Parey, Ambrose, 316.

Parliament, 59, 70, 95, 100. *See* Long Parliament.

Pascal, 112, 207, 324.

Passion, legitimacy, of, 49, 59. *See* Reason and passion.

Patriarchs, the, 177.

Pattison, Mark, 50, 249–50.

Paul, Saint, 259–61, 275, 276.

dePauly, Jean, 284 n, 287 n, 292 n.

People, Milton's distrust of the, 46–47, 81, 86–87, 90, 93, 102–03, 191.

Peters, Hugh, 216.

*Phædo* (Plato's), 17.

Pharaoh, 180 n.

Philaras, Leonard, 329.

Phillips, Edward, 4, 12, 282 n.

Physical love, when legitimate, 156. *See* Sensuality.

Pico della Mirandola, 280 n, 281.

Plan of being, 125–31.

Plato, 17–18, 75, 324, 345.

Pliny, 316.

Political evil, Milton's conception of, 82.

Political ideas in Milton, 137, 181–97, 278; in Augustine, 278.

Political liberty, Milton on. *See* Liberty.

Polygamy, Milton on, 182; among the ancient Hebrews, 182.

Pompen, F. A., 255 n, 351.

Powell, Anne, 350.

Powell, Mary, 49–70, *passim;* 228.

Predestination, Milton on, 23, 62, 75, 129, 180. *See* Free Will.

*Prelatical Episcopacy, Of,* 30, 39–40, 264–65.

Presbyterians, Milton's relations to the, 41, 47, 48, 63, 70–79, 83.

Pride, Milton's, xv, xvi, xvii, 1, 5, 6, 9, 27, 47, 49, 52, 105, 106, 203–04, 214, 220, 238; as the motive of the Fall, 274; Satan's, 214.

Priests, Milton's hatred of, 11, 78, 83–85, 182–83, 196, 268.

*Prolusiones*, 6.

Psycho-analysis, 51.

Psychology, Milton's, 149–71.

Puritanism, Milton's relations to, xiii, 1, 2, 6, 7, 12, 13–14, 21, 75, 105.

Puritans, the, ideals of, 21; failure of, 104; represented by Samson, 237.

Raleigh, Sir Walter, 50, 204, 217, 250.
Ramsay, R. L., 343.
Rand, E. K., 347.
Randolph, T., 16 n.
Ranelagh, Lady, 168 n.
Raphael, 122, 129, 138, 150, 154, 156, 170, 294.
Raschi, 255.
*Ready and easy Way to establish a free Commonwealth*, 31; quoted, 99–103, 214.
Reason and passion, the theme of in Milton, 19, 149–55, 170–71, 221, 233; in Renaissance thought, 56 n, 249.
*Reason of Church Government urged against Prelacy, The*, 11, 25–28, 30, 41–44, 183, 206, 265.
Redemption as the return of reason, 171.
Reformation, the, 21, 262, 272; not mentioned in *Paradise Lost*, 34, 196.
*Reformation in England, Of*, 30, 33–39, 265–66.
Regeneration as the triumph of reason over passion, 155.
*Regii sanguinis clamor ad cœlum*, 92.
Reincarnation in the *Zohar*, 283.
Religion, Milton's attitude to, 2–3, 11, 80, 95–96, 172–80.
Religious liberty, 182–83.
Restoration, the, 46, 81, 104, 106, 214, 215.
Resurrection, the, 147–48, 199, 200.
"Retraction," God's, 123–25, 131, 133, 149, 198, 285, 286–89, 292, 298; in Fludd, 302; in *Man's Mortality*, 317.
Reuchlin, J., 281.
Revelation, Milton's belief in a double, 204.
Roman Catholic Church, Milton's hatred of, 11, 62, 95–96, 176, 184.
Rousseau, J. J., 2.
Royal Society, the, 324.

Salmasius, 88, 90–92, 227, 228, 267, 341.
*Samson Agonistes*, 44, 204, 221, 236–43; freedom from dogma, 207;

quoted, 130, 165–66, 236, 238, 240, 241, 242–43, 337.
Satan, 16, 83, 126, 127, 129, 130, 154, 170, 171, 175, 177, 179, 180, 196, 210, 211, 212, 213, 257, 259, 261; as Passion, 151, 155; as a type of the tyrant, 190; character of, 214–19, 350; Fall of, 262; in *Paradise Regained*, 234; Milton's attitude toward, 214–29; not the hero of *Paradise Lost*, 219; origin of, 271; rebellion of, 208.
Scale of beings, theme of, in Milton, 138–39, 148, 305–08; in Fludd, 305–08.
Schelling, F. W. J., 123, 124.
Schöffler, H., 351.
Schopenhauer, A., 124.
Scotus, 206.
Scriptures. *See* Bible.
"Second Creation," 171, 172–80.
*Second Defence*. See *Defensio secunda*.
Selden, John, 301.
Sensuality as the Fall, 55, 57, 58, 152–55, 269, 275, 294; in the Fall of Satan and the rebel angels, 216, 254, 256, 263; in Milton's nature, 57; legitimate when under the control of intelligence, 19, 155–59, 261, 276, 294.
Sephiroth, the, 285, 290.
Sexual shame as a consequence of the Fall, 153.
Shakespeare, W., 163 n, 268.
Shekhina, 285, 288.
Shelley, P. B., 2, 207, 299.
Sherburn, George, 344.
Sherwin, P. F., 346.
Sin, 143, 144; the daughter of Satan, 155, 216, 284; and Death, allegory of, 144, 208.
Solemn League and Covenant, 24.
Son, the, 117, 134, 200; as the Creator, 118, 136, 145; as the sole manifestation of the Father, 120; as Reason, 151, 155; as the Demiurge, 120, 290; creation of, 119. *See* Christ.
Sonnets, Milton's, 71, 72.
"Sons of God," 117–18, 176, 177, 257, 258, 274.

Soul, Milton's doctrine of the. *See* Mortalism.
Smart, J. S., 7–8, 16 n, 342.
"Smectymnuus," 32, 40. See *Apology for Smectymnuus.*
Spenser, Edmund, 41, 75, 206, 218 n, 249, 343.
Spinoza, 323.
Spirit, definition of, 144; no distinction between matter and, 141.
Squires, V. P., 333.
Stage, Milton's love of the, 7.
Stern, A., 349.
Stevens, D. H., 344.
Stoicism, 302, 348. *See* Neo-Stoicism.
Stoll, E. E., 344.
Strafford, Earl of, 23.
Sulpitius Severus, 267.
Sumner, C. R., 113 n, 116, 130 n, 217, 259 n, 321 n.
Symbolism in Milton's poetry, 210–12.
Syncellus, Georgius, 254–56.

Temperance, Milton's praise of in *Comus,* 16.
*Tenure of Kings and Magistrates,* 30; quoted, 81–85, 188, 190.
Tertullian, 263, 265, 266, 267, 269, 321.
*Tetrachordon,* 30, 59, 73; quoted, 63–68, 132, 158, 159, 167, 168, 205, 266–67, 291.
Thaler, A., 345.
Theology, Milton's attitude to, 114, 121.
Thévenot, Doctor, 329.
Thompson, E. N. S., 342, 343, 344, 345, 346.
Thought, originality of Milton's. *See* Originality.
*Tikunē Zohar,* vi, 287–89, 302 n.
Toleration, Milton's advocacy of, 11, 23, 42, 95.
*Treatise of Christian Doctrine.* See *De doctrina Christiana.*
*Treatise of Civil Power in Ecclesiastical Causes,* 31; quoted, 95–96, 183.

Trelawny, E. J., xv.
Trinity, Milton on the, 37, 47, 105, 116, 238.
*Triumphs of Oriana, The,* 4.
*True Religion, Heresy, Schism, Toleration, Of,* 31.
Tupper, J. W., 346.
Tyranny, Milton's conception of, 83, 189.

Unity of body and soul in Milton's thought, 18, 19, 57–58, 141, 146, 282 n; of God, 116, 117; of man and God, 49.
Universities, Milton on the, 43, 97, 268.
Urania, Milton's invocation to, 291.
Usher, Archbishop, 39.

Vane, Sir Harry, 93, 216.
Veldkamp, J., 352.
Vicarious atonement, 178.
Virgil, 13.
Virgin birth, 177.
Virgin Mary. *See* Mary.
Voltaire, 284.
Voysin, Joseph, 281.

Wagner, R., 300.
Walton's Bible, 252–53, 255.
War in heaven, the, 208, 228, 263.
Westminster Assembly, 63.
Whitman, Walt, 299.
Williams, T. J., 329 n.
Windelband, W., 124.
Wisdom of Solomon, 249, 261.
Woman, Milton's conception of, 7, 64, 154, 159–70, 296, 345; Meredith on, 326.
Wotton, Sir Henry, 12.
Wrighter, Clement, 310, 312.

Young, Edward, 350.
Young, Thomas, 32.

Zohar, the, vi, 124, 251 n, 281–300, 302 n.
Zoroaster, 302.